TSI Study Guide

TSI Assessment Test Prep and Practice Questions

for Texas Success Initiative Exam

Miller Test Prep

Updated for Texas Success Initiative Assessment 2.0 (TSIA2)

TSI Study Guide: TSI Assessment Test Prep and Practice Questions for Texas Success Initiative Exam

Copyright 2024, 2022, 2020, 2018 © Miller Test Prep

Updated for Texas Success Initiative Assessment 2.0 (TSIA2) in 2024/09

Email: MillerTestPrep@outlook.com

ALL RIGHTS RESERVED

No part of this publication may be reproduced, distributed, or transmitted in any form or by any means, including photocopying, recording, or other electronic or mechanical methods, without the prior written permission of the publisher, except in the case of brief quotations embodied in critical reviews and certain other non-commercial uses permitted by copyright law.

This book is provided "as is," without warranty of any kind, either expressed or implied, including, but not limited to, the implied warranties of merchantability, fitness for a particular purpose, or non-infringement. While every effort has been made to ensure the accuracy and completeness of the information contained herein, the author and publisher assume no responsibility for any errors, omissions, or inaccuracies. The reader is advised to verify the information independently before making any decisions based on it.

Trademark Notice: TSI and TSIA2 are used throughout this book solely to refer to the Texas Success Initiative and Texas Success Initiative Assessment 2.0, which are administered by the Texas Higher Education Coordinating Board. We are not affiliated with or endorsed by the Texas Higher Education Coordinating Board, and we do not hold any trademark rights to the TSI or TSIA2 names. All references to TSI and TSIA2 are for informational purposes only and are the property of their respective trademark holders. This book is intended to help students prepare for the TSIA2 test by providing relevant study material and practice questions. Miller Test Prep has made every effort to ensure the accuracy and quality of the content in this book to aid in your test preparation.

Printed in the United States of America

ISBN: 978-1950159376

Table of Contents

INTRODUCTION — 1
- Your Guide to Using This Book — 1
- Overview of the TSIA2 Exam — 2
- Ace the TSIA2: Strategies for Success — 6
- TSIA2 30-Day Test Prep Study Plan — 8
- Success Skills for Test Day — 10
- Conquer Test Anxiety — 11

PART I: TSIA2 READING — 12
- Introduction — 12
- ELAR Reading Question Types — 16
- TSIA2 ELAR Reading Practice Questions — 30
- Answer Key — 36

PART II: TSIA2 WRITING — 38
- Introduction — 38
- Development — 39
- Organization — 42
- Effective Language Use — 45
- Standard English Grammar Conventions — 48
- Conventions of Usage — 57
- Conventions of Punctuation — 61
- TSIA2 Writing Test Practice Questions — 64
- Answer Key — 68

PART III: TSIA2 ESSAY — 70
- Introduction — 70
- Tips and Strategies — 70
- Essay Structure — 72
- Sample Essay and Analysis — 73

PART IV: TSIA2 MATHEMATICS — 77
- Introduction — 77

§1: QUANTITATIVE REASONING — 79
- Whole Number Operations — 79
- Fraction Operations — 82
- Decimal Operations — 89
- Percentage — 93
- Number Comparisons and Equivalents — 97
- Pre-Algebra Concepts — 102

§2. ALGEBRAIC REASONING — 110

- Evaluating Algebraic Expressions — 110
- Operations of Algebraic Expressions — 111
- Linear Equations — 113
- Setting Up Algebra Word Problems — 117
- Linear Applications and Graphs — 119

§3 GEOMETRIC AND SPATIAL REASONING — 127

- Perimeter and Circumference — 127
- Pythagorean Theorem — 127
- Distance Formula — 128

§4 PROBABILISTIC AND STATISTICAL REASONING — 130

- Calculating Probability — 130
- Descriptive Statistics — 131

§5 ALGEBRA & GEOMETRY FUNDAMENTALS — 135

- Factoring — 135
- Functions — 140
- Quadratic Equations and Inequalities — 145
- Polynomial Functions and Equations — 146
- Radical Functions — 154
- Rational Functions — 156
- Exponential Functions and Equations — 158
- Logarithmic Functions and Equations — 161
- Geometry Concepts for Algebra — 163
- Trigonometry — 169

§6 TSIA2 MATHEMATICS TEST PRACTICE QUESTIONS — 174

- Mathematics Practice Questions — 174
- Answer Key — 183

PART V: PRACTICE TESTS — 186

TSIA2 PRACTICE TEST 1 — 186

- English Language Arts and Reading (ELAR) — 186
- Mathematics — 195
- Practice Test 1 Answer Key — 200

TSIA2 PRACTICE TEST 2 — 205

- English Language Arts and Reading (ELAR) — 205
- Mathematics — 215
- Practice Test 2 Answer Key — 219

INTRODUCTION

YOUR GUIDE TO USING THIS BOOK

This book is designed to help students of all backgrounds, skill levels, and learning styles succeed in the TSIA2 exam. Whether you're a first-time test-taker or need specific accommodations, here is a guide on how to use this book effectively for your personal success.

Understanding the Structure

The book is organized into clear sections, each addressing a different part of the TSIA2 exam—Reading, Writing, Essay, and Mathematics. Each section starts with an introduction to the topics covered, followed by key concepts, practice questions, and answer keys. This structure is intended to allow flexibility, so you can focus on the areas that need the most improvement.

Planning and Time Management

Break your study time into chunks. For your convenience, this book includes a 30-day study plan to get most students ready in a month's time to be ready for the TSIA2 exam.

Using Practice Tests Effectively

For included practice tests, time yourself to replicate real test conditions. After completing a test, immediately check your answers using the provided answer key to identify areas of strength and weakness.

After each practice test, go beyond just checking answers. Revisit sections where you made errors and spend additional time studying those concepts. If necessary, revisit the respective sections in the book, such as the "Pythagorean Theorem" or "Effective Language Use".

Targeted Study Based on Performance

- Weak Areas: If you find you struggle with a particular type of question (e.g., geometry in the mathematics section or grammar in writing), focus your review on those specific areas. Use the targeted sections like "Conventions of Usage" or "Quadratic Equations" to strengthen your knowledge.

- Strong Areas: For the areas where you excel, maintain your skills by revisiting the relevant practice questions occasionally, but avoid over-focusing on these sections. This will leave more time to improve in your weaker areas.

Frequent Review and Reinforcement

Regularly review the content and practice questions you've already completed. Revisiting the material will reinforce learning and help you retain information long-term. Our 30-day study plan utilizes well-timed repetition as a key tool to help readers retain knowledge.

Personalize Your Approach

Remember that everyone's learning process is unique. Adapt this book to your specific needs and adjust the study strategies to what works best for you. The more personalized your approach, the more effective your study sessions will be.

By using this guide along with the book's structured sections, practice exercises, and answer keys, you can optimize your test prep experience and build confidence for the TSIA2 exam. Now, let's get the fun started!

Overview of the TSIA2 Exam

Welcome to the next step in your educational journey! As you prepare to take the TSIA2, you're embarking on an exciting path that will help shape your academic future.

The Texas Success Initiative (TSI) is a mandate that requires all public colleges and universities in Texas to evaluate the readiness of all incoming undergraduate students who are not exempt from enrolling in freshman-level academic courses. Students can qualify for exemptions in various ways, such as achieving college readiness benchmarks on standardized tests like the SAT®, ACT®, or completing a high school College Preparatory Course successfully. After January 11, 2021, Students who do not qualify for an exemption must take the Texas Success Initiative Assessment 2.0 (TSIA2), which is an update of the Texas Success Initiative Assessment (TSIA).

TSIA2 is a test used to evaluate the college readiness of non-exempt students, as mandated by the Texas Success Initiative. The TSIA2 assesses preparedness for college-level coursework in English language arts and reading (ELAR) and mathematics, which are essential for success in other college courses. Academic advisers and counselors use the TSIA2 results, along with your academic background, goals, and interests, to place you in appropriate courses that match your level of achievement.

The TSIA2 either certifies you as "college ready" in a subject area or provides a diagnostic profile of your academic strengths and weaknesses, allowing for targeted instruction to help you succeed in college-level courses.

The TSIA2 is not timed. Students are allowed to take as much time as they need to complete each section of the assessment. This untimed format is designed to reduce test anxiety and allow students to carefully consider their answers, ensuring that the results accurately reflect their knowledge and skills.

The TSIA2 harnesses computer-adaptive technology to tailor its questions to your individual proficiency. The complexity of subsequent questions is directly influenced by the accuracy of your previous answers. As you answer each question, the system evaluates your performance and selects subsequent questions that match your demonstrated proficiency level. This means that if you answer a question correctly, the next question may be more challenging, whereas if you answer incorrectly, the following question may be easier. This adaptive approach aims to more accurately assess your skill level in the tested areas.

Who Should Take the TSIA2

The Texas Success Initiative Assessment 2.0 (TSIA2) is taken by incoming undergraduate students at Texas public institutions of higher education who do not qualify for an exemption. Students can be **exempt** from taking the TSIA2 through various qualifications, including:

- Standardized Test Scores: Meet the minimum college readiness standard on the SAT®, ACT®, or the English III/Algebra II STAAR End-of-Course high school tests;

- College Preparatory Courses: Successful completion of a high school College Preparatory Course in English language arts and mathematics.

- Advanced Placement (AP) or International Baccalaureate (IB) Exams: Sufficient scores on relevant AP or IB exams that meet the institution's criteria for college readiness.

- Previous College Coursework: Completion of college-level coursework in relevant subjects (e.g., English and Math) at an accredited institution with a grade that meets the institution's requirements for readiness.

- Military Service: Veterans, active-duty military personnel, and reservists who have served for at least three years preceding enrollment.

- Other Assessments: Scores on the STAAR (State of Texas Assessments of Academic Readiness) End-of-Course exams, as well as other state-approved assessments.

- Other Exemptions: Various other state-approved criteria may apply, including certain professional or educational achievements and specific institutional agreements.

For a complete list of exemptions and detailed criteria, students should refer to their institution's guidelines or the Texas Higher Education Coordinating Board's official documentation on TSIA2 exemptions.

Sections of the TSIA2

Every assessment within the TSIA2 test is structured as a multiple-choice exam, with the sole exception being the TSIA2 essay section, where your writing skills are evaluated through an essay. Here are the three TSIA2 test sections:

TSIA2 ELAR

On TSIA2, you will begin with the multiple-choice College Readiness Classification (CRC) Test. This test includes 30 questions covering four subcategories within two content areas:

- **Reading:** These questions assess your ability to comprehend and analyze literary, informational, and argumentative texts, including paired passages.
- **Writing:** These questions evaluate your skills in revising and editing sentences, paragraphs, and early drafts of essays.

If you do not meet the college readiness benchmark on the CRC Test, you will then take the multiple-choice English language arts and reading (ELAR) Diagnostic Test. This test contains 48 questions, divided equally between reading and writing-focused questions. The Diagnostic Test aims to provide detailed information on your strengths and weaknesses in reading and writing. Advisers will use these results to recommend appropriate courses or interventions to prepare you for college-level coursework.

TSIA2 Essay

The TSIA2 Essay Test, alongside the multiple-choice ELAR component, determines your college readiness in reading and writing. You will write a 300- to 600-word essay in response to a randomly selected prompt. Your essay will be evaluated based on six key criteria:

- Purpose and Focus: Clarity and coherence in addressing the issue.
- Organization and Structure: Logical ordering and connection of ideas.
- Development and Support: Adequate development and support of ideas.
- Sentence Variety and Style: Control of vocabulary, voice, and sentence structure.
- Mechanical Conventions: Use of Standard English conventions.
- Critical Thinking: Ability to communicate a viewpoint and reasoned relationships among ideas.

No dictionaries or external resources are allowed, but you may request plain scratch paper to plan your essay, which will be collected after the test session.

TSIA2 Mathematics

Non-exempt students will start with the multiple-choice Mathematics College Readiness Classification (CRC) Test, consisting of 20 questions across four content areas:

- Quantitative Reasoning: Calculating ratios, proportions, percentages, and interpreting linear equations.

- Algebraic Reasoning: Solving various equations, evaluating functions, and solving contextual algebraic problems.
- Geometric and Spatial Reasoning: Unit conversion, solving geometric problems, performing transformations, and applying right triangle trigonometry.
- Probabilistic and Statistical Reasoning: Classifying data, creating data representations, computing probabilities, and describing measures of data center and spread.

If you do not meet the benchmark, you will take the multiple-choice Mathematics Diagnostic Test, which includes 48 questions, with 12 questions from each content area mentioned above. This test helps identify your strengths and weaknesses in mathematics. Advisers use these results to recommend suitable courses or interventions to help you succeed in college-level mathematics.

Note: Handheld calculators are not permitted during the TSIA2 Mathematics Test. Some questions will provide pop-up calculators, such as basic, square root, and graphing calculators (TI-84). For accommodated tests (e.g., paper-and-pencil, braille, or audio), you may use a square root calculator.

TSIA2 Registration and Testing: What You Need to Know

It is a good idea to contact the advising or testing office of the institution you plan to attend. They will provide specific instructions on registration, testing dates, and locations. Some institutions may require or offer an information session to explain the TSIA2 process and its importance.

To register for the test, follow the online registration instructions provided by your institution's advising or testing office. If online registration is unavailable, you may need to register at the advising or testing office. Be aware that there may be a fee for taking the TSIA2, so confirm the amount and payment methods with your institution.

Preparing for the TSIA2 is key to your success. Make use of study guides, like this one, practice tests, and other resources available online or through your institution. Concentrate on your weaker areas to boost your performance.

On the test day, arrive at the testing center on time with the required identification and materials. Confirm the list of acceptable IDs and items you can bring from the testing office. Some institutions may offer an online proctoring option for the TSIA2, so check with your institution for details and requirements. Remember that the TSIA2 is untimed, so take your time to read and answer each question carefully.

In most cases, you will receive your TSIA2 scores immediately after completing the test. Schedule a session with your academic adviser or counselor to discuss your results. They will help you understand your scores and recommend appropriate courses or interventions based on your performance.

If you have any uncertainties about the registration process or the test itself, don't hesitate to contact the advising or testing office for clarification. Keep track of any deadlines or additional requirements set by your institution to ensure a smooth testing process. After taking the test, make sure to follow up with your adviser to plan your course schedule based on your TSIA2 results.

Administration of the TSIA2

The TSIA2 is typically administered digitally on a computer. Its computer-adaptive nature means that the test adjusts the difficulty level of questions based on the test-taker's responses. Testing can be done at designated testing centers, including some high schools and college campuses. Some colleges may offer remote testing options as well.

Because the TSIA2 tests are untimed, the duration varies. The amount of time spent on each section will depend on the individual. Some students may complete a section in as little as 30 minutes, while others may take over an hour.

It's not always necessary to take all sections of the TSIA2 in one sitting. Some colleges may schedule different parts of the test on different days. It can be helpful for those who prefer to focus on one subject at a time, reducing test fatigue.

On test day, you will need to bring a valid form of identification. Check with the institution for specific ID requirements, as these can vary. Personal items such as mobile phones, calculators, or other electronic devices are typically not allowed in the testing area.

In most cases, educational institutions deliver the TSIA2 electronically, where you will be supplied with scratch paper. Calculators are not permitted for the mathematics sections; however, an on-screen calculator will become available for select questions within the test interface. If your institution offers the paper-based version of the TSIA2, you may use a basic four-function calculator provided by the school for certain parts of the math test. More advanced calculators, like scientific or graphing calculators, are not allowed regardless of the test format.

Outcomes and Implications of TSIA2 Scores

The TSIA2 is a computer-based test that provides immediate feedback upon completion of each section. As soon as you finish, you can request the testing center to print your TSIA2 score report. The TSIA2 employs a scaled scoring system, where your raw score—the number of questions you answered correctly—is converted into a scaled score. This method accounts for question difficulty and ensures a consistent scoring standard.

The following are College Readiness Benchmarks for tests taken on or after 2021/01/11. Students who meet or exceed the established benchmarks are deemed "college ready." This designation allows them to enroll in any introductory college course, such as English composition, history, government, or college algebra, without the need for remedial classes.

- Mathematics: a minimum score of 950 or less than 950 and a diagnostic level 6.

- ELAR: a minimum score of 945 on the multiple-choice section with an essay score of 5-8, or less than 945 on the multiple-choice section, a diagnostic level of 5 or 6, and an essay score of 5-8.

These benchmarks may change in the future. You can find the latest information at this link: https://tea.texas.gov/academics/college-career-and-military-prep/the-tsia-texas-success-initiative-assessment. This link may be subject to change. If it has changed, you can still find relevant information at https://tea.texas.gov.

After completing the assessment, you will receive one of the following score levels: Basic, Proficient, and Advanced.

- Basic: indicates that your performance needs to improve significantly in the content area.

- Proficient: indicates you have demonstrated skill in the content area, but there's room for improvement.

- Advanced: indicates that you have well-developed skills in the content area.

Along with these descriptors, you will receive an explanation detailing your strengths and weaknesses.

Using Your Scores

You can use these scores to send to your college of choice immediately, and they will remain available in the TSIA2 student portal for future use, such as if you decide to transfer to another school. Your TSIA2 score determines your level of college curriculum readiness, but your advisor will ultimately decide your course placement. This decision may include remedial courses or direct entry into college-level courses, depending on your scores and other factors such as your high school GPA and academic records. Advisors will also consider your declared major, if applicable, in the decision-making process.

Retaking the TSIA2

If you are satisfied with your enrollment status, placement, or options, you can proceed to enroll as appropriate. If you receive a low score and are not satisfied with your placement, you can retake the exam. Retakes are available year-round, but your college may have specific guidelines about when you can complete it. It is advisable to discuss your test results and options with your college advisor. Remember, you are more likely to improve your score on a retake if you study before taking the exam again.

Developmental Courses and Placement

If you choose not to retake the exam, your advisor will place you in remedial courses or the appropriate level of courses based on your TSIA2 results. It is possible to perform well in some sections and poorly in others; your course placement will be affected only in those content areas—whether math, reading, or writing-heavy courses. Performing well on the TSIA2 can allow you to place into college-level courses without the need for remedial classes, saving you time and money. Developmental courses should be seen as an opportunity for growth, not a setback, and many colleges offer resources such as tutoring, study workshops, and additional practice tests to help you improve.

Understanding the logistics of the TSIA2, from registration to scoring, can help you approach the test with greater confidence and a clear plan for success.

ACE THE TSIA2: STRATEGIES FOR SUCCESS

You know you will have to take the TSIA2. No matter how good a student you have been in the past, those butterflies in your stomach flutter anyway. Luckily, you still have a few weeks or months to prepare. Now what?

Your performance on the test will be largely determined by 1) how well you've studied the relevant materials in the past and 2) how well you familiarize and prepare for the test in the weeks and months prior to the test.

Based on our own test-taking experiences and scientific studies of test preparation, memorization, and cognitive psychology, we summarized the following strategies to facilitate and optimize your test preparation.

Choose the Right Test Preparation Tool

Test preparation tools can include courses, books, tutors, flash cards, and so on. Depending on your individual needs and current readiness, the best tool or combination of tools can be different. You are the most qualified person to assess what's best for yourself. When chosen properly, the right tool(s) can save you considerable time and enhance your test performance.

This book strives to strike the right balance between comprehensiveness and conciseness. We provide sufficient coverage to enable you to pass the test with a comfortable safety margin or earn a high score, but keep things relatively concise and to the point to help you get ready for the test as quickly as feasible.

Study the Preparation Materials with Systematic Repetition

We ourselves have been tested countless times in academic and professional settings. Based on those experiences and scientific research, we know that learning is more effective when repeated in spaced-out sessions.

Information repeatedly learned over a spaced-out period allows a learner to better remember and better recall the information being learned. In fact, strategically spaced repetition has been scientifically proven to better encode information into long-term memory.

When applying this learning principle, you will want to be systematic about test preparation: First, start early so that you do not have to cram right before the test. Second, while studying new materials, methodically review the older materials you studied a few days ago, well before your memory begins to fade. Using this strategy, you can go through the exam preparation materials at an aggressive rate and still maintain satisfactory retention because you repeatedly reinforce your fading memories.

Another highly beneficial practice can also be helpful: as you take practice tests, take note of those questions you answered incorrectly, or you answered correctly but want to review again anyway. Then write down the page number and question number for each. In the days and weeks that follow, you can systematically revisit the questions multiple times so that you can commit the current information to memory.

On the following page, you'll find a customized plan for a typical student to be well-prepared for the TSIA2 test in 30 days, which utilizes the systematic repetition technique.

Apply Memorization Techniques

Rule number one for memorization is comprehension. A good understanding will go a long way in ensuring long-term memory and effective recall. However, rote memorization is still invariably needed in almost all studies. In such situations, the application of various memorization techniques can help tremendously with retaining information effectively.

Many books have been written on this subject. But most advice boils down to two techniques: imagination and association. These techniques are beyond the scope of this book, but a quick Google search will generate ample resources. You will be amazed how handy these techniques can be in test preparation and beyond.

Take Practice Tests

Taking practice tests is beneficial on multiple fronts:
- Helps familiarize you with the format, coverage, and difficulty level of the test.
- Helps you apply the knowledge you have learned in a different context, reinforcing memory retention.
- Helps you learn from having to figure out the correct answer since you'll probably run into questions where you don't know the answer, or you answer incorrectly.
- Boosts your confidence and eases your nervousness when taking the actual exam thanks to performing increasingly better on practice exams.
- Consequently, taking practice tests is an integral part of preparing for any test.

Devote Yourself

For tests with set dates that you have no choice over, plan early and leave yourself enough time to prepare.

For those tests that you can choose a test date, you have your choice of two diametrically different approaches to prepare:
- **Approach #1.** Devote every hour you can to preparing for the exam, and then take it as soon as you feel ready.
- **Approach #2.** Fall prey to all the distractions in life, and study the materials at your leisure, halfheartedly in a drawn-out process. Procrastinate until you have your back against a wall and must take the test.

The more drawn-out the process, the more time you will have to spend reinforcing fading memories. In the end, you spend more total hours on exam preparation if you adopt the second approach.

Thus, in test preparation, if you would like to reduce the cumulative amount of "pain" you must endure and increase your odds of scoring well, then the best approach is to completely commit yourself to a single-minded, intensive preparation period. You can then take the exam when you feel confident and ready.

TSIA2 30-Day Test Prep Study Plan

The 30-day study plan in the following page is designed to help you prepare effectively for the TSIA2 exam while balancing your time and energy. Here's how you can optimize your study sessions by following the schedule:

1. Daily Focus and Goal Setting

Each day of the 30-day plan is intentionally focused on one or two core areas—Reading, Writing, Mathematics, and Essay preparation. By dedicating specific days to each section, you avoid overloading yourself and maintain a steady, focused progression. Ensure you set realistic goals for each session, such as completing a chapter or mastering a set of practice questions.

2. Efficient Time Management

- Study Blocks: Allocate 1–2 hours per day to your studies, breaking them into shorter, focused blocks (e.g., 30–45 minutes per block). Use techniques like the Pomodoro method (25 minutes study, 5 minutes break) to stay focused and avoid burnout.

- Prioritize Weak Areas: If you know certain sections are more challenging for you (e.g., math or essay writing), plan to spend more time on those days.

3. Balancing Study and Review

- Initial Study: During the first two weeks, focus on learning and practicing new content (e.g., reading strategies, grammar rules, math operations). This will build your foundational skills and familiarity with test concepts.

- Review Periods: The second half of the month includes dedicated review days. These are critical for reinforcing knowledge and identifying areas where you may need additional practice. Use these days to go over incorrect answers from practice tests, review key formulas, or refine your essay-writing techniques.

4. Practice Tests and Test Simulation

- Practice Under Real Conditions: On Day 21 and Day 28, take full-length practice tests in one sitting, replicating test-day conditions. This will help you gauge your readiness and stamina for the actual exam.

- Analyze Your Performance: Use the review days following each practice test to analyze your mistakes and review the correct answers. Look for patterns in your errors—whether it's certain types of math problems or recurring grammar mistakes—and focus on improving those areas.

5. Rest and Recharge

- Planned Breaks: Day 23 is a scheduled break in the middle of your study plan. Use this day to relax and recharge. Taking breaks is important for maintaining mental clarity and preventing burnout, especially during intensive test prep.

- Daily Breaks: Remember to schedule short breaks during your study sessions to maintain focus and retain information more effectively. Even a 5-minute break can help reset your mind.

6. Building Confidence for Test Day

- Final Reviews: The last few days are dedicated to reviewing all major sections, including essay writing, math concepts, and key reading strategies. These days are designed to boost your confidence by reinforcing what you've learned throughout the month.

- Positive Mindset: Use these final days to cultivate a positive mindset. Remind yourself of how much progress you've made, and trust in the preparation you've done.

30-Day Study System

Day 1	Day 2	Day 3	Day 4	Day 5
Intro & Reading	Reading	Take Reading Test	Writing	Writing
Day 6	**Day 7**	**Day 8**	**Day 9**	**Day 10**
Take Writing Test	Essay	Math §1	Math §2	Math §3
Day 11	**Day 12**	**Day 13**	**Day 14**	**Day 15**
Math §4	Math §5	Math §5	Math §5	Review Math §1-5
Day 16	**Day 17**	**Day 18**	**Day 19**	**Day 20**
Math Practice Q's	Review Reading	Review Writing	Review Math	Review Math
Day 21	**Day 22**	**Day 23**	**Day 24**	**Day 25**
Practice Test 1	Review Practice Test 1	Take a Break!	Review Reading	Review Writing
Day 26	**Day 27**	**Day 28**	**Day 29**	**Day 30**
Review Math	Review Math	Practice Test 2	Review Practice Test 2	Review Essay

I'm Ready!

By sticking to this study plan, managing your time effectively, and focusing on both learning and review, you'll be well-prepared to tackle the TSIA2 exam with confidence.

SUCCESS SKILLS FOR TEST DAY

Excelling in the TSIA2 test requires not just a good grasp of the subject matter but also effective test-taking strategies and the ability to manage test anxiety. Before you embark on the journey of preparation, it's imperative to understand what's expected of you. Different schools may require different sections of the TSIA2. Check with your institution to confirm which parts of the TSIA2 you must take. This information is typically available on the college's website or through its admissions office. Once you know the requirements, you can tailor your study plan accordingly.

Schedule Your Test

Strategically planning when to take the TSIA2 test can give you an edge. Consider your schedule and current workload—choose a time when you're least likely to be stressed by other obligations. Some students prefer to take the test after a period of intensive study, while others may opt for a date that allows them to retake sections if necessary. Ensure you know the deadlines and give yourself enough time to prepare.

Take "Easy" Test Sections First

When taking the TSIA2 in one sitting, the standard order of the sections is predetermined. Typically, the test starts with the English Language Arts and Reading (ELAR) section, followed by the Mathematics section. This sequence ensures a consistent testing experience for all examinees.

However, if you prefer to take the sections in a different order, you have the flexibility to take the sections separately on different dates. By scheduling the sections individually, you can choose the order that works best for you.

If you choose to take the TSIA2 sections on different dates to get the order you prefer, your strategy for the order in which to tackle the test sections should be based on self-assessment. If you're more confident in English, starting with the ELAR section could be a morale booster, setting a positive tone for the rest of the exam. Conversely, if math is your strong suit, leading with that might get you in the right headspace. It's a personal choice, so choose the sequence that you feel will maximize your performance.

It's helpful to go into the TSIA2 with a growth mindset. Most institutions allow you to retake the test after a certain period if you don't achieve the desired score in a particular section. Knowing this should alleviate some pressure—your first attempt isn't all-or-nothing. Check with your institution for specific retake policies.

Get Comfortable with CAT

The TSIA2 is a computer-adaptive test (CAT), meaning that the difficulty of the questions is based on your previous answers. Familiarize yourself with this format by using CAT practice tests. As you won't be able to return to a question once you've moved on, it's crucial to find a balance between not rushing and not lingering too long on any single question.

In contrast to paper-based exams, where you can skip questions and return to them later, digital tests lock you into answering each question as it appears; there's no option to leave it unanswered and revisit it afterward. However, incorrect answers do not result in point deductions. Therefore, if you find yourself completely unable to answer a question, it's advisable to take your best shot at guessing and proceed to the next question.

Navigating Multiple-Choice Questions

With four possible answers for every question, the TSIA2 offers a chance at scoring points even when you're unsure of the correct answer. Educated guessing is a skill you can develop. Look for contextual clues within the question and eliminate the most obviously incorrect answers to improve your odds of guessing correctly. Since there's no penalty for wrong answers, it's to your advantage to answer every question.

CONQUER TEST ANXIETY

Dealing with test anxiety is a crucial skill that can significantly impact one's academic and professional life. Test anxiety is a type of performance anxiety that occurs when an individual feels an intense fear or panic before, during, or after an examination. It can manifest through various symptoms, including nervousness, difficulty concentrating, negative thoughts, physical symptoms such as headaches or nausea, and even panic attacks. Fortunately, there are effective strategies to manage and overcome test anxiety, ensuring that it doesn't hinder one's ability to perform to the best of their abilities.

Test anxiety can stem from fear of failure, lack of preparation, previous negative experiences, or high pressure to perform well. Identifying the root cause is essential in developing a targeted approach to manage anxiety.

One of the most effective ways to reduce test anxiety is thorough preparation. Begin studying well in advance of the test date. This allows ample time to understand the material, reducing the likelihood of feeling overwhelmed as the test approaches. Create a study plan that breaks down the material into manageable sections. Use organizers, such as outlines, flashcards, or mind maps, to make the study process more efficient and less daunting.

Simulating test conditions can help alleviate anxiety. Practice with timed quizzes or tests in a quiet environment. This not only helps with time management but also makes the actual test environment feel more familiar.

Mindset and Attitude Adjustments

Transform negative thoughts into positive affirmations. Instead of thinking, "I'm going to fail," tell yourself, "I'm prepared and will do my best." Positive thinking can enhance self-confidence and reduce nervousness. Furthermore, accept that it's okay to be nervous and that feeling anxious doesn't mean you will perform poorly. Recognize that anxiety can sometimes motivate you to prepare better.

Relaxation Techniques

Deep breathing exercises can be effective in managing physical symptoms of anxiety. Techniques such as the 4-7-8 method, where you inhale for four seconds, hold your breath for seven seconds, and exhale for eight seconds, can help calm the nervous system.

The Progressive Muscle Relaxation technique can also help. This involves tensing and then slowly relaxing each muscle group in the body to reduce the physical symptoms of stress and anxiety.

During the Test

The TSIA2 test offers a unique and significant advantage over other tests: you are not timed and hence don't have to perform under time pressure. So, take your time and don't rush through. If you find yourself becoming anxious, pause for a moment, take a few deep breaths, and refocus on the question in front of you. Avoid dwelling on what you might have gotten wrong or what's coming next.

Test anxiety is a common challenge that many face, but it doesn't have to be a barrier to success. By understanding its causes, implementing effective study and preparation strategies, adopting relaxation techniques, and seeking support when needed, individuals can overcome test anxiety. Remember, the goal is not to eliminate anxiety completely but to manage it effectively so that it doesn't interfere with performance.

Part I: TSIA2 Reading

Introduction

The Texas Success Initiative Assessment 2.0 (TSIA2) is a comprehensive placement test designed to assess students' readiness for college-level coursework in Texas. Specifically, the English Language Arts and Reading (ELAR) section of the TSIA2 evaluates a student's proficiency in reading and writing, crucial skills necessary for academic success in higher education.

The TSIA2 ELAR test is structured to measure your abilities in two key areas: reading comprehension and writing skills. The **reading component** includes a variety of passages and questions designed to assess your ability to understand, analyze, and synthesize written material. This section covers a range of texts, including literary works, informational texts, and argumentative pieces, ensuring a thorough evaluation of your reading proficiency.

The **writing component** of the TSIA2 ELAR test focuses on your ability to revise and edit written content. It includes questions that assess your skills in sentence structure, grammar, and the organization of ideas. Additionally, the test includes an **essay section**, where you are required to write a coherent and well-structured essay in response to a given prompt. This essay evaluates your ability to articulate your thoughts clearly, develop arguments, and use standard written English effectively.

The TSIA2 ELAR test is untimed, allowing you to take the necessary time to read, analyze, and respond to each question thoughtfully. Computer-adaptive technology ensures that the difficulty of the questions adjusts based on your responses, providing a more accurate measure of your skills.

A test taker will encounter the TSIA2 ELAR Diagnostic Test if they do not meet the college readiness benchmark on the initial College Readiness Classification (CRC) Test. The CRC Test is the first part of the TSIA2 ELAR assessment, which includes multiple-choice questions focused on reading and writing skills. The additional Diagnostic Test aims to provide detailed information about the test taker's strengths and weaknesses in ELAR. The Diagnostic Test is designed to identify specific areas where the test taker may need further development and support.

You will not encounter the Diagnostic Test if you score above the then-current college readiness benchmark on the initial College Readiness Classification (CRC) Test. This book's focus is the CRC Test portion of the TSIA2.

In Part I of this book, we'll focus on TSIA2's reading component. We'll discuss the writing component and essay section in Part II, and III of this book.

Reading Skills Being Tested

The TSIA2 ELAR reading component includes reading-focused test questions that assess a student's ability to analyze and understand both literary and informational texts. These questions are divided into two primary categories:

Literary Text Analysis

- Explicit Information: Students are expected to identify and understand ideas that are clearly stated in literary texts.

- Inferences: This involves drawing reasonable conclusions based on the information provided in the text.

- Author's Craft: Students analyze the author's word choice, text structure, purpose, audience, and perspective to understand how these elements contribute to the overall meaning.

- Vocabulary: Students determine the meaning of words and phrases in context within literary texts.

Informational Text Analysis and Synthesis

- Main Ideas and Supporting Details: Students identify main ideas and comprehend information that is explicitly stated and clearly indicated in informational texts.
- Inferences (Single-Passage): This involves drawing reasonable conclusions based on the information provided in a single passage of informational text.
- Author's Craft: Similar to literary text analysis, this involves analyzing the author's word choice, text structure, purpose, and audience to understand the meaning in informational texts.
- Vocabulary: Students determine the meaning of words and phrases in context within informational texts, and for diagnostic purposes, they also apply decoding skills.
- Synthesis: Students draw reasonable connections between two related argumentative texts, determine rhetorical relationships, analyze commonalities, and examine claims and counterclaims.

Reading-Focused Questions Overview

A complete TSIA2 ELAR session involves 30 questions, equally divided between reading and writing. These questions are presented in an integrated manner, without any interruptions or clear separations between the reading and writing components. The test starts with reading-focused questions, beginning with the Literary Text Analysis section, followed by writing-focused questions, starting with the Essay Revision and Editing section.

There are a total of 15 reading-focused questions, with the following structure:

- Literary Text Analysis: 1 long passage with 4 questions focused on analyzing literary texts.
- Informational Text Analysis and Synthesis: 11 questions including:
    - Synthesis (Paired Argumentative Passages): 2 paired passages with 1 question for each paired passages.
    - Various Informational Text Analysis Types: 9 questions selected algorithmically from other informational text categories.

TSIA2 Passage Types

Long Literary Passage

The TSIA2 ELAR starts with a long literary passage, accompanied by a set of four questions. This passage is typically extracted from a fiction book but can represent a broad spectrum of genres, themes, and writing styles. This passage and its corresponding questions are designed to challenge and engage the reader on multiple levels. They require the students to immerse themselves into the story, understand the nuanced voices of characters, and grasp the subtle undercurrents of the plot and character dynamics.

This passage assesses the student's ability to quickly adapt to different writing styles and discern the various perspectives that literature often presents. Depending on whether the passage is a first-person narrative, inviting readers into the intimate thoughts of a character, or a third-person omniscient perspective, offering a bird's-eye view of the unfolding storyline, students must adjust their analytical lens accordingly.

The TSIA2 ELAR challenges you to quickly recognize the main characters and deduce how their relationships and differences drive the narrative forward. Understanding these character dynamics is crucial, as it will help you navigate the passage and confidently answer the accompanying questions.

When reading this passage, always look for 'what's at stake' within the narrative by asking questions such as: What are the characters striving for? What challenges do they face? What factors create the conflict/obstacle, and how is the situation resolved?

Medium-Length Paired Argumentative Passage

Following the long literary passage, you'll read two paired medium-length passages. Each pair is on a single topic, with each passage within the pair presenting distinct viewpoints. This pair of passages is followed by one question. With two pairs (a total of four passages), you will run into a total of two questions related to paired passages.

Here is an example of a paired passage: one passage might explore the benefits of a new environmental policy, while the second passage could discuss the potential drawbacks of the same policy. This structure is designed to test your ability to understand, compare, and analyze different perspectives on the same subject.

The paired passage format helps gauge your ability to integrate and synthesize information from multiple sources, an essential skill for academic success. To prepare effectively, focus on practicing with diverse reading materials and honing your ability to identify main ideas, supporting details, and the relationships between different viewpoints.

Short Informational Discrete Passage

An "informational discrete passage" in the context of reading comprehension tests like the TSIA2 refers to a standalone text that presents factual, non-fiction content on a specific topic. Unlike literary passages, which may explore themes, characters, and narratives through fiction, informational discrete passages aim to convey knowledge, data, or insights about real-world subjects such as history, science, technology, social sciences, or current events.

The key characteristics of an informational discrete passage include:

- Factual Content: The passage provides accurate information about a particular subject without the inclusion of fictional elements.

- Standalone Text: It is "discrete" in the sense that it is self-contained and does not require prior knowledge or context from other texts to be understood. Each passage is complete in itself.

- Objective Tone: Typically, these passages maintain an objective, neutral tone, focusing on delivering information rather than persuading the reader or exploring an author's personal narrative.

- Assessment of Comprehension Skills: Questions based on these passages test the reader's ability to understand and interpret factual information. This includes identifying main ideas, supporting details, understanding vocabulary in context, making inferences, and summarizing the passage.

Each of these passages will be followed by one question.

Passage Genres: Literary and Informational

TSIA2 passages generally fall into two broad genres: literary (fiction) and informational (non-fiction). Understanding these genres and the subtypes within informational texts is useful for test-takers to navigate the passages effectively.

Literary (Fiction) Passages

Literary passages are fictional narratives that come from novels, short stories, and dramas. These texts are characterized by their use of language to evoke emotions, their development of complex characters, and often, their exploration of universal themes through plot and setting. Literary texts demand an understanding of various elements such as:

- Narrative Voice: The perspective from which the story is told, which can be first-person, second-person, or third-person.
- Character Development: How characters are presented and evolve through the story, their motivations, relationships, and growth or change.
- Plot and Structure: The sequence of events and how they are organized within the narrative.
- Themes: The underlying messages or moral questions the text addresses.
- Literary Devices: The use of metaphors, similes, alliteration, irony, and other stylistic elements to enhance the storytelling.

Informational (Non-Fiction) Passages

Informational passages convey factual information about the world. Unlike literary texts, they are intended to inform, explain, or persuade rather than to entertain. They encompass a range of text types, including:

Narrative Non-Fiction

Although narrative non-fiction tells true stories, it employs many of the same techniques as fiction, such as character development and a structured plot. Examples include:

- Biographies: The life story of a person, told by someone else.
- Autobiographies: The story of a person's life, told by that person.
- Historical Accounts: Descriptions of historical events presented in a narrative format.

Expository Texts

Expository texts are explanatory in nature. They describe a topic in detail and are structured to educate the reader about a specific subject. Types of expository texts include:

- Textbooks: Provide detailed information on particular subjects.
- How-to Guides: Instruct the reader on ways to perform certain tasks.
- Articles: Focus on specific topics, providing explanations and insights.

Persuasive Texts

Persuasive texts aim to convince the reader to adopt a particular viewpoint or take a specific action. They include:

- Editorials: Articles that represent the opinion of the editor or publisher.
- Speeches: Written to persuade an audience on particular issues.
- Advertisements: Crafted to persuade consumers to purchase a product or service.

Argumentative Texts

Closely related to persuasive texts, argumentative writings present a viewpoint on a debatable issue, supported by evidence and reasoning. These include:

- Essays: Formal writings that articulate a position on a particular topic, supported by analysis and evidence.
- Legal Documents: Writings that argue for a particular interpretation of the law.
- Critical Reviews: Offer assessments of works, such as books or films, backed by critical reasoning.

Understanding these different genres and sub-genres can help test-takers identify them and adjust their reading strategies accordingly. For instance, literary passages require an appreciation of nuance and metaphor, whereas informational texts call for a more analytical approach, focusing on argument structure and factual details. Recognizing these distinctions can enhance a student's ability to interpret and analyze passages effectively on reading comprehension tests.

ELAR READING QUESTION TYPES

In this chapter, we will review the various types of questions that appear on the TSIA2 ELAR: questions about information and ideas, questions about rhetoric, questions comparing two passages, and vocabulary questions, and so on.

1. Questions Regarding Central Ideas and Themes

The ability to determine central ideas and themes in a passage is pivotal for a test taker preparing for the TSIA2 ELAR. This skill assesses your capacity to grasp the essence of what you read, identifying the main point or message the author intends to communicate and the underlying concepts or insights that recur throughout the text.

Understanding the central idea and themes is crucial because it forms the backbone of comprehension. It's about seeing beyond the words to grasp the 'why' and 'what' of the text. This ability is foundational, enhancing your reading comprehension and preparing you for academic success.

Strategies for Success:

- **Preview and Predict:** Start by examining titles, headings, and introductory sentences to determine the passage's main focus.
- **Note Repetitions:** Pay attention to ideas, phrases, or motifs repeated throughout the text; these often indicate key themes.
- **Summarize:** Try to encapsulate the passage's main point in a single sentence. This exercise forces you to distill the essence of what you've read.
- **Ask Questions:** While reading, continually ask yourself, "What's the main point here?" and "What themes are emerging?"
- **Context Clues:** Use context clues around unfamiliar words or concepts to understand their importance to the central idea or themes.

Application in Test Preparation:

To prepare for this question type, engage with a wide range of reading materials. After reading a piece, practice writing a brief summary of the central idea and list out potential themes. Discuss these with peers or mentors to explore different perspectives and interpretations. Utilize practice tests to familiarize yourself with how the TSIA2 frames these questions, and review explanations for both correct and incorrect answers to deepen your understanding.

Common Pitfalls and How to Avoid Them:

- **Getting Lost in Details:** Don't let minor details distract you from the overall message. Always tie specifics back to the main idea or themes.

- **Overgeneralization:** Avoid too broad interpretations. Ensure your understanding of the central idea or themes is specific and supported by the text.

- **Misinterpreting the Text:** This can happen if you rush or skim too quickly. Take your time to fully engage with the passage, rereading complex or dense parts.

Example Passage 1

The most notable distinction between living and inanimate things is that the former maintain themselves by renewal. A stone when struck resists. If its resistance is greater than the force of the blow struck, it remains outwardly unchanged. Otherwise, it is shattered into smaller bits. Never does the stone attempt to react in such a way that it may maintain itself against the blow, much less so as to render the blow a contributing factor to its own continued action. While the living thing may easily be crushed by superior force, it nonetheless tries to turn the energies which act upon it into means of its own further existence. If it cannot do so, it does not just split into smaller pieces (at least in the higher forms of life), but loses its identity as a living thing.

As long as it endures, it struggles to use surrounding energies in its own behalf. It uses light, air, moisture, and the material of soil. To say that it uses them is to say that it turns them into means of its own conservation. As long as it is growing, the energy it expends in thus turning the environment to account is more than compensated for by the return it gets: it grows. Understanding the word "control" in this sense, it may be said that a living being is one that subjugates and controls for its own continued activity the energies that would otherwise use it up. Life is a self-renewing process through action upon the environment. (*Democracy and Education*, by John Dewey)

Question: The main idea of this passage is to:

A) Highlight the resilience of inanimate objects to external forces.

B) Illustrate the mechanisms through which living things utilize environmental elements.

C) Argue that living things maintain themselves by renewal.

D) Discuss the environmental factors affecting the growth of living organisms.

Answer: C) Argue that living things maintain themselves by renewal.

Explanation: The passage presents a clear distinction between living and inanimate objects, emphasizing that the defining characteristic of living beings is their ability to maintain and renew themselves. This is contrasted with inanimate objects like stones, which do not have the capability to use external forces to their advantage or to renew themselves in the face of destruction. The central argument revolves around the concept of self-renewal as a unique and defining feature of life, making option C the correct answer. It encapsulates the passage's main point about the intrinsic capacity of living organisms to harness and transform environmental energies for their own continued existence and growth.

Example Passage 2

In this Autobiography I shall keep in mind the fact that I am speaking from the grave. I am literally speaking from the grave, because I shall be dead when the book issues from the press. I speak from the grave rather than with my living tongue, for a good reason: I can speak thence freely. When a man is writing a book dealing with the privacies of his life—a book which is to be read while he is still alive—he shrinks from speaking his whole frank mind; all his attempts to do it fail, he recognizes that he is trying to do a thing which is wholly impossible to a human being. The frankest and freest and privatest product of

the human mind and heart is a love letter; the writer gets his limitless freedom of statement and expression from his sense that no stranger is going to see what he is writing.
(*The Autobiography of Mark Twain*, by Mark Twain)

Question: The main purpose of this passage is to

A) Emphasize the limitations that living authors face when writing autobiographies.

B) Argue the superiority of love letters as forms of expression.

C) Illustrate the challenges of writing about one's private life for public consumption.

D) Explain the author's decision to write as if speaking from the grave in his autobiography.

Answer: D) Explain the author's decision to write as if speaking from the grave in his autobiography.

Explanation: The passage primarily focuses on the author's rationale for adopting a unique narrative perspective in his autobiography — that of speaking from the grave. This approach is chosen to achieve a level of frankness and freedom not possible when one is constrained by the considerations and repercussions of speaking as a living person. While the passage touches upon the nature of writing about private matters and compares it to the freedom found in love letters, these points serve to support the main argument rather than constitute the central idea themselves. Thus, the correct answer is D, as it directly addresses the author's intention to use posthumous narration as a means to express himself without reservation.

2. Questions Regarding Details in the Passage

Detail-oriented questions on the TSIA2 ELAR evaluate your ability to identify and understand specific information within the text. These questions test your ability to pick out facts, examples, and other particulars that support the main idea or themes of the passage.

Being adept at locating details is essential for thorough comprehension. It enables you to gather evidence, understand the structure of arguments, and appreciate the nuances of the narrative or exposition. This skill is crucial for academic research, critical analysis, and practical decision-making.

Strategies for Success:

- **Active Reading and Mental Notes:** As you read, note where the key facts, names, dates, and specific information are mentioned. In a computer-based test, you won't be able to underline the text, but mental notes will still help you quickly locate details when answering questions.

- **Practice Skimming:** Improve your skimming skills to quickly locate information within the text without having to read everything thoroughly a second time.

- **Understand Question Types:** Familiarize yourself with how detail questions are phrased. Knowing if a question asks for a fact, an example, or an explanation can guide you on what to look for.

- **Context Is Key:** Always consider the detail within the passage's context to ensure correct interpretation.

Application in Test Preparation:

Engage with texts across a variety of subjects and formats. After reading, challenge yourself to recall specific details without looking back at the text. Use practice tests to hone your ability to find and interpret details.

Common Pitfalls and How to Avoid Them:

- **Overlooking Details:** Important details can be easily missed if you read too quickly. Slow down and ensure you're fully processing the information.

- **Confusing Similar Details:** Pay attention to the nuances that differentiate similar pieces of information within the text to avoid mixing them up.

- **Relying Too Much on Memory:** Don't assume you remember all the details correctly. Since the TSIA2 test has no time constraints, double-check the passage to confirm your answers.

Example Passage 1

The *Endurance* steamed along the front of this ice-flow for about seventeen miles. The glacier showed huge crevasses and high pressure ridges, and appeared to run back to ice-covered slopes or hills 1000 or 2,000 ft. high. Some bays in its front were filled with smooth ice, dotted with seals and penguins. At 4 a.m. on the 16th we reached the edge of another huge glacial overflow from the ice-sheet. The ice appeared to be coming over low hills and was heavily broken. The cliff-face was 250 to 350 ft. high, and the ice surface two miles inland was probably 2,000 ft. high. (*South!*, by Ernest Shackleton)

Question: According to the passage, which of the following is not true?

A) The Endurance traveled along the front of the ice-flow for approximately seventeen miles.

B) The glacier was devoid of any crevasses and pressure ridges.

C) Seals and penguins were spotted on some smooth ice areas in front of the glacier.

D) The ice surface two miles inland from the cliff-face was estimated to be around 2,000 ft. high.

Answer: B) The glacier was devoid of any crevasses and pressure ridges.

Explanation: The passage describes the Endurance's journey along the front of an ice-flow, detailing the presence of "huge crevasses and high pressure ridges" in the glacier. This directly contradicts option B, which falsely claims that the glacier was devoid of crevasses and pressure ridges. Options A, C, and D are all supported by the passage: A) states the distance the Endurance traveled along the ice-flow, C) mentions the wildlife observed on the smooth ice, and D) provides an estimation of the ice surface's height two miles inland. Therefore, B is the correct answer as it is the only statement not corroborated by the passage, making it untrue according to the provided text.

Example Passage 2

The dock was still for a moment. Then a barrel toppled from a pile of barrels, and a figure moved like a bird's shadow across the opening between mounds of cargo set about the pier. At the same time two men approached down a narrow street filled with the day's last light. The bigger one threw a great shadow that aped his gesticulating arms behind him on the greenish faces of the buildings. Bare feet like halved hams, shins bound with thongs and pelts, he waved one hand in explanation, while he rubbed the back of the other on his short, mahogany beard. (*The Jewels of Aptor*, by Samuel R. Delany)

Question: According to the passage, which is the most accurate description of the bigger man?

A) He was quietly observing from the shadows, unnoticed.

B) He carried a barrel on his shoulder as he walked.

C) He was barefoot, with his shins wrapped, and had a short mahogany beard.

D) He was wearing heavy boots and a long coat as he gestured animatedly.

Answer: C) He was barefoot, with his shins wrapped, and had a short mahogany beard.

Explanation: The passage vividly describes the bigger man's appearance and actions as he walks down a narrow street. It specifically mentions that his "bare feet like halved hams, shins bound with thongs and pelts," indicating that he is barefoot and has his shins wrapped. Additionally, it describes him as having a "short, mahogany beard," which he rubs with the back of his hand. These details collectively match option C, making it the most accurate description of the bigger man according to the passage. Options A, B, and D do not accurately reflect the details provided; A suggests he was hiding, B incorrectly mentions him carrying a barrel, and D describes attire not mentioned in the passage. Therefore, C is the correct answer.

3. Summarizing

Summarizing questions test your ability to distill a passage's main ideas, key details, and overall essence into a concise statement. This skill is fundamental to reading comprehension, requiring you to understand both the broader context and specific elements of the text.

The ability to summarize is invaluable across all academic disciplines and in everyday life. It allows you to efficiently communicate the core of what you've read, ensuring that you, and those you share information with, grasp the essential points without needing to digest the entire text.

Strategies for Success:

- **Identify Main Ideas:** Focus on understanding the central idea or thesis of the passage. This is often introduced in the opening sentences and concluded in the final paragraph.

- **Highlight Supporting Details:** Recognize which facts, examples, or arguments support the main idea. These are crucial for a well-rounded summary.

- **Eliminate Non-Essential Information:** Learn to distinguish between crucial details and filler content. Summaries should omit anecdotes, descriptive passages, and secondary points unless they're vital for understanding the main idea.

- **Use Your Own Words:** Practice paraphrasing the passage's content. This ensures you truly understand what you've read and can articulate it independently.

- **Structure Your Summary:** A coherent summary logically follows the flow of the original text, presenting ideas in the order they appeared.

Application in Test Preparation:

Practicing with a diverse range of texts is key. After reading a passage, try to write a summary of about three to four sentences. Compare your summaries with the original text to refine your ability to capture the essence succinctly. Engaging in group study sessions where you share and discuss summaries can also enhance your understanding and ability to communicate the central ideas.

Common Pitfalls and How to Avoid Them:

- **Being Too Verbose:** A common mistake is including too much detail. Remember, a summary should be brief and to the point.

- **Misrepresenting the Text:** Ensure your summary accurately reflects the passage. Avoid introducing personal interpretations or biases.

- **Skipping Over the Conclusion:** The author's concluding thoughts often encapsulate the central message; make sure these are included in your summary.

Example Passage 1

The development within the young of the attitudes and dispositions necessary to the continuous and progressive life of a society cannot take place by direct conveyance of beliefs, emotions, and knowledge. It takes place through the intermediary of the environment. The environment consists of the sum total of conditions which are concerned in the execution of the activity characteristic of a living being. The social environment consists of all the activities of fellow beings that are bound up in the carrying on of the activities of any one of its members. It is truly educative in its effect in the degree in which an individual shares or participates in some conjoint activity. By doing his share in the associated activity, the individual appropriates the purpose which actuates it, becomes familiar with its methods and subject matters, acquires needed skill, and is saturated with its emotional spirit. "
(*Democracy and Education*, by John Dewey)

Question: Which of the following provides the best summary of the passage?

A) The development of societal attitudes in the young is best achieved through solitary study and reflection.

B) The primary role of the environment is to provide physical conditions necessary for individual survival.

C) The most effective method of education is the Direct transmission of knowledge and values from one generation to the next.

D) Young individuals develop necessary societal attitudes through engagement in shared activities within their social environment.

Answer: D) Young individuals develop necessary societal attitudes through engagement in shared activities within their social environment.

Explanation: This passage emphasizes the importance of the social environment in the educative process, particularly how shared or conjoint activities within this environment facilitate the development of attitudes, dispositions, and skills necessary for the life of a society. It argues against the notion of education through direct conveyance of beliefs and knowledge, instead highlighting the role of participatory activities in fostering educational growth. The passage clearly states that the educative effect is maximized when an individual partakes in communal activities, thereby absorbing the collective purposes, methods, emotional spirit, and skills. Therefore, option D provides the best summary of the passage, capturing the essence that the development of societal attitudes and dispositions in the young occurs through active participation in the social environment's activities. Options A, B, and C misrepresent the passage's content by suggesting alternative methods or focuses of education that the author did not emphasize.

Example Passage 2

As the sun went down and the evening chill came on, we made preparation for bed. We stirred up the hard leather letter-sacks, and the knotty canvas bags of printed matter (knotty and uneven because of projecting ends and corners of magazines, boxes and books). We stirred them up and redisposed them in such a way as to make our bed as level as possible. And we did improve it, too, though after all our work it had an upheaved and billowy look about it, like a little piece of a stormy sea. Next we hunted up our boots from odd nooks among the mailbags where they had settled, and put them on. Then we got down our coats, vests, pantaloons and heavy woolen shirts, from the arm-loops where they had been swinging all day, and clothed ourselves in them—for, there being no ladies either at the stations or in the coach, and the weather being hot, we had looked to our comfort by stripping to our underclothing, at nine o'clock in the morning. All things being now ready, we stowed the uneasy Dictionary where it would lie as quiet as possible, and placed the water-canteens and pistols where we could find them in the dark. Then we smoked a final pipe, and swapped a final yarn; after which, we put the pipes, tobacco and bag of coin in snug holes and caves among the mailbags, and then fastened down the coach curtains all around, and made the place as "dark as the inside of a cow," as the conductor phrased it in his picturesque way. It was certainly as dark as any place could be—nothing was even dimly visible in it. And finally, we rolled ourselves up like silkworms, each person in his own blanket, and sank peacefully to sleep. (*Roughing It*, by Mark Twain)

Question: Which of the following most accurately describes what the author did before sleeping?

A) They rearranged the mailbags to create a more comfortable sleeping area and dressed in warm clothing.

B) They extinguished the campfire and ensured all mailbags were securely stowed in the coach.

C) They checked the security of the coach and set up a perimeter for protection.

D) They prepared a meal and cleaned up the dining area before settling down for the night.

Answer: A) They rearranged the mailbags to create a more comfortable sleeping area and dressed in warm clothing.

Explanation: The passage showcases the author and companions' resourcefulness while preparing for bed on a coach journey. They addressed the discomfort of their makeshift bed made from mailbags, rearranging them to achieve as level a surface as possible. Despite their efforts, the bed still appeared uneven. Acknowledging the evening chill, they retrieved and donned their clothing, which had been stored away due to the day's heat, to ensure warmth through the night. These actions, demonstrating their ability to adapt to their environment, directly correspond to option A, highlighting the dual focus on improving sleeping comfort through the adjustment of the mailbags and dressing in warm clothing to counteract the cold. Options B, C, and D introduce activities (extinguishing fires, setting up a perimeter, preparing meals, and cleaning) not mentioned in the passage, making A the most accurate description of the author's pre-sleep activities.

4. Understanding Relationships and Making Inferences

This type of question evaluates your ability to understand the relationships between various elements within the text and to make logical inferences based on the provided information. It requires a deeper level of comprehension, moving beyond the literal content to grasp the implied meanings and connections.

The skill of making inferences and understanding relationships is crucial for real-world problem-solving and critical thinking. It allows you to read between the lines, draw conclusions from subtle cues, and connect the dots in complex situations. This skill is invaluable in academics, professional settings, and everyday life, where not everything is stated explicitly.

Strategies for Success:

- **Look for Clues:** Pay attention to the text's tone, word choice, and any hints the author might give to imply relationships or to set the groundwork for inferences.

- **Connect Ideas:** Identify how different parts of the passage relate to each other through cause and effect, contrast, or similarities.

- **Read Actively:** Ask questions as you read. Consider what is stated and what can be reasonably assumed. Question why the author included certain details and what they signify.

- **Use Background Knowledge:** Apply your own knowledge and experiences to understand unstated aspects of the passage. This can help fill in gaps and make informed inferences.

- **Practice Predicting:** Try to anticipate the author's direction or the conclusion of arguments or narratives. Such attempts prepare you to make inferences and understand relationships.

Application in Test Preparation:

Engage with a wide variety of reading materials, including those that are complex or outside your comfort zone. After reading, practice articulating the relationships you've identified and the inferences you've made. Discussing texts with others can also reveal different perspectives and deepen your understanding. Utilize practice tests to familiarize yourself with these questions' format and refine your analytical skills.

Common Pitfalls and How to Avoid Them:

- **Overreaching:** Be cautious not to extend your inferences beyond what is reasonably supported by the text. Your conclusions should always be grounded in the passage.

- **Ignoring the Context:** Every inference or relationship identified should be contextual. Avoid making assumptions based on external knowledge not supported by the passage.

- **Overlooking Subtlety:** The most crucial connections or implications are often subtle. Ensure you don't gloss over these finer points in your reading.

Example Passage 1

Once upon a time Jeremiah the prophet had asked for only one thing, that he might get away from that strange cityful of perverse men to whom it was his hard lot to be the mouthpiece of a God they were forgetting. He was tired of them. "O that I had in the wilderness a lodging place of wayfaring men that I might leave my people and go from them." Well, time passed on. The people got no wiser, and Jeremiah's burden certainly got no lighter. But the very chance he prayed for came. He had a clear and honorable opportunity to go to the lodge in the wilderness, or anywhere else he liked, away from the men who had disowned his teaching. His work was done apparently, and he had failed. Yet with the door standing invitingly open, see what Jeremiah did! He "went and dwelt among the people that were left in the land." He had his chance and he did not take it! (*A Day at a Time*, by Archibald Alexander)

Question: Which of the following does this passage imply about Jeremiah?

A) Jeremiah eventually abandoned his people due to their persistent disregard for his teachings.

B) Despite his frustrations and the opportunity to leave, Jeremiah chose to stay with his people.

C) Jeremiah found solace and success in solitude, away from the city and its perverse inhabitants.

D) The people eventually embraced Jeremiah's teachings, leading to a harmonious relationship.

Answer: B) Despite his frustrations and the opportunity to leave, Jeremiah chose to stay with his people.

Explanation: The passage describes Jeremiah's deep-seated desire to escape from a difficult situation where he felt his message was not being received by a people increasingly disconnected from their faith. Despite his frustrations and the clear opportunity to leave for a quieter life in the wilderness—an opportunity he had explicitly wished for—Jeremiah decides against taking this path. When presented with a real chance to abandon the very people who had disregarded his teachings, he instead chooses to remain among them. This decision underlines a sense of duty or commitment to these people despite the personal toll it had taken on him. The passage does not suggest that he abandoned his people (A), found success in solitude (C), or that his teachings were embraced, leading to harmony (D). Instead, it clearly illustrates Jeremiah's dedication to his role and people by staying with them against his earlier desires to leave, making option B the correct and most accurate interpretation.

Example Passage 2:

In the old days Hortons Bay was a lumbering town. No one who lived in it was out of sound of the big saws in the mill by the lake. Then one year there were no more logs to make lumber. The lumber schooners came into the bay and were loaded with the cut of the mill that stood stacked in the yard. All the piles of lumber were carried away. The big mill building had all its machinery that was removable taken out and hoisted on board one of the schooners by the men who had worked in the mill. The schooner moved out of the bay toward the open lake carrying the two great saws, the traveling carriage that hurled the logs against the revolving, circular saws and all the rollers, wheels, belts and iron piled on a hull-deep load of lumber. Its open hold covered with canvas and lashed tight, the sails of the schooner filled and it moved out into the open lake, carrying with it everything that had made the mill a mill and Hortons Bay, a town. (*The End of Something*, by Ernest Hemingway)

Question: What is the likely fate of the town of Hortons Bay?

A) It will experience a revival as a tourist destination.

B) It will become a thriving fishing community.

C) It will grow into a major industrial city.

D) It will likely decline or become abandoned.

Answer: D) It will likely decline or become abandoned.

Explanation: The passage vividly depicts Hortons Bay's transition from a bustling lumbering town to a place stripped of its defining industry. With the removal of the mill's machinery, including the saws and other equipment vital for its lumber operations, and the transportation of these resources out of town, the narrative strongly implies that Hortons Bay's economic foundation has been dismantled. The specific mention that "everything that had made the mill a mill and Hortons Bay, a town" was carried away leaves little room for interpreting a future for Hortons Bay that involves economic prosperity or community sustainability in its current form. Options A, B, and C suggest potential futures that are not supported by the passage's depiction of the town's deindustrialization and the essential elements of its identity and economy being physically removed. Therefore, the most logical conclusion is option D.

5. Questions Related to a Passage's Rhetoric

In writing, rhetoric refers to the art of using language effectively and persuasively to communicate ideas, argue a point, or influence an audience. It involves the strategic selection and organization of words, phrases, and overall textual structure to achieve a specific purpose. This can include convincing readers of a particular viewpoint, motivating them to take action, evoking an emotional response, or simply informing them in a clear and engaging manner.

Mastering the analysis of a passage's rhetoric is essential for test-takers preparing for the TSIA2 ELAR. This type of question evaluates your ability to understand how an author's choice of words, structure, point of view, and overall argumentation contribute to the effectiveness and persuasiveness of the text. It's about discerning not just what the author says, but how they say it and to what end.

Rhetorical analysis lies at the heart of advanced reading comprehension. It enables you to critically engage with texts, recognizing the techniques authors use to shape their readers' thoughts and feelings. This skill is required across academic disciplines where the power of persuasion and the strength of arguments often hinge on rhetorical strategies.

Strategies for Success:

- **Analyze Word Choices**: Focus on the author's diction. Consider how the choice of words affects the passage's tone and influences the reader's perception.

- **Dissect Text Structure:** Identify the structure (e.g., argument, narrative, compare and contrast) and evaluate how it supports the author's purpose. Does the structure enhance the clarity or impact of the argument?

- **Examine Point of View:** Consider the narrative voice and perspective. How does the point of view shape the information presented and the reader's engagement with the text?

- **Determine the Purpose**: Assess why the author wrote the passage. Is it to inform, persuade, entertain, or a combination of these? How do the rhetorical choices align with this purpose?

- **Evaluate Arguments:** Scrutinize how the author builds their argument. Look for the use of evidence, reasoning, and persuasive techniques. Are the arguments logical and well-supported?

Application in Test Preparation:

To prepare for rhetorical analysis questions on the TSIA2, immerse yourself in various texts, paying particular attention to the author's rhetorical choices. Practice identifying the purpose, structure, and point of view of each text you read. Analyze how these elements work together to create a coherent and persuasive piece. Utilize practice tests, specifically focus on questions that ask you to analyze rhetoric, and review the rationales for answers to deepen your analytical skills.

Common Pitfalls and How to Avoid Them:

- **Overlooking the Rhetorical Context:** Remember that every text is written for a reason. Missing the context can lead to a superficial understanding of the passage.

- **Focusing Solely on Content:** While the what is important, the how — the rhetorical strategies used — is equally crucial for fully comprehending the text.

- **Ignoring the Effect on the Audience:** Consider the intended audience and how the text is designed to affect them. Such considerations can provide valuable insights into the author's rhetorical choices.

Example Passage 1:

Two more rounds went by, in which King was parsimonious of effort and Sandel prodigal. The latter's attempt to force a fast pace made King uncomfortable, for a fair percentage of the multitudinous blows showered upon him went home. Yet King persisted in his dogged slowness, despite the crying of the young hotheads for him to go in and fight. Again, in the sixth round, Sandel was careless, again Tom King's fearful right flashed out to the jaw, and again Sandel took the nine seconds count.
(*A Piece of Steak*, by Jack London)

Question: How do you describe the fighting style of the two boxers?

A) Both boxers preferred a fast-paced and aggressive approach.

B) King was conservative with his energy, while Sandel was more reckless and aggressive.

C) Sandel was cautious and strategic, whereas King relied on sheer power.

D) Both boxers fought cautiously, avoiding taking risks.

Answer: B) King was conservative with his energy, while Sandel was more reckless and aggressive.

Explanation: The passage contrasts the fighting styles of the two boxers, King and Sandel, during their match. King is described as "parsimonious of effort," meaning he was careful and conservative with his energy, choosing not to expend it wastefully. In contrast, Sandel is depicted as "prodigal," indicating he was reckless and lavish with his efforts, trying to force a fast pace and throwing numerous blows, many of which landed. Despite the pressure and the audience's demands for a more aggressive approach, King maintained his deliberate and slow strategy, waiting for the right moment to strike effectively, as seen in the sixth round when his powerful right-hand punch knocked Sandel down. Therefore, option B is the correct answer.

Example Passage 2:

I have heard an experienced counsellor say that he never feared the effect upon a jury of a lawyer who does not believe in his heart that his client ought to have a verdict. If he does not believe it his unbelief will appear to the jury, despite all his protestations, and will become their unbelief. This is that law whereby a work of art, of whatever kind, sets us in the same state of mind wherein the artist was when he made it. That which we do not believe we cannot adequately say, though we may repeat the words never so often. (*Essays*, by Ralph Waldo Emerson)

Question: What's the author's attitude about belief and conviction?

A) Belief and conviction in one's assertions are not essential for persuading others.

B) A person's unbelief in their own statements can be easily concealed from others.

C) Sincere belief and conviction are fundamental to influencing the beliefs of others.

D) Repetition and persistence are the most effective methods for convincing others.

Answer: C) Sincere belief and conviction are fundamental to influencing the beliefs of others.

Explanation: The passage argues that a lawyer's lack of genuine belief in a client's right to a verdict will be transparent to the jury, despite attempts to assert the contrary, and will sway the jury towards unbelief as well. The author further draws a parallel to the creation of art, suggesting that the audience is put in the same state of mind as the creator, which underscores the importance of authentic belief and conviction in both law and art. This indicates the author's stance that true belief and conviction in one's own assertions are key to effectively influencing the beliefs of others, making option C the correct answer. Options A, B, and D do not align with the author's viewpoint as presented in the passage.

Example Passage 3:

Sun Tzŭ said: Raising a group of a hundred thousand men and marching them great distances entails heavy loss on the people and a drain on the resources of the State. The daily expenditure will amount to a thousand ounces of silver. There will be commotion at home and abroad, and men will drop down exhausted on the roads. A great many families will be impeded in their labor. Hostile armies may face each other for years, striving for the victory which is decided in a single day. This being so, to remain in ignorance of the enemy's condition simply because one grudges the outlay of a hundred ounces of silver in honors and emoluments, is the height of inhumanity. One who acts thus is no leader of men, no present help to his sovereign, no master of victory. (*The Art of War*, by Sun Tzŭ)

Question: How did the author build his argument?

A) By comparing the costs of war to the benefits of peace.

B) By listing the high economic and social costs of war to demonstrate its toll on a nation.

C) By providing historical examples of successful wars that were worth their cost.

D) By appealing to the common people's desire for wealth and prosperity.

Answer: B) By listing the high economic and social costs of war to demonstrate its toll on a nation.

Explanation: The author constructs his argument by detailing the burdensome costs associated with waging war, such as the "heavy loss on the people" and the "drain on the resources of the State." He quantifies the daily expenditure and describes the societal disruptions and the physical toll on those conscripted to fight. Furthermore, he discusses the foolishness of not understanding the enemy's condition, which he equates to inhumanity and poor leadership. By elaborating on the specific consequences and potential futility of war, Sun Tzu underscores the gravity of the decision to go to war and the importance of strategic knowledge. This approach corresponds with option B, as he lists both economic and social costs to build his case against thoughtless warfare.

Example Passage 4:

In the great Central Valley of California there are only two seasons—spring and summer. The spring begins with the first rainstorm, which usually falls in November. In a few months the wonderful flowery vegetation is in full bloom, and by the end of May it is dead and dry and crisp, as if every plant had been roasted in an oven.

Then the lolling, panting flocks and herds are driven to the high, cool, green pastures of the Sierra. I was longing for the mountains about this time, but money was scarce and I couldn't see how a bread supply was to be kept up." (*My First Summer in the Sierra*, by John Muir)

Question: Which of the following best describes the relationship of the two paragraphs?

A) The first paragraph outlines a problem, and the second paragraph provides a solution.

B) The first paragraph describes a setting, and the second paragraph introduces a personal conflict.

C) The first paragraph provides historical context, while the second paragraph discusses present implications.

D) The first paragraph presents a scientific explanation, and the second paragraph provides the data to support it.

Answer: B) The first paragraph describes a setting, and the second paragraph introduces a personal conflict.

Explanation: The first paragraph sets the scene by describing the climate and seasons in the Central Valley of California, explaining the transition from spring to summer and the resulting changes in the landscape. The second paragraph shifts the focus to the narrator's personal circumstances. It introduces a conflict: the narrator's desire to go to the mountains and the financial constraint that inhibits this desire. The link between the two paragraphs is the change in seasons, which affects both the natural world and the narrator's yearnings. Option B is correct.

6. Questions Comparing Two Passages

The TSIA2 ELAR includes a section where you're asked four questions about two related passages. Within this set, two questions will task you with comparing the passages. It's common for students to struggle with these comparative questions. To become comfortable with the comparative questions on the TSIA2 ELAR, focus on identifying similarities and differences in facts and arguments. Practicing with a variety of texts can improve your ability to quickly discern the underlying connections and contrasts. Additionally, summarizing the main points in each passage and making mental notes of your comparative observations is also a helpful technique during an exam.

Example Passages: Read the passages below and answer the question based on what is stated or implied in the passages.

Passage 1

Genetically engineered (GE) foods, recognized for their safety by leading scientific and regulatory bodies like the FDA and WHO, undergo rigorous evaluations, ensuring they pose no greater risk than conventional foods. This technology allows for precise genetic modifications to enhance nutritional value, reduce allergens, and improve crop resilience, thereby increasing yields while decreasing the need for harmful chemicals. The result is a significant contribution to global food security and sustainability.

Moreover, GE crops can be biofortified to address nutritional deficiencies in developing countries, offering an efficient path to combat global malnutrition. The extensive testing of GE foods before market release further underscores their safety, making them an indispensable tool in the quest to sustainably meet increasing food demands. Embracing GE technology is essential for improving agricultural outcomes, ensuring food security, and minimizing environmental impact, thereby supporting a future where food production is safe, efficient, and sustainable.

Passage 2

Genetic engineering in food production, while lauded for its potential to improve crop yields and nutritional value, raises significant concerns regarding safety and environmental impact. Central to the debate is the lack of long-term studies on the effects of genetically engineered (GE) foods on human health. Critics argue that altering the genetic makeup of crops could result in unforeseen health consequences for humans.

Environmental consequences are equally alarming. The introduction of GE crops engineered to be herbicide-resistant has led to an increase in herbicide use, contributing to the emergence of "superweeds" resistant to conventional control methods. This necessitates the development of more potent, potentially more hazardous herbicides.

Finally, genetically engineered crops can cross-pollinate with wild relatives, leading to unintended ecological ramifications. The irreversible nature of these genetic interventions means that once the "genie is out of the bottle," there may be no turning back, posing a risk to global food security and natural ecosystems.

Question 1. Which choice best describes the relationship between Passage 1 and Passage 2?

A) Both passages argue for the safety and necessity of GE foods.

B) Passage 1 presents the benefits of GE foods, while Passage 2 discusses potential risks and concerns.

C) Passage 2 reinforces the arguments made in Passage 1 about the environmental benefits of GE foods.

D) Both passages are neutral, providing an objective overview of GE food technology.

Answer: B) Passage 1 presents the benefits of GE foods, while Passage 2 discusses potential risks and concerns.

Explanation: Passage 1 focuses on the advantages and safety of genetically engineered foods, emphasizing their contribution to food security and sustainability. In contrast, Passage 2 highlights the safety and environmental concerns associated with genetically engineered foods, such as potential health effects, increased herbicide use, and ecological risks. Therefore, the relationship between the two passages is one of contrast, with each presenting opposing views on the subject of GE foods.

Question 2. Based on the information in the two passages, on which of the following points about genetic engineering are the two authors most likely to agree?

A) Genetic engineering unequivocally improves global food security.

B) Long-term studies on GE foods' effects are unnecessary.

C) Genetic modifications can increase crop yields.

D) All genetic interventions are reversible and pose no long-term risks.

Answer: C) Genetic modifications can increase crop yields.

Explanation: Both passages mention the potential of genetic engineering to improve crop yields—Passage 1 in the context of its benefits and Passage 2 as part of the debate on its safety and environmental impact. Despite their differing viewpoints on other aspects of GE foods, this is a common ground where both authors acknowledge the technology's capacity to enhance agricultural productivity.

7. Vocabulary Questions

In the TSIA2 ELAR, 2 to 4 out of the 20 questions are dedicated to assessing vocabulary. These questions are designed to evaluate your understanding and application of vocabulary in various contexts. The format of these questions varies, with some being embedded within the context of a passage while others are structured as fill-in-the-blank questions.

Passage-based Vocabulary Questions

These questions are integrated within reading passages, similar to other comprehension questions you have encountered in this chapter. A passage is provided, and you are asked to answer questions that hinge on understanding certain vocabulary used in the text. This setup allows you to leverage the surrounding context to infer the meanings of unfamiliar words, making educated guesses possible even if the precise definition of a word isn't known to you.

Example Passage

(1) The country near the mouth of the river is wretched in the extreme: on the south side a long line of perpendicular cliffs commences, which exposes a section of the geological nature of the country. (2) The strata are of sandstone, and one layer was remarkable from being composed of a firmly-cemented conglomerate of pumice pebbles, which must have travelled more than four hundred miles, from the Andes. (3) The surface is everywhere covered up by a thick bed of gravel, which extends far and wide over the open plain. (4) Water is extremely scarce, and, where found, is almost invariably brackish. (5) The vegetation is scanty; and although there are bushes of many kinds, all are armed with formidable thorns, which seem to warn the stranger not to enter on these inhospitable regions.
(The Voyage of the Beagle, by Charles Darwin)

Question 1: In sentence 4, "brackish" mostly nearly means

A) Boiling

B) Fresh

C) Salty

D) Clear

Answer: C) Salty

Explanation: "Brackish" refers to water that has more salinity than freshwater but not as much as seawater, making "salty" the correct meaning. From the context, one can also rule out A, B, or D, even if one is not familiar with the word "brackish".

Question 2: In sentence 5, "inhospitable" most nearly means?

A) Welcoming

B) Unfriendly

C) Populated

D) Sheltered

Answer: B) Unfriendly

Explanation: "Inhospitable" refers to an environment that is harsh and difficult to live in, thus "unfriendly" is the term that most closely matches the meaning in this context.

TSIA2 ELAR Reading Practice Questions

In this chapter, you'll apply the reading skills you've honed to a practice set designed to reflect the real TSIA2 Test. You'll tackle 15 questions that simulate the test's format and content. Once you've completed them, or if you encounter any difficulties along the way, you can turn to the end of the chapter for detailed explanations of each answer to help you understand and learn.

Instructions

The TSIA2 ELAR comprises 15 reading-focused and 15 writing-focused multiple-choice questions, adding up to a total of 30 questions. The following are 15 reading-focused multiple-choice questions only. These questions evaluate your comprehension skills by determining your ability to understand both explicitly stated and implied information within a passage or a pair of passages. Some of these questions will include sentences with missing words or phrases, which you must complete by selecting the appropriate option.

While these Practice questions are not a replica of an actual TSIA2 test, they are structured to give you a similar experience and help you familiarize yourself with it. Taking this test does not predict or ensure any particular score on the actual test.

Read the passage(s) below and answer the question based on what is stated or implied in the passage(s).

> (1) When the world rang with the tale of Arctic gold, and the lure of the North gripped the heartstrings of men, Carter Weatherbee threw up his snug clerkship, turned the half of his savings over to his wife, and with the remainder bought an outfit. (2) There was no romance in his nature—the bondage of commerce had crushed all that; he was simply tired of the ceaseless grind, and wished to risk great hazards in view of corresponding returns. (3) Like many another fool, disdaining the old trails used by the Northland pioneers for a score of years, he hurried to Edmonton in the spring of the year; and there, unluckily for his soul's welfare, he allied himself with a party of men.
>
> (4) There was nothing unusual about this party, except its plans. (5) Even its goal, like that of all the other parties, was the Klondike. (6) But the route it had mapped out to attain that goal took away the breath of the hardiest native, born and bred to the vicissitudes of the Northwest. (7) Even Jacques Baptiste, born of a Chippewa woman and a renegade voyageur (having raised his first whimpers in a deerskin lodge north of the sixty-fifth parallel, and had the same hushed by blissful sucks of raw tallow), was surprised. (8) Though he sold his services to them and agreed to travel even to the never-opening ice, he shook his head ominously whenever his advice was asked.
>
> (9) Percy Cuthfert's evil star must have been in the ascendant, for he, too, joined this company of argonauts. (10) He was an ordinary man, with a bank account as deep as his culture, which is saying a good deal. (11) He had no reason to embark on such a venture—no reason in the world save that he suffered from an abnormal development of sentimentality. (12) He mistook this for the true spirit of romance and adventure. (13) Many another man has done the like, and made as fatal a mistake.
> (*The Sea-Wolf*, by Jack London)

Question 1: Based on the passage, which of the following best describes Carter Weatherbee's motivation to leave his job?

A) He was lured by the romance of adventure.

B) He desired to risk great hazards for potential gains.

C) He was following the well-trodden trails of pioneers.

D) His wife encouraged him to seek fortune in the Klondike.

Question 2: Which of the following best describes Percy Cuthfert's character in the last paragraph?

A) Adventurous and well-experienced

B) Sentimental and with a misguided sense of adventure

C) Financially savvy and risk-averse

D) Pragmatic and uninterested in wealth

Question 3: What can be inferred about Jacques Baptiste's attitude towards the men's plan?

A) He was enthusiastic and supportive.

B) He was indifferent to the risks involved.

C) He was surprised and skeptical.

D) He was eager to offer his advice.

Question 4: As used in sentence 6, "vicissitudes" most nearly means _____.

A) Boredom

B) Changes

C) Monotony

D) Ease

Passage 1:

Artificial Intelligence (AI) is a major technological advancement offering significant benefits across various sectors. In healthcare, AI aids early disease detection and personalized medicine, enhancing life quality. AI-powered educational tools provide personalized learning experiences. In industries, AI optimizes operations, cuts costs, and boosts productivity. For environmental conservation, AI monitors climate change, manages resources, and predicts natural disasters. Daily life is improved with smart devices, and in creative fields, AI spurs innovation. AI's potential to address global challenges like healthcare disparities and climate crisis is immense, amplifying human potential and making it an essential tool for humanity's future.

Passage 2:

Artificial Intelligence (AI) presents serious risks despite its advancements. Autonomous weapons could unpredictably revolutionize warfare, raising ethical concerns about machine-based life-and-death decisions. AI's data processing threatens privacy, leading to high surveillance levels. It can erode human agency by making decisions for individuals. AI's potential biases could result in unfair outcomes in healthcare and criminal justice. Superintelligent AI systems might surpass human control, posing existential threats. These risks highlight the need for strict ethical standards and regulatory oversight to balance AI's potential benefits with safeguarding humanity's future.

Question 5: The author of Passage 1 would most likely disagree with the author of Passage 2 about

A) the role of AI in improving healthcare.

B) the ethical concerns of autonomous weapons.

C) the impact of AI on human privacy.

D) the necessity of regulatory oversight for AI development.

Passage 1:

The multiverse hypothesis posits that our universe is just one of many, each with its own distinct physical laws and constants. This theory emerges from interpretations of quantum mechanics and cosmic inflation models, suggesting that different regions of space-time may have expanded at different rates, leading to separate, non-interacting universes. This concept provides potential explanations for the fine-tuning observed in our universe, as well as the quantum phenomena that seem random and unpredictable. By proposing a vast number of parallel universes, the multiverse hypothesis offers a compelling framework for understanding the complexities and peculiarities of our own cosmos.

Passage 2:

The multiverse hypothesis, while intriguing, faces significant scientific criticism due to its lack of empirical testability. Critics argue that a theory must be verifiable to be scientifically valid, and the multiverse concept inherently defies observational verification. Moreover, it introduces more questions than it answers, complicating rather than simplifying our understanding of the universe. Many scientists view the multiverse as speculative, resting more on theoretical mathematics than on concrete evidence. Without the ability to observe or interact with these other universes, the multiverse hypothesis remains an abstract idea rather than a robust scientific theory.

Question 6: The authors of both passages probably would characterize the multiverse hypothesis as being:

A) Empirically validated

B) Theoretically intriguing

C) Mathematically trivial

D) Easily observable

The military force of the U.S.T. *Buford* is in command of a Colonel of the United States Army, tall and severe-looking, about fifty. In his charge are a number of officers and a very considerable body of soldiers, most of them of the regular army. Direct supervision over the deportees is given to the representative of the Federal Government, Mr. Berkshire, who is here with a number of Secret Service men. The Captain of the Buford takes his orders from the Colonel, who is the supreme authority on board. (*The Bolshevik Myth*, by Alexander Berkman)

Question 7: Which of the following conclusions about the command structure on board of *Buford* can most reasonably be drawn from the passage?

A) The Colonel and Mr. Berkshire share equal authority on the Buford.

B) The Secret Service men are in charge of the military operations.

C) The Colonel is the supreme authority on board the Buford.

D) Mr. Berkshire commands the military personnel and the Captain.

The word "idealism" is used by different philosophers in somewhat different senses. We shall understand by it the doctrine that whatever exists, or at any rate whatever can be known to exist, must be in some sense mental. This doctrine, which is very widely held among philosophers, has several forms, and is advocated on several different grounds. The doctrine is so widely held, and so interesting in itself, that even the briefest survey of philosophy must give some account of it. (*The Problems of Philosophy*, by Bertrand Russell)

Question 8: What's the author's attitude about the "doctrine" in this passage?

A) Dismissive

B) Critical

C) Neutral

D) Supportive

In the summer of 1857, Russell, Majors & Waddell were sending a great many trains across the plains to Salt Lake with supplies for General Johnston's army. Men were in great demand, and the company was paying teamsters forty dollars per month in gold. An old and reliable wagon master, named Lewis Simpson—who had taken a great fancy to me, and who, by the way, was one of the best wagon-masters that ever ran a bull train—was loading a train for the company, and was about to start out with it for Salt Lake. He asked me to go along as an "extra hand." The high wages that were being paid were a great inducement to me, and the position of an "extra hand" was a pleasant one. All that I would have to do would be to take the place of any man who became sick, and drive his wagon until he recovered. I would have my own mule to ride, and to a certain extent I would be a minor boss.
(*The Life of Buffalo Bill*, by William F. Cody)

Question 9: What can be inferred from this passage about the author's likely next course of action?

A) The author will decline the offer due to the risks involved.

B) The author will accept the offer because of the high wages and responsibilities.

C) The author will negotiate for a higher salary.

D) The author will recommend someone else for the position.

The first impression, on seeing the correspondence of the horizontal strata on each side of these valleys and great amphitheatrical depressions, is that they have been hollowed out, like other valleys, by the action of water; but when one reflects on the enormous amount of stone, which on this view must have been removed through mere gorges or chasms, one is led to ask whether these spaces may not have subsided. But considering the form of the irregularly branching valleys, and of the narrow promontories projecting into them from the platforms, we are compelled to abandon this notion. To attribute these hollows to the present alluvial action would be preposterous; nor does the drainage from the summit-level always fall, as I remarked near the Weatherboard, into the head of these valleys, but into one side of their bay-like recesses. Some of the inhabitants remarked to me that they never viewed one of those bay-like recesses, with the headlands receding on both hands, without being struck with their resemblance to a bold seacoast. (The Voyage of the Beagle, by Charles Darwin)

Question 10: According to the passage, how does the author view the role of alluvial action in shaping the observed geography?

A) As the predominant force.

B) As negligible or non-contributory.

C) As causing subsidence in the valleys.

D) As influencing the drainage from the summit.

> When the party came out of the Yellowstone, Adams went on alone to Seattle and Vancouver to inspect the last American railway systems yet untried. They, too, offered little new learning, and no sooner had he finished this debauch of Northwestern geography than with desperate thirst for exhausting the American field, he set out for Mexico and the Gulf, making a sweep of the Caribbean and clearing up, in these six or eight months, at least twenty thousand miles of American land and water. (*The Education of Henry Adams*, by Henry Adams)

Question 11: The primary purpose of the passage is to_____

A) critique the American railway systems.

B) illustrate the extent of Adams' travels across America.

C) compare different geographic regions of America.

D) highlight the inadequacies of American geography.

> Descartes determined that he would believe nothing which he did not see quite clearly and distinctly to be true. Whatever he could bring himself to doubt, he would doubt, until he saw reason for not doubting it. By applying this method he gradually became convinced that the only existence of which he could be quite certain was his own. He imagined a deceitful demon, who presented unreal things to his senses in a perpetual phantasmagoria; it might be very improbable that such a demon existed, but still it was possible, and therefore doubt concerning things perceived by the senses was possible.
> (*The Problems of Philosophy*, by Bertrand Russell)

Question 12: Which of the following best describes what "phantasmagoria" means in the passage?

A) A systematic method of doubt

B) A state of clear and distinct truth

C) A deceptive, shifting sequence of illusions

D) A demon's improbable existence

> Shirley was, I believe, sincerely glad of being relieved from so burdensome a charge as the conduct of an army must be to a man unacquainted with military business. I was at the entertainment given by the city of New York to Lord Loudoun, on his taking upon him the command. Shirley, though thereby superseded, was present also. There was a great company of officers, citizens, and strangers, and, some chairs having been borrowed in the neighborhood, there was one among them very low, which fell to the lot of Mr. Shirley. Perceiving it as I sat by him, I said, "They have given you, sir, too low a seat." "No matter," says he, "Mr. Franklin, I find a low seat the easiest."
> (*The Autobiography of Benjamin Franklin*, by Benjamin Franklin)

Question 13: The passage's author conveys Shirley's attitude by

A) highlighting his relief at no longer being in command.

B) describing his discomfort at the social event.

C) illustrating his humility in accepting a lower seat.

D) emphasizing his displeasure with Lord Loudoun.

I grew convinced that truth, sincerity and integrity in dealings between man and man were of the utmost importance to the felicity of life; and I formed written resolutions, which still remain in my journal book, to practice them ever while I lived. Revelation had indeed no weight with me, as such; but I entertained an opinion that, though certain actions might not be bad because they were forbidden by it, or good because it commanded them, yet probably these actions might be forbidden because they were bad for us, or commanded because they were beneficial to us, in their own natures, all the circumstances of things considered. And this persuasion, with the kind hand of Providence, or some guardian angel, or accidental favorable circumstances and situations, or all together, preserved me, through this dangerous time of youth, and the hazardous situations I was sometimes in among strangers, remote from the eye and advice of my father, without any willful gross immorality or injustice, that might have been expected from my want of religion. (*The Autobiography of Benjamin Franklin*, by Benjamin Franklin)

Question 14: How was the passage's author convinced of his belief in truth, sincerity, and integrity?

A) Through religious teachings and revelation.

B) By reflecting on personal experiences and documenting his commitment in written resolutions.

C) By the influence of his father's advice.

D) Due to the favorable outcomes of his actions.

From the great secular games celebrated by Philip to the death of the emperor Gallienus, there elapsed twenty years of shame and misfortune. During that calamitous period, every instant of time was marked, every province of the Roman world was afflicted, by barbarous invaders and military tyrants, and the ruined empire seemed to approach the last and fatal moment of its dissolution. The confusion of the times and the scarcity of authentic memorials oppose equal difficulties to the historian, who attempts to preserve a clear and unbroken thread of narration. Surrounded with imperfect fragments, always concise, often obscure, and sometimes contradictory, he is reduced to collect, to compare, and to conjecture: and though he ought never to place his conjectures in the rank of facts, yet the knowledge of human nature, and of the sure operation of its fierce and unrestrained passions, might, on some occasions, supply the want of historical materials.
(*The History of the Decline and Fall of the Roman Empire*, by Edward Gibbon)

Question 15: The passage's author will most likely agree with which of the following methods in dealing with the lack of reliable historical accounts?

A) Ignoring the less reliable fragments of history.

B) Recreating details to form a continuous narrative.

C) Relying on archaeological evidence.

D) Collecting, comparing, and conjecturing based on available fragments.

ANSWER KEY

Q1: B) He desired to risk great hazards for potential gains.

Explanation: Sentence 2 explains that Carter Weatherbee was tired of the constant grind and wanted to take significant risks for the possibility of equally significant returns.

Q2: B) Sentimental and with a misguided sense of adventure

Explanation: The last paragraph characterizes Percy Cuthfert as a man who embarks on the venture due to an "abnormal development of sentimentality," mistaking it for a spirit of true adventure. This suggests that his sense of adventure may be misguided. The meaning of "with a bank account as deep as his culture" is ambiguous here. The word "deep" here could mean "deep" or "shallow" due to a lack of context.

Q3: C) He was surprised and skeptical.

Explanation: In sentences 7 and 8, Jacques Baptiste's surprise at the plans and his ominous head shaking when asked for advice suggest skepticism towards the men's plan.

Q4: B) Changes

Explanation: "Vicissitudes" refers to changes or variations occurring in the course of something, which aligns with the challenges described in sentence 6.

Q5: B) the ethical concerns of autonomous weapons.

Explanation: The author of Passage 1 emphasizes the benefits of AI, including advancements in healthcare, without mentioning ethical concerns about autonomous weapons, which are a primary focus in Passage 2.

Q6: B) Theoretically intriguing

Explanation: Both passages recognize the multiverse hypothesis as an interesting theoretical concept, even though they differ on its scientific validity and testability.

Q7: C) The Colonel is the supreme authority on board the Buford.

Explanation: The passage explicitly states that "The Captain of the Buford takes his orders from the Colonel, who is the supreme authority on board," indicating that the Colonel holds the highest command over all operations and personnel on the Buford.

Q8: C) Neutral

Explanation: The author describes the doctrine of idealism as "widely held" and "interesting," and mentions the need to discuss it in a survey of philosophy, suggesting a neutral, objective attitude toward the subject.

Q9: B) The author will accept the offer because of the high wages and responsibilities.

Explanation: The passage mentions the high wages and the appealing nature of the "extra hand" position as significant inducements for the author, suggesting he is likely to accept the offer.

Q10: B) As negligible or non-contributory.

Explanation: The author explicitly mentions that attributing the formation of hollows to current alluvial action would be "preposterous," indicating a view that alluvial action plays a minimal or no role in shaping these geographical features.

Q11: B) illustrate the extent of Adams' travels across America.

Explanation: The passage details Adams' extensive travels from the Yellowstone to Seattle, Vancouver, and then on to Mexico and the Caribbean, emphasizing the broad scope of his geographic exploration within America.

Q12: C) A deceptive, shifting sequence of illusions

Explanation: In the passage, "phantasmagoria" refers to the array of unreal things that Descartes imagined a deceitful demon presented to his senses, indicating a misleading or illusory spectacle.

Q13: C) illustrating his humility in accepting a lower seat.

Explanation: Shirley's response to the low seat, "No matter, Mr. Franklin, I find a low seat the easiest," suggests humility and acceptance, which the author conveys through this anecdote from the social event.

Q14: B) By reflecting on personal experiences and documenting his commitment in written resolutions.

Explanation: The author states that he grew convinced of the importance of truth, sincerity, and integrity and formed written resolutions to practice them, indicating that his convictions were reinforced by personal reflection and commitment documented in his journal.

Q15: D) Collecting, comparing, and conjecturing based on available fragments.

Explanation: The author describes his method of dealing with scarce and unreliable historical records by collecting, comparing, and making educated guesses (conjectures) from available fragments, clearly stating this approach in the passage.

PART II: TSIA2 WRITING

INTRODUCTION

The Texas Success Initiative Assessment 2.0 (TSIA2) English Language Arts and Reading (ELAR) section has three components: reading, writing, and essay. The writing component is designed to evaluate a student's proficiency in written communication. This component assesses various skills critical for success in college-level coursework.

The writing-focused multiple-choice questions concentrate on revising and editing, requiring students to improve the development, organization, and expression of ideas in early drafts of essays. These questions also test the ability to apply Standard English conventions, including grammar, punctuation, and usage.

Students will encounter tasks that ask them to complete or correct sentences to ensure clarity and adherence to standard grammar rules. This part of the test assesses the ability to identify and correct errors in written passages, focusing on enhancing overall coherence and readability.

Writing Skills Being Tested

The TSIA2 ELAR writing component includes test questions that can be divided into two primary categories:

Essay Revision and Editing

The Essay Revision and Editing section requires students to revise and edit prose texts to improve their development, organization, and rhetorical word choice. Additionally, students must ensure that the text conforms to the conventions of standard written English grammar, usage, and punctuation. This section emphasizes several key areas:

- Development: Students will make necessary revisions to enhance the development of the text.
- Organization: Students will improve the organization of the text to ensure logical flow and coherence.
- Effective Language Use: Students will revise the text to improve the rhetorical use of language, making it more persuasive and clearer.
- Standard English Conventions: This involves editing the text to conform to the conventions of standard written English grammar, usage, and punctuation.

Sentence Revision, Editing, and Completion

With these questions, students will edit and complete sentences to ensure they conform to standard written English conventions. This includes addressing various aspects such as:

- Conventions of Grammar: Students will revise sentences to ensure they follow standard grammar rules.
- Conventions of Usage: This involves editing sentences to ensure correct word usage and adherence to English language standards.
- Conventions of Punctuation: Students will revise punctuation to ensure clarity and correctness.

Additionally, diagnostic tests will include tasks on:

- Conventions of Spelling and Capitalization: This includes ensuring correct spelling and proper capitalization in sentences.

- Purpose and Organization: Students will make effective decisions regarding the appropriateness of written material for a given purpose and audience, as well as the organization of the content.
- Sentence Combining: This involves combining two sentences into a more effective single sentence, enhancing clarity and coherence.

These questions collectively assess a student's ability to revise and edit written material, ensuring it meets high standards of clarity, coherence, and correctness.

Writing-Focused Questions Overview

A complete TSIA2 ELAR session involves 30 questions, equally divided between reading and writing. These questions are presented in an integrated manner, without any interruptions or clear separations between the reading and writing components. The test starts with reading-focused questions, beginning with the Literary Text Analysis section, followed by writing-focused questions, starting with the Essay Revision and Editing section.

There are a total of 15 writing-focused questions, with the following structure:

- Essay Revision and Editing: 1 long passage with 4 questions aimed at revising and editing essays.
- Sentence Revision, Editing, and Completion: 11 questions chosen algorithmically from all varieties of sentence revision, editing, and completion tasks.

DEVELOPMENT

In the TSIA2 test, questions related to **development** evaluate a test taker's skill in refining and enhancing text to meet a specific rhetorical purpose. This evaluation is structured around three key elements: proposition, support, and focus. **Proposition** involves structuring the text around clear central ideas or arguments, ensuring that the claims made are compelling and well-presented. **Support** requires test takers to fortify these claims with relevant details, facts, or statistics that enhance the argument's credibility. **Focus** demands the careful consideration of each piece of information included, requiring additions or deletions to maintain the text's relevance to the intended topic and purpose. Mastery of these components help produce coherent, persuasive, and purpose-driven writing.

Proposition

TSIA2 questions on proposition demand that you grasp a text or paragraph's central theme or main idea and assess how revisions could enhance or obscure this theme. The main idea is often presented in the first sentence, with subsequent sentences providing supporting details to expand on this central concept. However, the main idea could also be located in a passage's middle or end.

Example 1

(1) George Stephenson, an English engineer, designed the first successful steam locomotive. (2) His creation, named Locomotion No. 1, played a crucial role in the Industrial Revolution. (3) It first ran on the Stockton and Darlington Railway in 1825. (4) The locomotive drastically reduced the time and cost of transporting goods and passengers. (5) Its success paved the way for the rapid expansion of railway networks worldwide.

Question: Which sentence contains the main idea of the paragraph?

A) Sentence 1

B) Sentence 2

C) Sentence 3

D) Sentence 5

Answer: A

Explanation: Sentence (1) introduces George Stephenson and his achievement of designing the first successful steam locomotive, which is the paragraph's central focus. This sentence sets the stage for the details that follow, making it the statement of the main idea.

Example 2

(1) Uluru, famously known as Ayers Rock, stands prominently in the heart of the Northern Territory's arid "Red Centre". (2) The rock is a large sandstone formation deeply sacred to the indigenous Anangu people. (3) Its striking appearance changes color dramatically at sunrise and sunset, shifting from terracotta to deep red and even purple. (4) In 1985, ownership of Uluru was officially returned to the Anangu, who now manage the land together with Parks Australia. (5) Uluru is not just a rock but a significant cultural landmark that embodies centuries of Aboriginal heritage.

Question: Which sentence contains the main idea of the paragraph?

A) Sentence 1

B) Sentence 2

C) Sentence 4

D) Sentence 5

Answer: D

Explanation: Sentence (5) encapsulates the paragraph's main idea by emphasizing Uluru's significance beyond its physical appearance, highlighting its cultural and historical importance. This sentence provides a summary perspective that encompasses all aspects mentioned in the previous sentences.

Support

Some of TSIA2's Expression of Ideas questions will ask test takers to enhance texts by ensuring that supporting details such as facts, statistics, and examples robustly back the central claims. This area focuses on refining content to bolster the strength and credibility of the passage's arguments or narratives. You are expected to add, revise, or retain information and ideas in order to support claims or points.

Example 1

(1) Hurricane Katrina, which struck in August 2005, is one of the most devastating natural disasters in U.S. history. (2) <u>It reached Category 5 status with winds exceeding 175 miles per hour.</u> (3) The storm caused catastrophic damage, particularly in New Orleans, Louisiana. (4) Levee breaches led to widespread flooding throughout the area. (5) The disaster resulted in over 1,800 deaths and billions of dollars in damages.

Sentence 2 is reproduced here.

It reached Category 5 status with winds exceeding 175 miles per hour.

Question: Which of the following provides the best detail to illustrate how powerful the hurricane was?

A) (as it is now)

B) It prompted a massive national and international response effort.

C) It originated from the merger of a tropical wave and the remnants of a tropical depression.

D) Florida Governor Jeb Bush declared a state of emergency before Hurricane Katrina's powerful landfall.

Answer: A

Explanation: Sentence (2), as it is now, specifically highlights the hurricane's intensity by detailing its Category 5 status and wind speeds exceeding 175 miles per hour, which directly reflects the storm's power.

Example 2

(1) The Great Pyramid of Giza was constructed over 4,500 years ago. (2) Originally built as a tomb for Pharaoh Khufu, it was once the tallest man-made structure in the world. (3) The pyramid is made of approximately 2.3 million blocks of stone, each weighing an average of 2.5 tons. (4) It originally stood at 481 feet tall, though it now reaches about 455 feet due to the loss of its outer casing stones. (5) The Great Pyramid attracts millions of visitors each year. (6) It stands as a testament to <u>Pharaoh Khufu's relentless pursuit of eternal life</u>.

Question: Which of the following best completes the sentence (6)?

A) (as it is now)

B) the skills of contemporary builders

C) ancient Egyptian engineering and religious achievement

D) the development of tourism in Egypt

Answer: C

Explanation: Option C, "ancient Egyptian engineering and religious achievement," is the correct answer as it aligns with the context provided in the passage about the pyramid's historical and cultural significance as an ancient structure, underscoring its purpose and the sophistication of its construction.

Focus

TSIA2 questions that test for focus will ask the test taker to modify, maintain, add, or remove content within the text to ensure it aligns closely with the topic's relevance and overall purpose.

Example

(1) Trade protectionism, often intended to shield domestic industries from foreign competition, can actually be detrimental to a country's economy. (2) By imposing tariffs and quotas, governments increase the cost of imports, leading to higher consumer prices and reduced marketplace choices. (3) This artificial inflation stymies competition and innovation within domestic industries, which might become complacent and less driven to improve. (4) Moreover, other countries may retaliate by imposing their own trade barriers, which can hurt domestic exporters and decrease overall trade volume. (5) In the long run, protectionism can isolate a country from global trade networks, hindering economic growth and technological advancement. (6) Thus, while protectionism aims to protect, it often ends up harming economic vitality and international competitiveness.

Sentence 4 is reproduced here.

Moreover, other countries may retaliate by imposing their own trade barriers, which can hurt domestic exporters and decrease overall trade volume.

Question 1: The writer is considering deleting sentence 4. Should the writer make this deletion?

A) Yes, because the sentence introduces irrelevant information.

B) Yes, because it contradicts the main argument of the passage.

C) No, because it illustrates the potential international consequences of protectionism.

D) No, because it focuses on domestic policies rather than international relations.

Answer: C

Explanation: Sentence 4 should not be deleted as it provides crucial information about international reactions to protectionism. It supports the overall argument that protectionism can negatively affect a country's economy. It highlights the potential for retaliation by other countries, which has a direct repercussion on domestic exporters and overall trade volume.

Question 2: The writer is considering modifying sentence 4. Which of the following modifications would be appropriate?

A) Other countries always refrain from retaliating by imposing their own trade barriers, which helps domestic exporters.

B) Moreover, friendly nations might support domestic policies by lowering their trade barriers, which can boost domestic exports and increase overall trade volume.

C) Moreover, other countries may retaliate by imposing their own trade barriers, which can harm domestic exporters and decrease overall trade volume.

D) Additionally, other countries tend to ignore trade protectionism, which has no real impact on global trade dynamics.

Answer: C

Explanation: Modification C is the most appropriate as it retains the original meaning and context of the sentence, reiterating the potential negative consequences of protectionism on international relations without changing the factual content or the tone of the passage. This modification ensures that the critical idea of retaliation by other countries, leading to harm for domestic exporters and a decrease in trade volume, remains clear and intact.

ORGANIZATION

The organization of a text critically influences how its content is perceived and understood. The TSIA2 writing test assesses a test taker's skill in structuring text to enhance clarity and impact. This involves arranging information and ideas in a logical sequence, whether it is chronological for narrating events or structured to unfold an argument for clarity in persuasion. Effective organization also entails crafting strong introductions that set clear expectations, and conclusions that succinctly encapsulate the main points. Furthermore, transitions play a vital role, guiding the reader through the text and signaling shifts in narrative or argumentative direction.

Logical Sequence

For questions related to logical sequence, the test taker will revise the text as necessary to present information and ideas in the clearest and most logical order.

Example

(1) The Battle of Trafalgar, a pivotal naval engagement, took place on October 21, 1805. (2) It was fought near the coast of Cape Trafalgar, located in southwestern Spain. (3) The battle was part of the larger Napoleonic Wars, which were raging across Europe at the time. (4) Vice Admiral Horatio Nelson commanded the British fleet of 27 ships. (5) Undeterred by the enemy's bigger fleet, Nelson's innovative tactics proved superior, leading to a decisive British victory. (6) The opposing French and Spanish fleets, on the other hand, comprised 33 ships and were numerically superior. (7) Tragically, Admiral Nelson was mortally wounded during the battle but lived long enough to learn of his fleet's victory.

Question: Which is the most logical placement for Sentence 5 (reproduced here)?

Undeterred by the enemy's bigger fleet, Nelson's innovative tactics proved superior, leading to a decisive British victory.

A) Where it is now

B) After Sentence 1

C) After Sentence 6

D) After Sentence 7

Answer: C

Explanation: Sentence 6 mentions the numerical superiority of the opposing fleets. Placing Sentence 5 after 6 highlights how Nelson's tactics overcame the larger French and Spanish fleets, creating a direct cause-effect relationship that underscores the significance of his innovative approach in achieving victory.

Introductions and Conclusions

Introductions, conclusions, and transitions serve as the framework that guides readers through the text, ensuring clarity and coherence. A well-crafted introduction sets the stage, offering a preview of what's to come, while a thoughtful conclusion provides closure, summarizing key points. The following examples illustrate how the TSIA2 normally measures your understanding of such organizational elements.

Example

(1) Gradualism is a core concept in geological theory, advocating that the Earth's features evolve through slow, continuous processes over long periods. (2) This idea contrasts with catastrophism, which suggests that sudden, catastrophic events have shaped the Earth's landscape. (3) James Hutton, in the late 18th century, first developed the concept extensively, proposing that processes like erosion and sedimentation occur gradually. (4) Gradualism has influenced geology by providing a framework to understand Earth's systems, suggesting that observing current natural processes helps explain ancient geological conditions. (5)

For instance, studying sediment deposition by rivers today helps geologists understand the formation of similar ancient layers. (6) Gradualism is founded on uniformitarianism, the idea that geological forces have been consistent through time.

(7) Nevertheless, the introduction of punctuated equilibrium in evolutionary biology, proposing rapid changes between periods of stability, has led to refinements in gradualism. (8) This adaptation incorporates both gradual changes and sudden geological events into current models. (9) Despite these modifications, gradualism remains foundational in geology, guiding modern scientific approaches. (10) Overall, its principle that Earth's features develop gradually <u>continues to face significant criticism and skepticism.</u>

Question 1: Which of the following, if added before Sentence 1, would serve as the best introduction to the passage?

A) James Hutton was a renowned 18th-century scientist.

B) Geological theories have evolved significantly over the centuries.

C) Many geological theories focus exclusively on catastrophic events.

D) Geologic change has fascinated humans from ancient times.

Answer: B

Explanation: Option B provides a general introduction that sets the stage for discussing gradualism and its contrast with other geological theories, fitting naturally with the theme of the passage.

Question 2: Which of the following most effectively completes Sentence 10 as a conclusion?

A) (as it is now)

B) demonstrates the evolving nature of scientific theories.

C) begs revisions to this theory.

D) continues to be a cornerstone of geological science.

Answer: D

Explanation: Option D directly complements the passage's theme by emphasizing that, despite refinements and adaptations, gradualism remains a fundamental and enduring aspect of geological science.

Transitions

In writing, effective transitions act as bridges, seamlessly connecting sections and ideas, thereby enhancing the document's logical flow and overall readability. Transition words and sentences guide readers from one thought to another, clarifying relationships between points or paragraphs.

Transition Words

Transition words help guide readers through a text by connecting ideas and paragraphs. They can be categorized based on the function they serve:

- **Additive Transitions**: These introduce additional information or indicate agreement with previously stated ideas. Examples include "furthermore," "moreover," "also," and "in addition."
- **Adversative Transitions**: These indicate conflict, contradiction, or dismissal, helping to show contrast between ideas. Examples include "however," "on the other hand," "although," and "nevertheless."
- **Causal Transitions**: These establish a cause-and-effect relationship between ideas. Examples include "because," "therefore," "thus," and "as a result."
- **Sequential Transitions**: These indicate a sequence or order of events or steps in a process. Examples include "first," "next," "then," and "finally."

Each category plays a specific role in structuring arguments and enhancing the clarity and flow of a text, making it easier for readers to follow the writer's thought process.

Example

(1) The British Museum in London was established in 1753 and is one of the world's oldest museums dedicated to human history, art, and culture. (2) It houses a vast collection of over eight million works, showcasing artifacts from all continents. (3) Consequently, it provides insight into human culture from its beginnings to the present. (4) Among its most famous exhibits are the Rosetta Stone and the Egyptian mummies. (5) <u>Therefore</u>, the museum is renowned for its expansive library, which was once part of the same institution before becoming part of the British Library.

Question: Which of the following is the best version of the underlined portion of sentence 5?

A) (as it is now)

B) Furthermore

C) Subsequently

D) Nevertheless

Answer: B

Explanation: Option B, *Furthermore* is the most appropriate transition word because it adds additional information about the British Museum's features, aligning well with this passage's positive and informative tone.

Transition Sentences

Transition sentences serve as bridges, linking sections of text to ensure coherence and guide the reader from one point to the next. Effective transition sentences can summarize previous information, introduce new concepts, or highlight contrasts, thereby enhancing the reader's understanding and engagement with the material.

Example

(1) Niels Bohr was a pioneering physicist known for his foundational contributions to understanding atomic structure and quantum theory. (2) Born in Copenhagen in 1885, he went on to develop the Bohr model of the atom, which introduced the theory that electrons travel in orbits around the atom's nucleus. (3) This model was crucial in the advancement of modern physics. (4) Moreover, Bohr's concept of complementarity became a central part of his contributions to quantum mechanics. (5) He received the Nobel Prize in Physics in 1922 for his groundbreaking work. (6) Bohr's legacy includes scientific achievements, his efforts to promote open scientific exchange, and his involvement in the development of nuclear weapons during World War II.

Question: Which of the following sentences, if placed after Sentence 5, creates the best transition to Sentence 6?

A) Bohr's theoretical advancements had little impact on his personal beliefs.

B) Bohr's interest in science began at a very young age.

C) Bohr also made significant contributions beyond theoretical physics.

D) Bohr retired shortly after receiving his Nobel Prize.

Answer: C

Explanation: Sentence C provides a natural segue into Sentence 6, which discusses Bohr's broader legacy, including scientific exchange and involvement in nuclear weapons development. It effectively connects his Nobel Prize-winning work to his other contributions.

EFFECTIVE LANGUAGE USE

On the TSIA2 writing test, Effective Language Use questions focus on text revision to enhance the language and achieve specific rhetorical objectives.

Precision

Precision questions require the test taker to refine the text to enhance the accuracy and suitability of word choices.

Example Question: Which word choice best enhances the precision of the underlined portion in the following sentence?

The speaker articulated his thoughts in a very clear manner.

A) lucidly

B) eloquently

C) vehemently

D) explicitly

Answer: A

Explanation: "Lucidly" specifically refers to clarity and ease of understanding, directly aligning with the description of the speaker's clear articulation, making it the most precise and contextually appropriate choice among the options.

Concision

Concision questions ask the test taker to edit the text to boost word choice efficiency by removing verbosity and redundancy.

Example Question: How can this sentence be revised to improve concision?

She completely eliminated all of the unnecessary and redundant information from her report.

A) She eliminated all the unnecessary information from her report.

B) She totally removed every bit of unnecessary and redundant information.

C) She removed all unnecessary information from her report.

D) She cleared out all the unnecessary and redundant details.

Answer: C

Explanation: Option C eliminates redundancy and wordiness effectively by using "all unnecessary information," succinctly conveying the same meaning as the original.

Style and tone

Style and tone are critical elements in writing that shape how content is perceived and understood. Style refers to the unique way an author uses words, structures sentences, and organizes ideas to convey meaning.

Writing styles can be put into the following main categories: **descriptive**, where vivid detail brings topics to life; **expository**, which explains or informs with clarity and precision; **narrative**, telling stories with a clear sequence of events; and **persuasive**, aimed at convincing readers of a particular viewpoint. Each style serves a unique purpose, shaping how content is presented and influencing the reader's understanding and engagement with the text.

Tone, on the other hand, conveys the author's attitude toward the subject and the audience. It ranges widely, including tones such as formal, informal, optimistic, pessimistic, serious, humorous, sarcastic, and respectful. The chosen tone can significantly affect how readers perceive and react to the content, shaping their emotional and intellectual engagement.

TSIA2 style and tone questions ask the test taker to adjust the text to better align the style and tone with the context of the text or to suit the intended purpose.

Example: Style Question

(1) Montreal, a city steeped in history and modern flair, boasts stunning views of the St. Lawrence River. (2) Its streets are lined with an eclectic mix of old stone facades and sleek, contemporary buildings. (3) The vibrant arts scene is palpable, with murals, galleries, and live music at every turn. (4) <u>The city's cuisine blends French and global influences.</u>

Question: Which of the following replacements for Sentence 4 best maintains the style of the rest of the passage?

A) Sadly, the city's infrastructure is crumbling under its own weight.

B) Many argue that the city's tax policies are overly complicated.

C) Despite its charm, Montreal struggles with high crime rates.

D) Strolling through Montreal, one encounters charming cafes and quaint bookshops.

Answer: D

Explanation: Sentence D continues the descriptive style, focusing on creating a vivid, sensory-rich image of Montreal's streets. It complements the first three sentences by adding details about the city's everyday street life, enhancing the cohesive descriptive narrative of the passage. The other options introduce a negative or argumentative tone.

Example: Tone Question

(1) The coral reefs off the coast of eastern Australia, notably the Great Barrier Reef, face a grim future. (2) Rising sea temperatures, driven by global warming, have led to widespread coral bleaching, a sign of severe stress. (3) Additionally, pollution and overfishing exacerbate the degradation, further threatening this vital ecosystem. (4) Efforts to mitigate these impacts have been insufficient, and without drastic measures, the reefs' decline may become irreversible. (5) It's a troubling outlook for one of the world's most biodiverse and beautiful natural treasures.

Question: Which of the following best describes the passage's tone about the coral reefs off the coast of eastern Australia?

A) Optimistic

B) Pessimistic

C) Neutral

D) Indifferent

Answer: B

Explanation: The passage uses phrases like "grim future," "severe stress," "insufficient efforts," and "troubling outlook," all of which contribute to a pessimistic tone, indicating concern and a negative outlook on the future of the coral reefs.

Syntax

Syntax refers to the rules and principles that govern the structure of sentences in a language, including word order, sentence length, punctuation, and the relationship between elements. TSIA2 Syntax questions require the test taker to employ diverse sentence structures to achieve specific rhetorical objectives.

Example 1

The baobab tree, often called the "Tree of Life," thrives across the African savannas with a lifespan that can reach over a thousand years. The baobab tree's bulbous trunk stores vast amounts of water.

Question: Which of the following best combines the two sentences into a single sentence?

A) The baobab tree, with a life span of over a thousand years, widely known as the "Tree of Life," thrives across African savannas and has a bulbous trunk that stores vast amounts of water.

B) The "Tree of Life," or baobab tree, can survive for over a thousand years, with its trunk uniquely adapted to store vast amounts of water.

C) Known as the "Tree of Life," the baobab tree flourishes across the African savannas by storing water in its large trunk.

D) Thriving on the African savannas, the baobab tree, often called the "Tree of Life," boasts a bulbous trunk and a long lifespan of more than a thousand years.

Answer: A

Explanation: Option A is the best choice as it maintains the original sentence order and information. It most faithfully captures the spirit and details of the original sentences.

Example 2

Ibuprofen is a widely-used anti-inflammatory drug, effectively reduces pain, fever, and inflammation, makes it a staple in many medicine cabinets.

Question: Which of the following is the best version of this sentence?

A) A widely-used anti-inflammatory drug, ibuprofen effectively, reduces pain, fever, and inflammation, a staple in many medicine cabinets.

B) Reduces pain, fever, and inflammation effectively, ibuprofen, a widely-used anti-inflammatory drug, is a staple in many medicine cabinets.

C) Ibuprofen, reducing pain, fever, and inflammation effectively, a widely-used anti-inflammatory drug, which makes it a staple in many medicine cabinets.

D) Ibuprofen, a widely-used anti-inflammatory drug, effectively reduces pain, fever, and inflammation, making it a staple in many medicine cabinets.

Answer: D

Explanation: Option D maintains the correct syntax, clearly stating the drug's uses and its status as a common item in medicine cabinets. The other options are syntactically jumbled, altering the natural flow of information.

STANDARD ENGLISH GRAMMAR CONVENTIONS

The TSIA2 Writing Test's questions on Standard English Conventions measure a student's proficiency in essential English grammatical principles. Grammar is the structural foundation of the English language, governing the composition of words, phrases, clauses, and sentences. It provides a set of rules and guidelines that help us communicate with clarity and effectiveness. Mastery of English grammar enables speakers and writers to express their thoughts accurately and makes their communication comprehensible to others.

Understanding English grammar involves various elements, including syntax (the arrangement of words and phrases to create well-formed sentences), morphology (the structure of words), and punctuation (the symbols that help clarify and modify meanings within texts). Additionally, grammar encompasses the correct use of verb tenses, conjugations, pronouns, prepositions, and conjunctions, which are crucial for maintaining sentence coherence and context. In this chapter, we will go over the fundamentals of English grammar.

Nouns, Verbs, and Subjects

Nouns are words that name people, places, things, or ideas. They are one of the primary elements of English sentences, serving as the subject or object within the sentence structure. Nouns can be classified further into categories such as common nouns (e.g., *dog, happiness*), proper nouns (e.g., *John, New York*), collective nouns (e.g., *bunch, herd*), and abstract nouns (e.g., *freedom, beauty*).

Examples:

- **Table** (common noun): The **table** is made of wood.
- **Jenny** (proper noun): **Jenny** moved to Boston.
- **Team** (collective noun): The **team** celebrates their victory.

Pronouns are used in place of nouns to avoid repetition and promote smooth sentence flow. Pronouns include personal pronouns (he, she, it, they), possessive pronouns (his, hers, theirs), reflexive pronouns (myself, themselves), and relative pronouns (who, which, that).
Examples:

- **She** is watching TV. (*She* replaces the noun.)
- This book is **hers**. (*Hers* indicates possession.)
- The man **who** called yesterday was my uncle. (*Who* connects clauses.)

Noun Phrases combine a noun with other words (usually modifiers and determiners) to function as a single unit within a sentence. These phrases provide detailed information about the noun.
Examples:

- The **big brown dog** barked loudly. (*big brown* modifies *dog*)
- **A slice of cheese** can be very filling. (*A slice of* specifies the amount.)

Verbs denote actions, occurrences, or states of being. They are vital for sentence formation as they link the subject to additional information about the subject.
Examples:

- **Runs**: The dog **runs** fast.
- **Seems**: She **seems** happy.
- **Is**: The book **is** on the table.

Subjects are the nouns or pronouns that perform the action of the verb or about which something is stated.
Examples:

- **Laura** likes to swim. (*Laura* is the subject taking action.)
- **It** is raining. (*It* is the subject in a state of being.)
- **Cars** need fuel to run. (*Cars* perform the action.)

Modifiers in Noun Phrases

Modifiers provide additional details about nouns, enhancing descriptions or specifying attributes to make sentences more informative and interesting. They can include adjectives, participial phrases, prepositional phrases, and relative clauses.
Examples:

- The **tall, mysterious man** entered the room. (Adjectives **tall** and **mysterious** modify *man*.)
- The house **with the red door** is mine. (The prepositional phrase **with the red door** modifies *house*.)
- Anyone **wanting to join** must register online. (Participle phrase **wanting to join** modifies *Anyone*.)

Subject-Verb Agreement

Subject-Verb Agreement ensures the verb matches the subject in number (singular or plural). This agreement is crucial for maintaining grammatical accuracy in English.
Examples:

- **The cat** sleeps. (*Cat* is singular; *sleeps* is singular.)

- **The dogs** bark. (*Dogs* is plural; *bark* is plural.)
- **The team** wins games. (*Team*, although collective, is treated as singular here.)

Sentence Boundaries

Understanding sentence boundaries includes identifying and correcting sentence fragments, run-on sentences, and comma splices, which can disrupt the flow of writing and confuse readers.

Sentence Fragments are incomplete sentences that lack a subject, verb, or complete thought. They often occur when a sentence has been cut off from its clause or is missing key components.

Examples:

- Walking through the park. (**Incorrect Example**: lacks a subject and verb)

    Corrected: She was walking through the park.

- After the movie was over. (**Incorrect Example**: lacks a main clause)

    Corrected: After the movie was over, we went to dinner.

Run-On Sentences: These occur when two or more independent clauses are joined without appropriate punctuation or conjunctions.

Examples:

- She runs every day she never feels tired. (**Incorrect Example**: lacks conjunction or punctuation)

    Corrected: She runs every day, but she never feels tired.

- It is late we should go home. (**Incorrect Example**: two independent clauses joined without a conjunction)

    Corrected: It is late, so we should go home.

Comma Splices: These happen when two independent clauses are incorrectly joined by a comma without a coordinating conjunction.

Examples:

- He completed his essay, he submitted it late. (**Incorrect Example**: comma splice)

    Corrected: He completed his essay, but he submitted it late.

- I enjoy hiking, my brother likes kayaking. (**Incorrect Example**: comma splice)

    Corrected: I enjoy hiking, and my brother likes kayaking.

Simple Sentence vs. Compound Sentence

A **simple sentence** contains one independent clause, which has a subject and a verb and expresses a complete thought. It is straightforward and concise, making it very effective for stating clear, uncomplicated ideas.

Examples:

- The dog barks. (One subject and one verb, expressing a complete idea.)
- Rain falls heavily. (A simple declaration with a subject and action.)

In contrast, a compound sentence is constructed by joining two or more independent clauses with the help of coordinating conjunctions, commonly remembered by the acronym FANBOYS (for, and, nor, but, or, yet, so). These conjunctions help to clarify the relationship between the clauses.

Examples:

- I tried to call you, **but** you didn't answer. (*But* introduces a contrast.)
- We can go to the cinema, ***or*** we can just stay home. (*Or* presents alternatives.)
- He must be sick, **for** he didn't eat anything. (*For* explains a reason.)

Each conjunction serves a unique purpose, enabling the writer to convey complex relationships and ideas within a single sentence effectively. 'And' adds; 'but' contrasts; 'or' offers choices; 'nor' negates; 'yet' and 'so' show consequences. Understanding how to use these conjunctions allows for precise and engaging writing, especially useful in constructing arguments or narratives that require nuanced expression.

Understanding the difference between simple and compound sentences allows for more dynamic and varied sentence structures, enhancing both the readability and interest of written communication.

Clauses and Phrases in a Sentence

In English grammar, **clauses** and **phrases** play crucial roles but serve different purposes. A **clause** is a group of words that contains a subject and a verb. Clauses can be independent (able to stand alone as a sentence) or dependent (cannot stand alone and must be attached to an independent clause).

Examples:

- She laughed. (Independent clause)
- Because I was late, (Dependent clause)
- If you see him, (Dependent clause)

A **phrase**, on the other hand, is a group of words that does not contain a subject-verb pairing capable of expressing a complete thought. Phrases provide additional information about subjects or objects within a sentence but cannot stand alone as a sentence.

Examples:

- Running quickly (a verb phrase describing how someone is running)
- In the morning (a prepositional phrase indicating when)
- Extremely tired (an adjective phrase describing a state)

By combining clauses and phrases effectively, writers can create sentences that are not only grammatically correct but also rich in detail and variety, thereby enhancing the narrative or expository quality of their writing.

Complex Sentences

A Complex sentence incorporates an independent clause and at least one dependent clause. The independent clause can stand alone as a complete sentence, but the dependent clause cannot, relying instead on the main clause to provide complete meaning. This structure is essential for conveying detailed, nuanced ideas and relationships within a sentence.

Examples:

- Although it was raining, we decided to go for a walk. (The dependent clause *Although it was raining* sets the context, while the independent clause *we decided to go for a walk* provides the main action.)

- She was late because her alarm didn't go off. (The independent clause *She was late* is the main point, and *because her alarm didn't go off* explains the reason.)

Complex sentences enhance writing by adding depth to the information presented, allowing for cause-and-effect relationships, conditions, contrasts, and reasons to be clearly expressed. They enrich narratives and arguments by linking related thoughts and ensuring that important details are highlighted effectively.

Main and Subordinate Clauses in Complex Sentences

In complex sentences, the main (or independent) clause contains the core idea or action, capable of standing alone as a complete sentence. The subordinate (or dependent) clause, however, adds necessary detail and context but cannot exist independently as it does not express a complete thought on its own.

Examples:

- You will succeed if you work hard. (Main clause: *You will succeed*; Subordinate clause: *if you work hard*.)
- Because the weather was bad, our flight was delayed. (Main clause: *our flight was delayed*; Subordinate clause: *Because the weather was bad*.)
- She returned the computer after she noticed it was damaged. (Main clause: *She returned the computer*; Subordinate clause: *after she noticed it was damaged*.)

Understanding the distinction between main and subordinate clauses is crucial for constructing sentences that are grammatically correct and logically structured. This knowledge aids in creating sentences that flow smoothly and convey information effectively.

Subordinate Clauses with Relative Pronouns in Complex Sentences

Subordinate clauses in complex sentences often begin with relative pronouns such as *who, which, that, whom,* and *whose*. These pronouns connect the clause to a noun or pronoun in the main clause, providing additional details about it.

Examples:

- The man who called you is waiting outside. (The relative pronoun *who* connects the subordinate clause *who called you* to *The man*, giving more information about him.)
- The book that I borrowed was fascinating. (The relative pronoun *that* links the subordinate clause *that I borrowed* to *The book*, specifying which book.)

Subordinate clauses allow for the inclusion of pertinent details without the need for multiple sentences, thereby keeping the discourse compact and focused.

Subordination and Coordination in Sentences

Subordination and coordination help structure ideas and arguments effectively by emphasizing the relationship between clauses.

Subordination

Subordination involves using a subordinate clause (a clause that cannot stand alone as a complete sentence) to provide additional information without disrupting the main clause. It shows a relationship of dependence and often introduces complex sentences. Subordinate clauses are introduced by subordinating conjunctions such as because, although, if, when, and while.

Examples:

- Although it was raining, we went for a hike. (*Although it was raining* is a subordinate clause that provides a condition.)

- I couldn't see her because she was hiding. (*Because she was hiding* gives the reason for the result: *I couldn't see her*.)
- She wanted to attend the meeting because she was sick. (**Incorrect Example**: The sentence improperly suggests she wanted to attend the meeting because she was sick, which is logically inconsistent.)

    Corrected: Because she was sick, she didn't want to attend the meeting.

Coordination

Coordination involves joining two or more clauses of equal importance using coordinating conjunctions (FANBOYS: for, and, nor, but, or, yet, so). This structure is used to build compound sentences, where each clause could stand as a complete sentence if separated.

Examples:

- We wanted to go swimming *but* it started to rain. (*But* is a coordinating conjunction that introduces a contrasting clause.)
- She can sing *and* she can dance. (*And* connects two independent clauses of equal importance.)
- He must hurry *or* he will miss the bus. (*Or* presents alternative outcomes.)
- I need to buy bread, *and* my shoes are old. (**Incorrect Example**: The sentence improperly uses the coordinating conjunction *and* to connect two unrelated ideas, which makes the sentence confusing and lacking coherence.)

    Corrected: I need to buy bread, *and* I need new shoes.

Understanding the use of subordination and coordination allows for the construction of more nuanced and varied sentences, enhancing both the clarity and the depth of written and spoken communication.

Parallel Structure

Parallel structure, or parallelism, refers to the use of consistent grammatical patterns within a sentence or among sentences. Using parallel structure improves readability and adds symmetry and balance to your writing.

Examples:

- She likes reading, writing, and skiing. (Parallel verbs ending in -ing show activities enjoyed by the subject.)
- Not only does he enjoy painting, but he also loves sculpting. (Parallel structure in a correlative conjunction setup enhances the flow.)
- She enjoys to swim, biking, and *to run*. (**Incorrect Example**: The sentence mixes infinitive forms ("to swim," "to run") with a gerund ("biking"), disrupting the parallel structure.)

    Corrected: She enjoys *swimming, biking*, and *running*.

Parallel structure can be applied in lists, comparisons, and contrasts, and across coordinated elements. It ensures that each element follows the same grammatical or structural pattern, which not only reinforces the rhythm of the text but also strengthens the relationships among ideas.

Modifier Placement

Correct placement of modifiers—words, phrases, or clauses that describe in sentences—is crucial for clear and precise communication. Misplaced modifiers can lead to ambiguous or unintentionally humorous sentences.

Examples:

- The student with all the answers, clearly confident, spoke up first in class. (Modifier *clearly confident* is correctly placed next to the noun it describes, the student.)
- She *almost* drove her kids to school every day. (**Incorrect Example**: The sentence suggests she almost decided to drive her kids but didn't.)

    Corrected: She drove her kids to school almost every day.

- They bought a puppy for my brother *called* Spike. (**Incorrect Example**: The sentence seems to suggest the brother is called Spike.)

    Corrected: They bought a puppy called Spike for my brother.

- Running quickly to the store, the rain started to fall. (**Incorrect Example**: The sentence incorrectly implies that the rain was running quickly to the store.)

    Corrected: As she was running quickly to the store, the rain started to fall.

Ensuring modifiers are close to the words they modify avoids confusion. This adherence to grammatical rules enhances the clarity and effectiveness of communication, making it easier for the reader or listener to understand the intended message.

Pronouns, Possessive Pronouns, and Possessive Nouns

Pronouns are versatile words used to replace nouns in sentences, helping to avoid repetitive mentions of the same nouns. They are essential for smoothing out sentences and making language flow more naturally. Pronouns must agree in number, gender, and person with the nouns they replace, known as their antecedents.

Examples:

- *She* went to *her* friend's house. (*She* replaces the name of the female person.)
- *They* asked if *they* could come over. (*They* replaces the names of the plural subjects.)

Pronouns include several types, such as personal (I, you, he, she, it, we, they), possessive (my, your, his, her, its, our, their), reflexive (myself, yourself, himself), and relative (who, whom, which, that). Each type serves different functions, allowing speakers to indicate possession, reflect the action back to the subject, or connect clauses. Mastery of pronoun use is crucial for effective communication, ensuring clarity and precision in expressing relationships and actions within sentences.

Pronoun-Antecedent Agreement

Pronoun-antecedent agreement is a key rule in English grammar that requires pronouns to agree with their antecedents in gender, number, and person. When this rule is not followed, it can lead to confusion and unclear writing.

Examples:

- *The student* lost *his* notebook. (*His* agrees with *the student* in number and gender.)
- *The children* love playing in *their* backyard. (*Their* agrees with *children* in number.)

This rule helps maintain clarity by ensuring that the pronoun clearly refers to a specific noun.

Possessive Nouns vs. Possessive Pronouns

Possessive nouns and possessive pronouns both indicate ownership, but they do so in different ways. Possessive nouns show ownership by adding an apostrophe and sometimes an s to the noun, whereas possessive pronouns replace the noun altogether and do not require an apostrophe.

Examples:

- *John's* book is on the table. (*John's* is a possessive noun.)
- That book is *mine*. (*Mine* is a possessive pronoun.)

Using possessive nouns and pronouns correctly is crucial for clear communication about ownership and relationships between entities. Possessive pronouns, such as my, your, his, her, its, our, and their, help to streamline sentences and enhance clarity by eliminating repeated mentions of the noun.

Possessive Nouns vs. Plural Nouns

Possessive nouns and plural nouns are often confused due to their similar forms, especially with nouns that end in s. However, their functions are different: possessive nouns indicate ownership, while plural nouns indicate more than one of a noun.

Examples:

- The *cat's* toys are scattered everywhere. (*cat's* is a possessive noun, indicating the toys belong to a cat.)
- The *cats'* toys are scattered everywhere. (*cats'* is a possessive noun, indicating the toys belong to the cats—more than one cat.)
- There are three *cats* in the house. (*cats* is a plural noun, indicating more than one cat.)

Understanding the distinction between possessive and plural nouns is essential for writing accurately and clearly. The apostrophe in possessive nouns plays a critical role, signaling a relationship of ownership, which is absent in plural nouns. Mastery of this aspect of grammar helps in preventing common errors and improving the overall quality of writing.

Possessive Determiners

Possessive determiners, also known as possessive adjectives, are a subset of determiners used to indicate ownership or association with a noun. These words sit before the nouns they modify and adjust according to the possessor rather than the object being possessed. Common possessive determiners include my, your, his, her, its, our, and their. They are essential for clarifying to whom or what something belongs, thereby providing clearer, more concise information in sentences.

Examples:

- *My* book is on the table. (*My* indicates that the book belongs to the speaker.)
- Is that *your* car parked outside? (*Your* specifies ownership of the car by the person being spoken to.)
- They can't find *their* keys. (*Their* shows that the keys belong to a group of people already mentioned.)

Possessive determiners are closely related to possessive pronouns, but unlike pronouns, they must be followed by a noun. They help avoid repetition by not needing to continually state the name of the owner and the object. For instance, instead of saying "John's book," you can say "my book" when speaking from John's perspective.

Noun Agreement

Noun agreement in English grammar primarily ensures that nouns match in number and gender where necessary, especially when they are directly linked in a sentence. Such links are most commonly observed in subjects with their predicates and in sentences where nouns interact with possessive pronouns or adjectives. Discrepancies in noun agreement can confuse readers and lead to misinterpretations of what is being communicated.

Examples:

- The list of items are on the desk. (**Incorrect Example**: The phrase list of items suggests a singular subject, but *are* is a plural verb.)

    Corrected: The list of items *is* on the desk.

- Each of the players have their own locker. (**Incorrect Example**: *Each* refers to individual members of a group and requires singular agreement.)

    Corrected: Each of the players *has* his or her own locker.

- A group of students were planning to meet in the library. (**Incorrect Example**: The collective noun *group* requires a singular verb when treated as a single entity.)

    Corrected: A group of students *was* planning to meet in the library.

When it comes to ensuring noun agreement, it's important to identify whether the noun is singular or plural and whether it is a collective noun that could be misleading. Collective nouns like group, team, and staff can be particularly tricky because they may imply plurality but often take singular verbs and pronouns when the group is considered a single unit. However, they can take plural verbs when the emphasis is on the individual members within the group.

In addition to verb agreement, noun agreement with possessive pronouns must also be considered. Singular nouns should be matched with singular possessive pronouns, and plural nouns should go with plural possessive pronouns unless the collective sense is overwhelmingly singular.

Pronoun Clarity

Pronoun clarity in English grammar refers to the clear and precise use of pronouns, ensuring that each pronoun clearly refers to a specific antecedent. An antecedent is the noun or noun phrase that a pronoun replaces, and when pronouns are used without clear antecedents, it can lead to ambiguity and confusion. Maintaining pronoun clarity is crucial for effective communication, as it ensures that the reader or listener understands exactly what or whom the pronouns are referring to in any given sentence.

Examples:

- When Sarah returned Ellen's book back to her, *she* felt relieved.

    Unclear: It's ambiguous whether *she* refers to Sarah or Ellen.

    Corrected: When Sarah returned Ellen's book back to her, Ellen felt relieved.

- Mark told John that *his* performance was excellent.

    Unclear: It's unclear whose performance is being praised — *Mark's* or *John's*.

    Corrected: Mark told John that John's performance was excellent.

- Jessica told Samantha that *she* needed to finalize the report by tomorrow.

    Unclear: It's ambiguous whether *she* refers to Jessica or Samantha.

    Corrected: Jessica told Samantha that Samantha needed to finalize the report by tomorrow.

To avoid such ambiguity, it is essential to ensure that the pronoun's antecedent is immediately clear to the reader. This can be achieved by placing the antecedent in a position close to the pronoun and making sure that it is the only possible noun that the pronoun could be referring to. If a sentence continues to be ambiguous, it is often better to repeat the noun rather than use a pronoun. Another effective method is to restructure the sentence to clarify which noun the pronoun is referring to.

Logical Comparison

Logical comparison in English grammar involves comparing like elements in a sentence to ensure that the comparison is meaningful and clear. Errors in logical comparison occur when dissimilar or unrelated elements are compared, which can create confusion and weaken the clarity of a statement. Here are some correct examples of logical comparison:

- She finds mathematics more challenging than physics.
- Playing the piano is as enjoyable as singing for him.
- The cost of living in New York is higher than in Boston.

Here are some examples of problematic logical comparison:

- Her cooking skills are better than any *chef*. (**Incorrect Example**: This comparison is illogical because it compares her cooking skills to any chef rather than to the *cooking skills* of any chef.)

    Corrected: Her cooking skills are better than those of any chef.

- Reading a book is more interesting than *to watch* a movie. (**Incorrect Example**: The comparison between the gerund *reading* and the infinitive *to watch* creates a mismatch.)

    Corrected: Reading a book is more interesting than *watching* a movie.

- The climate in Iceland is more predictable than *Greenland*. (**Incorrect Example**: This comparison illogically juxtaposes the climate of one place with another place itself rather than with the *climate* of the other place.)

    Corrected: The climate in Iceland is more predictable than the *climate* in Greenland.

In constructing logical comparisons, it is essential to match grammatical structures and ensure that the elements being compared are of the same kind or category. This means comparing nouns to nouns, phrases to phrases, and clauses to clauses, as well as maintaining parallel structures in comparisons that involve actions or qualities. Using comparisons correctly enhances the readability and persuasiveness of writing.

CONVENTIONS OF USAGE

Conventional expression in English grammar refers to using phrases and sentence structures that align with Standard Written English norms. These norms include idiomatic expressions, correct preposition use, and commonly accepted phrasing that native speakers recognize as standard or typical. Here are some examples of conventional English expression:

- She looks forward to meeting you. (Instead of: She looks forward *for* meeting you.)
- They agreed to the proposal. (Instead of: They agreed *with* the proposal.)
- He is responsible for the error. (Instead of: He is responsible *of* the error.)

Here are some examples of inappropriate expressions defying conventional English expression:

- She made a decision *of going* to the university. (**Incorrect Example**: The phrase *made a* *decision of going* is awkward and non-standard.)

> **Corrected**: She decided to go to the university.

- I am interested *for* learning new languages. (**Incorrect Example**: The preposition *for* is incorrectly used with the expression interested.)

  Corrected: I am interested in learning new languages.

- He *should of* completed the project on time. (**Incorrect Example**: *should of* is a common spoken error that stems from the contraction *should've* but is incorrect in written form.)

  Corrected: He should have completed the project on time.

Conventional expressions ensure that the language remains consistent and understandable across various contexts. For non-native speakers and learners of English, familiarizing themselves with these conventional expressions is crucial, as they often differ significantly from literal or direct translations from other languages.

Who vs. Whom vs. Whoever vs. Whomever

Understanding when to use *who, whom, whoever, and whomever* can be one of the trickier aspects of English grammar, particularly because the usage of *whom* and *whomever* is becoming less common in casual conversation.

Who and Whom

Who and *whom* are relative pronouns, but *who* is used as a subject or subject complement, while *whom* is used as an object of a verb or a preposition.

Examples:

- *Who* is going to the store? (*Who* is the subject of the verb is going.)
- *Whom* did you see? (*Whom* is the object of the verb did see.)
- To *whom* should I address the letter? (*Whom* is the object of the preposition to.)

A simple trick to determine whether to use *who* or *whom* is to mentally substitute *he/she* (for *who*) or *him/her* (for *whom*) in the sentence. If *he* or *she* fits, use *who*. If *him* or *her* fits, use *whom*.

Whoever and Whomever

Whoever and *whomever* follow similar rules but are used in clauses that can act as the subject or object within a larger sentence. *Whoever* is used as the subject, and *whomever* as the object in their respective clauses.

Examples:

- Give it to *whoever* asks for it first. (*Whoever* is the subject of the verb asks.)
- Give it to *whomever* you see first. (*Whomever* is the object of the verb see.)
- *Whoever* made the cake deserves a compliment. (*Whoever* is the subject of the verb made.)

In complex sentences, it's crucial to analyze the clause where *whoever* or *whomever* appears to ensure correct usage. Remember, *whoever* acts like *who* (and thus like *he* or *she*), and *whomever* acts like *whom* (and thus like *him* or *her*).

Practical Usage

In modern informal English, particularly in American English, the use of *whom* and *whomever* is declining, often replaced by *who* and *whoever* in common speech. This trend is not typically penalized in casual contexts but might be considered incorrect in formal writing or standardized testing environments.

Here are additional examples to clarify their uses in sentences:

- *Who* knows the best route to Cambridge?
- With *whom* were you speaking last night?
- *Whoever* wins the race will get a prize.
- I will vote for *whomever* you recommend.

Inappropriate Shifts in Verb Tense

Inappropriate shifts in verb tense within a sentence or between sentences disrupt the flow of writing and can confuse the reader about when actions are happening. Consistent verb tense helps maintain clarity and coherence in narrative and expository writing.

Examples:

- Yesterday, we went to the beach and swim in the ocean. (**Incorrect Example**: The sentence incorrectly shifts from the past tense *went* to the present tense *swim*.)

    Corrected: Yesterday, we *went* to the beach and *swam* in the ocean.

- She starts to make dinner, and then she will call her friend. (**Incorrect Example**: The shift from present tense *starts* to future tense *will call* is inappropriate as the actions are sequential.)

    Corrected: She starts to make dinner, and then she calls her friend.

These corrections illustrate how maintaining the appropriate verb tense throughout a passage is essential for readability and ensuring temporal consistency.

Inappropriate Shifts in Verb Voice and Mood

Shifting unnecessarily between the active and passive voice or between different moods (indicative, imperative, subjunctive) within a narrative can make the text difficult to follow and diminish its stylistic coherence.

Examples:

- The cake was made by Maria, and she decorates it. (**Incorrect Example**: The sentence starts in passive voice and shifts to active voice without clear reason.)

    Corrected: Maria made the cake, and she decorated it.

- If he were richer, he buys a big house. (**Incorrect Example**: The sentence uses the subjunctive mood *were* then incorrectly shifts to the indicative mood *buys*.)

    Corrected: If he were richer, he would buy a big house.

Using a consistent voice and mood throughout sentences ensures that the writing remains unified and that the tone or intent is not unintentionally altered.

Inappropriate Shifts in Pronoun Person and Number

It is important to maintain consistent pronoun person and number within and between sentences to avoid confusion and ensure that the writing clearly reflects the intended subjects or objects.

Examples:

- When one tries to learn a language, you need to practice regularly. (**Incorrect Example**: The sentence shifts from third-person *one* to second-person *you*.)

    Corrected: When one tries to learn a language, one needs to practice regularly.)

- If a student wants to succeed, they should study hard. (**Incorrect Example**: Shifts from singular *a student* to plural *they*.

    Corrected: If students want to succeed, they should study hard. Or alternatively: If a student wants to succeed, he or she should study hard.

- Everyone should bring their own lunch, and it should be nutritious. (**Incorrect Example**: Shifts from *their* implying plural to *it* implying singular.)

    Corrected: Everyone should bring his or her own lunch, and it should be nutritious.

Frequently confused words

Frequently confused words often resemble each other in spelling or pronunciation but differ significantly in meaning. Some TSIA2 questions will test your knowledge regarding their differences. Below is a list of such words. This list is by no means exhaustive though.

Accept vs. Except:	Accept (verb): To receive or agree to something. Except (preposition): Excluding or other than.
Advice vs. Advise:	Advice (noun): Recommendations or guidance. Advise (verb): To recommend or inform.
Affect vs. Effect:	Affect (verb): To influence something. Effect (noun): The result or outcome of a cause. Effect (verb): To cause something to happen.
Allude vs. Elude:	Allude (verb): To suggest or call attention to indirectly. Elude (verb): To evade or escape from.
Capital vs. Capitol:	Capital (noun, adjective): A city that serves as a seat of government or capital used in financial contexts. Capitol (noun): A building in which a legislative body meets.
Complement vs. Compliment:	Complement (noun, verb): Something that completes or goes well with something. Compliment (noun, verb): A praise or flattering remark.
Desert vs. Dessert:	Desert (noun): A barren area of land or to abandon. Dessert (noun): The sweet course eaten at the end of a meal.
Discreet vs. Discrete:	Discreet (adjective): Careful and prudent in one's speech or actions, especially in order to keep something confidential. Discrete (adjective): Individually separate and distinct.
Elicit vs. Illicit:	Elicit (verb): To draw out a response or reaction. Illicit (adjective): Forbidden by law, rules, or custom.

Ensure vs. Insure:	Ensure (verb): To make certain or guarantee. Insure (verb): To protect against risk by paying an insurance premium.
Farther vs. Further:	Farther (adjective, adverb): More distant in space. Further (adjective, adverb): Additional or to a greater extent.
Fewer vs. Less:	Fewer (adjective): Used with countable nouns (e.g., fewer apples). Less (adjective): Used with uncountable nouns (e.g., less water).
Principal vs. Principle:	Principal (adjective, noun): Main or head of a school. Principle (noun): A fundamental truth or proposition.
Lead vs. Led:	Lead (verb, present tense): To guide or be in charge. Led (verb, past tense of lead): Guided or was in charge.
Loose vs. Lose:	Loose (adjective): Not tightly fixed or secure. Lose (verb): To be deprived of or cease to have.
Stationary vs. Stationery:	Stationary (adjective): Not moving Stationery (noun): Writing materials, such as paper, envelopes, and pens.
Weather vs. Whether:	Weather (noun): The state of the atmosphere. Whether (conjunction): Expressing a doubt or choice between alternatives.
Your vs. You're:	Your (possessive adjective): Belonging to or associated with the person or people being addressed. You're (contraction): You are.

CONVENTIONS OF PUNCTUATION

The TSIA2 test section on Conventions of Punctuation assesses a test taker's ability to edit and correct written text to align with the rules of Standard Written English punctuation.

End-of-sentence Punctuation

End-of-sentence punctuation indicates the conclusion of a statement, question, or exclamation. The correct use of periods, question marks, and exclamation points helps convey the intended tone and clarity of the message.

Examples:

- She enjoys reading mystery novels (**Incorrect Example**: Missing period.)

    Corrected: She enjoys reading mystery novels.

- Are you coming to the party (**Incorrect Example**: Missing question mark.)

    Corrected: Are you coming to the party?

- What an incredible view (**Incorrect Example**: Missing exclamation point.)

    Corrected: What an incredible view!

Using the correct end-of-sentence punctuation based on the context and intent of the sentence is essential for effective communication. It helps ensure that statements are delivered with the appropriate emphasis and that questions and exclamations are properly identified, thus preventing misunderstandings.

Within Sentence Punctuation

Punctuation within sentences, such as colons, semicolons, dashes, and ellipses, clarifies the structure of complex thoughts and indicates pauses or breaks.

Examples:

- He bought all the ingredients eggs, milk, flour, and sugar. (**Incorrect Example**: Missing commas in a series.)

    Corrected: He bought all the ingredients: eggs, milk, flour, and sugar.

- We will go to the beach we will have a picnic. (**Incorrect Example**: Run-on sentence.)

    Corrected: We will go to the beach; we will have a picnic.

- It's true I saw him there. (**Incorrect Example**: Missing dash for emphasis.)

    Corrected: It's true—I saw him there.

Appropriate use of within-sentence punctuation like colons and semicolons helps manage the flow of information and emphasizes connections or separations between ideas. Dashes can add emphasis or introduce additional thoughts, while ellipses can indicate trailing thoughts or omitted material.

Possessive Nouns and Pronouns

Possessive nouns and pronouns show ownership and are crucial for clarifying who or what something belongs to. It's important to distinguish these from plural forms, which indicate quantity.

Examples:

- The cats bowls are full. (**Incorrect Example**: Missing possessive apostrophe.)

    Corrected: The cats' bowls are full.

- Its a beautiful day. (**Incorrect Example**: Contraction mistaken for possessive.)

    Corrected: It's a beautiful day.

- Their going to their places. (**Incorrect Example**: Misuse of "their" for "they're".)

    Corrected: They're going to their places.

Items in a Series

Correct punctuation in a series involves using commas to separate items listed in a sentence, ensuring clarity and flow.

Examples:

- We need to order paper, pens notebooks, and erasers. (**Incorrect Example**: Missing commas)

    Corrected: We need to order paper, pens, notebooks, and erasers.

- In the summer I enjoy swimming, biking and hiking. (**Incorrect Example**: Missing commas to separate the items in a series.)

    Corrected: In the summer, I enjoy swimming, biking, and hiking.

The following example effectively and correctly uses semicolons to separate items in a complex list where each item itself contains commas.

- She visited Paris, France; Rome, Italy; and Berlin, Germany.

In this example, commas are used within each list item to separate the city from the country, which is standard when listing geographical locations. Semicolons are then used to separate each of these list items from one another. This is the correct approach when items in a list contain commas, as it helps prevent confusion and maintains clarity by clearly delineating each item.

Nonrestrictive and Parenthetical Elements

Nonrestrictive and parenthetical elements provide additional information without altering the fundamental meaning of the sentence and are typically set off by commas, parentheses, or dashes.

Examples:

- My brother, who lives in New York, is visiting us (**Correct**: Nonrestrictive clause.)
- We will go to the beach (if it doesn't rain) this weekend (**Correct**: Parenthetical element.)
- My friend Steve who is a lawyer is coming tonight (**Incorrect Example**: Missing commas to set off a nonrestrictive clause.)

    Corrected: My friend Steve, who is a lawyer, is coming tonight.

- We decided on the movie an action film without much debate (**Incorrect Example**: Missing commas around a nonrestrictive appositive.)

    Corrected: We decided on the movie, an action film, without much debate.

Hyphenation Conventions

Hyphenation is used to avoid ambiguity or to form a single idea from multiple words, especially in compound modifiers.

Examples:

- A well-known author will visit (**Correct**: Hyphenation for compound adjective before a noun)
- It is a hotly-debated topic. (**Incorrect Example**: In modern punctuation conventions, hyphens are not used in adverb-adjective modifiers when the adverb ends in -*ly*.)

    Corrected: It is a hotly debated topic.

- She is a small business owner. (**Incorrect Example**: Without a hyphen, it implies that the business owner is small.)

    Corrected: She is a small-business owner.

- They entered a high stakes game. (**Incorrect Example**: Missing hyphen in a compound adjective.)

    Corrected: They entered a high-stakes game.

Unnecessary Punctuation

Unnecessary punctuation can clutter writing and confuse readers. Recognizing and removing superfluous punctuation helps streamline the text.

Examples:

- We need to cut costs, by reducing unnecessary expenses. (**Incorrect Example**: Unnecessary comma before "by".)

    Corrected: We need to cut costs by reducing unnecessary expenses.

- We visited the zoo, and saw many interesting animals. (**Incorrect Example**: Unnecessary comma before the coordinating conjunction.)

    Corrected: We visited the zoo and saw many interesting animals.

TSIA2 Writing Test Practice Questions

In this chapter, you'll apply the writing skills you've honed to a practice set designed to reflect the real TSIA2 ELAR Test's writing-focused questions. The TSIA2 ELAR comprises 15 reading-focused and 15 writing-focused multiple-choice questions, for a total of 30 questions. The following are 15 writing-focused multiple-choice questions only.

These 15 questions simulate the test's format and content. Once you've completed them, or if you encounter any difficulties along the way, you can turn to the end of the chapter for detailed explanations of each answer to help you understand and learn.

Instructions for questions 1-4

Review the following initial draft of an essay and select the best response to the question or the most suitable completion of the statement.

---

(1) Marine biologists are the stewards of the sea, dedicated to exploring and understanding life in the world's oceans. (2) Through rigorous research, they study the delicate interactions of marine organisms, shedding light on the dynamics of underwater ecosystems. (3) Their work ranges from the analysis of microscopic plankton to the tracking of the majestic blue whale.

(4) A significant portion of a marine biologist's career is spent in the field, often aboard research ships or diving underwater to collect data firsthand. (5) Back in the lab, they meticulously analyze their findings, often using sophisticated statistical models to interpret complex data. (6) They might spend hours cataloging the biodiversity of a single rock pool or mapping the vast, open waters of the pelagic zone.

(7) Marine biologists are also at the forefront of conservation efforts, playing a crucial role in protecting endangered species and habitats. (8) They assess the timelines of human activity, such as pollution, and develop strategies to mitigate its effects.

(9) Their expertise is not limited to fieldwork: marine biologists must also be adept at employing various scientific instruments and techniques to study life forms that are often elusive or difficult to observe. (10) They also need to be proficient communicators, translating scientific jargon into understandable language for the public, stakeholders, and policymakers.

(11) Marine biologists may specialize in a particular branch, like marine ecology or marine mammalogy, becoming experts in niche fields. (12) Their academic contributions, often published in scientific journals, are pivotal in advancing our knowledge of marine science.

(13) Although the job can entail challenging conditions and remote expeditions, it is the passion for discovery and conservation that fuels marine biologists. (14) Their work is essential, not just for scientific advancement but for ensuring the health and sustainability of our planet's marine environments. (15) In essence, marine biologists are the ocean's advocates, tirelessly working to understand and protect its complex and life-sustaining systems.

Question 1: Which is the best version of the underlined portion of sentence 8 (reproduced below)?

They assess the <u>timelines</u> of human activity, such as pollution, and develop strategies to mitigate its effects.

A) (as it is now)

B) history

C) repercussions

D) profitability

Question 2: Which is the best version of the underlined portion of sentence 9 (reproduced below)?

Their expertise is not limited to fieldwork: marine biologists must also be adept at employing various scientific instruments and techniques to study life forms that are often elusive or difficult to observe.

A) (as it is now)

B) fieldwork;

C) fieldwork,

D) fieldwork-

Question 3: Which is the best version of the underlined portion of sentence 13 (reproduced below)?

Although the job can entail challenging conditions and remote expeditions, it is the passion for discovery and conservation that fuels marine biologists.

A) (as it is now)

B) Because

C) Since

D) Unless

Question 4: Which is the most logical placement for sentence 5 (reproduced below)?

Back in the lab, they meticulously analyze their findings, often using sophisticated statistical models to interpret complex data.

A) (as it is now)

B) After sentence 6

C) After sentence 8

D) Before sentence 13

Instructions for questions 5-15

Choose the best version of the quoted part of the sentence. If you think the original sentence is best, choose the first answer.

Question 5: Because she traveled extensively through Europe and Asia, this provided her with rich material for her art.

A) this provided her with

B) she had

C) it provided her with

D) she therefore had

Question 6: Dog training a method sometimes used in behavior therapy.

A) a method sometimes used

B) which is a method used sometimes

C) is a method used

D) method that is used sometimes

Question 7: The travelers enjoyed the scenic view while the boat cruised down the river. They took many photos.

A) the boat cruised down the river. They

B) cruising down the river, they

C) the boat cruising down the river, they

D) the boat was cruising down the river, they

Question 8: The recipe called for tomatoes, the most popular ingredient in Mediterranean cuisine.

A) the most popular ingredient

B) being the most popular ingredient

C) as the most popular ingredient

D) which is the most popular ingredient

Question 9: The students who studying late at night tend to perform well on exams.

A) who studying late at night

B) who often study late at night

C) because they study late at night

D) they study late at night

Question 10: Due to the heavy snowfall, and several schools being closed.

A) and several schools being

B) several schools were

C) with several schools being

D) several schools are hence

Question 11: The committee decided to postpone the meeting until everyone were able to attend.

A) were able to

B) be able to

C) was able to

D) are able to

Question 12: The teacher usually gives us a quiz if we finished the lesson early.

A) if we finished

B) when finishing

C) whenever we are finishing

D) as long as we finish

Question 13: Laughing loudly and waving to the crowd, <u>the mayor's speech</u> captivated everyone.

A) the mayor's speech

B) the speech by the mayor

C) the crowd was

D) the mayor

Question 14: The two scientists presented their findings at the conference where <u>its</u> implications were hotly debated.

A) its

B) one's

C) the

D) their

Question 15: The city has implemented new policies to ensure <u>their</u> financial stability.

A) their

B) its

C) one's

D) it's

Answer Key

Q1: C) repercussions

Explanation: The correct answer is "repercussions," as it fits with the context of sentence 8 provided in the passage. The sentence discusses the role of marine biologists in evaluating the negative impacts ("repercussions") of human activities like pollution and creating strategies to reduce those effects.

Q2: B) fieldwork;

Explanation: The colon is used to introduce an explanation or elaboration of what is stated before it, e.g., a list of items. A semicolon (;), on the other hand, is typically used to connect two independent clauses that are closely related but could stand as sentences on their own. In this case, the second clause is an independent clause, not an extension of the first, which makes the semicolon the appropriate choice.

Q3: A) (as it is now)

Explanation: *Although* is the correct answer because it introduces a concessive clause, indicating that despite the challenging conditions and remote expeditions, marine biologists are motivated by their passion for discovery and conservation. The use of *although* correctly sets up a contrast between the challenges of the job and the driving passion.

Q4: B) After sentence 6

Explanation: Placing Sentence 5 after Sentence 6 allows for a smooth continuation of the theme of fieldwork. Sentence 6 discusses field activities such as cataloging biodiversity, which still pertains to data collection. Following this with Sentence 5, which deals with the analysis of such data back in the lab, creates a more logical and seamless flow of activities from collection to analysis.

Q5: B) she had

Explanation: "She had" correctly joins the dependent and independent clauses, providing a complete and grammatically correct sentence.

Q6: C) is a method used

Explanation: "Is a method used" provides the verb necessary to complete the sentence, ensuring it is not a fragment.

Q7: A) the boat cruised down the river. They

Explanation: Answer A) correctly avoids a comma splice and maintains proper sentence structure.

Q8: A) the most popular ingredient

Explanation: "The most popular ingredient" is a concise appositive phrase that correctly provides additional information about tomatoes.

Q9: B) who often study late at night

Explanation: "Who often study late at night" is a relative clause that properly modifies "students" and provides relevant information.

Q10: B) several schools were

Explanation: "Several schools were" correctly provides a main verb, making the sentence complete and avoiding a fragment.

Q11: Answer: C) was able to

Explanation: The correct answer is C) because *everyone* is a singular indefinite pronoun that takes a singular verb.

Q12: D) as long as we finish

Explanation: "As long as we finish" indicates a condition that must be met for the action to occur, ensuring logical consistency in the sentence.

Q13: D) the mayor

Explanation: "The mayor" correctly follows the modifying phrase, ensuring the sentence logically attributes the actions to the right subject.

Q14: Answer: D) their

Explanation: The correct answer is D) because the antecedent findings is plural, and their is the appropriate possessive pronoun to use with plural antecedents. This ensures subject-pronoun agreement.

Q15: Answer: B) its

Explanation: The correct answer is B) because the word *city* is a singular noun and requires a singular possessive pronoun. *Its* is the appropriate possessive pronoun to use with singular nouns to show possession.

PART III: TSIA2 ESSAY

INTRODUCTION

The Texas Success Initiative Assessment 2.0 (TSIA2) includes a critical essay component designed to evaluate the writing proficiency of students entering college. This component aims to determine whether students are college-ready or require additional developmental education. The essay test is structured to assess overall writing ability, ensuring that students can effectively express their ideas in written form.

The TSIA2 Essay Test involves a single constructed-response prompt, which includes a brief text or passage for the students to read. This passage is not meant to test reading comprehension but rather to provide context for the writing assignment. The prompt typically presents an issue or question, such as, "Has technology enhanced students' educational experiences or become distractions?", or "Should environmental regulations prioritize environmental protection and sustainability or economic growth and development?" Students are then required to write a 300–600-word essay responding to the prompt, developing a point of view, and supporting their position with appropriate reasoning and examples drawn from their experiences, studies, or observations.

The essays are evaluated on a holistic scale from 1 to 8, with specific criteria guiding the scoring process. These criteria include purpose and focus, organization and structure, development and support, sentence variety and style, mechanical conventions, and critical thinking. Essays that are too short, off-topic, or written in a language other than English receive a score of zero.

Holistic scoring considers the overall effectiveness of the essay in conveying ideas clearly and logically. A score of 1 indicates severe flaws in the writing, including a lack of viable points of view, disorganization, and numerous grammatical errors. In contrast, a score of 8 demonstrates a clear and insightful development of the point of view, strong organization, varied sentence structure, and mastery of language mechanics.

TIPS AND STRATEGIES

Scoring well on the TSIA2 Essay requires solid writing skills, careful planning, and strategic execution. Here are some essential tips to help you achieve a high score:

1. Understand the Prompt

Read the prompt carefully to understand what is being asked. Make sure you address all parts of the prompt in your response. Identify the main issue or question and consider your position on the topic. Misinterpreting the prompt can lead to an off-topic response, significantly impacting your score. Spend a few minutes analyzing the prompt to ensure you understand it thoroughly. Consider what kind of response is required—whether it's an argumentative, expository, or descriptive essay.

2. Plan Your Essay

Before you start writing your TSIA2 essay, it is crucial to outline your ideas to ensure a coherent and well-structured response. Spend a few minutes brainstorming and organizing your thoughts. This preparation helps you create a clear outline, which includes your thesis statement, main points, and examples you plan to use. A well-organized outline serves as a roadmap, keeping you focused and ensuring your essay flows logically from one point to the next. This step is essential for structuring your essay and preventing writer's block, as you will have a clear plan to follow.

When planning your essay, remember that your score is based on your writing skills, not your opinion. Do not worry if you choose a position that seems less commonly held; the scorer will not lower your score based on personal bias. What matters is how well you articulate and support your argument. Stick to your chosen stance throughout the essay, even if you start to doubt it partway through—if you have planned your essay well, this shouldn't happen in the first place. Avoid changing your position or taking a middle-of-the-road approach, as this can make your essay appear indecisive and weak. Stay committed to your initial viewpoint and develop it fully.

By outlining your essay and sticking to your position, you can write a focused and persuasive essay that demonstrates your ability to think critically and communicate effectively.

3. Develop a Strong Thesis Statement

Craft a clear thesis statement that presents your main argument or point of view. The thesis statement should be included in your introduction and guide the direction of your essay. A strong thesis statement clearly articulates your stance on the issue and provides a roadmap for your essay. It helps the reader understand your position and the main points you will discuss.

4. Use Specific Examples

Support your thesis with specific examples and evidence. Draw from your experiences, studies, or observations to strengthen your argument. Detailed examples make your essay more convincing and demonstrate your ability to apply reasoning. Using concrete evidence helps illustrate your points and makes your arguments more credible.

5. Organize Your Essay

Structure your essay with a clear introduction, body paragraphs, and a conclusion. Each paragraph should focus on a single idea that supports your thesis. Use transitions between paragraphs to maintain a smooth flow. An organized essay is easier to follow and demonstrates clear logical progression. Each paragraph should start with a topic sentence, followed by evidence or examples, and conclude with a sentence that ties it back to your thesis.

6. Maintain Focus and Clarity

Stay on topic throughout your essay. Avoid tangential information that does not directly support your thesis. Be concise and clear in your writing to ensure your ideas are easily understood. Maintaining focus helps keep your essay coherent and ensures that every sentence contributes to your argument. Clarity in writing involves using straightforward language and avoiding unnecessary jargon or complex sentence structures.

7. Use Varied Sentence Structure

Vary your sentence structure to make your writing more engaging. Use a mix of simple, compound, and complex sentences to enhance readability and maintain the reader's interest. Varied sentence structures can help emphasize different points and keep the reader engaged. This technique also demonstrates your writing versatility and ability to manipulate language effectively.

8. Adhere to Standard English Conventions

Check your grammar, spelling, and punctuation. Errors can distract the reader and undermine your credibility. Proofread your essay to correct any mistakes and ensure it adheres to the conventions of standard written English. Proper grammar, spelling, and punctuation are essential for clarity and professionalism in writing. Consistent errors can significantly lower your score.

9. Show Critical Thinking

Demonstrate critical thinking by analyzing different perspectives and addressing counterarguments. This shows depth in your reasoning and strengthens your essay. Critical thinking involves evaluating evidence, questioning assumptions, and presenting well-reasoned arguments. Addressing counterarguments shows that you have considered multiple viewpoints and are prepared to defend your position.

ESSAY STRUCTURE

Successfully structuring your TSIA2 essay is crucial to ensuring clarity and coherence. Below is a general template or framework that you can follow to organize your thoughts and present them effectively.

Introduction

1. **Hook**: Start with an engaging sentence to grab the reader's attention. This could be a relevant quote, a provocative question, or a brief anecdote related to the essay topic.
2. **Context**: Provide a brief background on the topic. This will help the reader understand the issue and set up your argument.
3. **Thesis Statement**: Clearly state your main argument or point of view. This statement should be specific and assertive, outlining the main points you will discuss in your essay.

Example: "Technology has rapidly transformed how we live, work, and communicate. While some argue that this progression leads to a more connected and efficient society, others believe it erodes our privacy and autonomy. This essay will argue that the benefits of technological advancements outweigh the drawbacks, focusing on improvements in healthcare, education, and communication."

Body Paragraphs

Each body paragraph should focus on a single main idea that supports your thesis. Use the following structure for each paragraph:

1. **Topic Sentence**: Start with a sentence that clearly states the main idea of the paragraph. This sentence should tie back to your thesis statement.
2. **Explanation**: Explain the main idea in more detail. Provide context or background information as needed.
3. **Evidence**: Support your main idea with specific examples, facts, statistics, or quotes. Ensure your evidence is relevant and strengthens your argument.
4. **Analysis**: Analyze the evidence and explain how it supports your main idea and thesis statement. Discuss any implications or significance.
5. **Transition**: End with a sentence that smoothly transitions to the next paragraph, maintaining the logical flow of your essay.

Example: "One of the most significant benefits of technology is its impact on healthcare. Advanced medical technologies like AI and telemedicine have revolutionized patient care. For instance, AI algorithms can predict patient outcomes and personalize treatment plans, leading to better health results. Telemedicine allows patients to consult with specialists without geographic limitations, increasing access to quality healthcare. These advancements improve patient outcomes and make healthcare more accessible and efficient."

Counterargument (Optional)

Including a counterargument can strengthen your essay by demonstrating that you have considered multiple perspectives. Follow this structure:

1. **Counterpoint**: Present a counterargument to your thesis or main points. This shows that you understand and acknowledge opposing views.
2. **Refutation**: Refute the counterargument by providing evidence or reasoning that disproves or mitigates it.

3. **Conclusion**: Reinforce your thesis by explaining why your argument remains valid despite the counterargument.

Example: "Some critics argue that technology diminishes human interaction and increases isolation. While it's true that excessive use of digital devices can lead to social withdrawal, technology also provides new ways to connect with others. Social media platforms and video conferencing tools enable people to maintain relationships and collaborate effectively, even across long distances. Therefore, when used responsibly, technology can enhance rather than hinder social interactions."

Conclusion

1. **Restate Thesis**: Begin by restating your thesis in different words to reinforce your main argument.
2. **Summarize Main Points**: Briefly summarize the main points of your essay, highlighting how they support your thesis.
3. **Closing Thought**: End with a strong closing sentence that leaves a lasting impression on the reader. This could be a call to action, a prediction, or a thought-provoking statement related to your topic.

Example: "In conclusion, while technology presents certain challenges, its benefits in healthcare, education, and communication are undeniable. We can create a more connected and efficient society by embracing technological advancements. As we move forward, it's crucial to balance innovation with mindful usage to maximize the positive impact of technology on our lives."

By following this framework, you can structure your TSIA2 essay clearly and organize it effectively, conveying your ideas and arguments. Practice writing essays using this template to become more comfortable with the structure and improve your writing skills.

SAMPLE ESSAY AND ANALYSIS

Sample Essay 1

Prompt: Social media has transformed the way people communicate and interact with each other. While some argue that social media has fostered greater connectivity and provided a platform for positive social change, others believe it has contributed to increased isolation, misinformation, and negative mental health effects. What is your perspective on the influence of social media on society? Do you think its impact has been more positive or negative? Use specific examples to support your argument.

Sample Essay—Social Media: A Double-Edged Sword

In today's digital age, social media has become an integral part of daily life, connecting billions of people worldwide. While some argue that social media has brought us closer and fostered positive social change, others contend that it has led to increased isolation, misinformation, and adverse mental health effects. Despite its benefits, the overall impact of social media on society has been more negative than positive.

One of the most significant negative impacts of social media is its contribution to misinformation. Platforms like Facebook and Twitter have become breeding grounds for false information and fake news. For instance, during the 2020 COVID-19 pandemic, numerous conspiracy theories about the virus's origin and vaccine misinformation spread rapidly on social media, causing public confusion and hesitancy. This dissemination of false information undermines public trust and can have dangerous real-world consequences.

Furthermore, social media has been linked to negative mental health outcomes. Studies have shown that excessive use of social media can lead to anxiety, depression, and loneliness. Many studies have found that limiting social media use significantly reduced feelings of loneliness and depression among participants. The constant exposure to curated, idealized images of others' lives can lead to unhealthy comparisons and a distorted sense of reality, exacerbating mental health issues.

While some argue that social media fosters connectivity and positive social movements, these benefits are often overshadowed by the platforms' detrimental effects. Although social media has enabled movements like #MeToo to gain global attention, it has also allowed for the proliferation of hate speech and cyberbullying. These negative interactions can cause significant emotional distress and perpetuate a culture of hostility and division.

In conclusion, although social media has the potential to connect people and drive positive change, its negative impacts on misinformation, mental health, and social interactions outweigh these benefits. As society becomes increasingly reliant on these platforms, it is crucial to address these issues to mitigate their harmful effects and foster a healthier digital environment.

Analysis

In this sample essay, the introduction starts with a hook that engages the reader by highlighting social media's integral role in modern society. The context provides a brief overview of the debate surrounding social media's impact, and the thesis statement clearly states the author's position that social media's impact has been more negative than positive.

Each body paragraph begins with a topic sentence that introduces the main point. The paragraphs provide explanations, evidence, and analysis to support these points. For example, the first body paragraph discusses misinformation on social media, using the COVID-19 pandemic as a specific example. The analysis explains how this evidence supports the thesis.

The optional counterargument paragraph presents a counterpoint about social media fostering connectivity and social movements, but then refutes it by highlighting the negative aspects such as hate speech and cyberbullying. This approach shows the complexity of the issue and strengthens the author's argument.

The conclusion restates the thesis in different words, summarizes the main points, and ends with a strong closing statement. This reinforces the essay's argument and leaves a lasting impression on the reader.

By following this structured framework and practicing writing essays on various prompts, you can develop the skills needed to excel in the TSIA2 essay section.

Sample Essay 2

Prompt: "Education is the most powerful weapon which you can use to change the world." — Nelson Mandela. Discuss how education can transform individuals and societies. Do you believe it is the key to positive change? Use specific examples to support your argument.

Sample Essay—Education: The Catalyst for Change

Nelson Mandela once said, "Education is the most powerful weapon which you can use to change the world." This profound statement highlights education's transformative power on individuals and societies. I firmly believe that education is the key to positive change, as it empowers individuals with knowledge, promotes social equality, and drives economic development.

One of the most significant ways education transforms individuals is by empowering them with knowledge and skills. An educated person is better equipped to make informed decisions, solve problems, and contribute meaningfully to society. For instance, consider the impact of education on health. Educated individuals are more likely to understand the importance of nutrition, exercise, and preventive healthcare, leading to healthier lifestyles and longer lifespans. Moreover, education fosters critical thinking and creativity, enabling individuals to innovate and drive progress in various fields.

Education also plays a crucial role in promoting social equality. Access to quality education can level the playing field, providing opportunities for all, regardless of socioeconomic background. For example, scholarships and financial aid programs enable students from low-income families to pursue higher education and achieve their dreams. By breaking down barriers to education, societies can reduce income inequality and promote social mobility. This, in turn, leads to a more just and equitable society where everyone has the chance to succeed.

Furthermore, education drives economic development by creating a skilled and knowledgeable workforce. Countries with high literacy rates and strong educational systems tend to have more robust economies. For instance, nations like Finland and South Korea, known for their excellent education systems, boast high levels of innovation and economic prosperity. Educated individuals are more likely to secure well-paying jobs, start businesses, and contribute to economic growth. In this way, education benefits individuals and strengthens the overall economy.

Critics may argue that other factors, such as political stability and access to resources, are equally important for societal change. While this is true, education serves as the foundation upon which other aspects of development are built. Without a well-educated population, it is challenging to achieve sustainable progress in any area. Education equips individuals with the tools they need to navigate and improve their circumstances, making it an essential element of positive change.

In conclusion, Nelson Mandela's assertion that "education is the most powerful weapon which you can use to change the world" holds true. Education empowers individuals, promotes social equality, and drives economic development, making it the key to positive change. By investing in education, societies can unlock the full potential of their citizens and create a brighter future for all.

Analysis

In this sample essay, the introduction starts with Nelson Mandela's quote, setting the stage for the discussion on the transformative power of education. The thesis statement clearly presents the author's position that education is the key to positive change.

Each body paragraph begins with a topic sentence that introduces the main idea. The paragraphs provide explanations, evidence, and analysis to support these points. For example, the first body paragraph discusses how education empowers individuals with knowledge and skills, using health as a specific example. The analysis explains how this empowerment leads to informed decision-making and innovation.

The essay also addresses potential counterarguments by acknowledging that other factors, such as political stability and access to resources, are important for societal change. However, it refutes this by emphasizing that education serves as the foundation for progress in all areas.

The conclusion restates the thesis in different words, summarizes the main points, and ends with a strong closing statement that highlights the overall benefits of education. This reinforces the essay's argument and leaves a lasting impression on the reader.

Sample Essay 3

Prompt: "Success is not final, failure is not fatal: It is the courage to continue that counts." — Winston Churchill. Discuss how perseverance in the face of failure can lead to success. Do you believe that persistence is more important than talent in achieving success? Use specific examples to support your argument.

Sample Essay—The Power of Perseverance

Winston Churchill once said, "Success is not final, failure is not fatal: It is the courage to continue that counts." This quote highlights the critical role of perseverance in achieving success. I firmly believe that persistence is more important than talent in reaching one's goals, as it fosters resilience, encourages learning from mistakes, and ultimately leads to long-term achievement.

One of the most significant ways perseverance contributes to success is by fostering resilience. Individuals who persist despite setbacks develop the strength to overcome obstacles. For example, Michael Jordan, widely regarded as one of the greatest basketball players of all time, was cut from his high school basketball team. Instead of giving up, he used this failure as motivation to improve his skills, eventually leading him to an illustrious career in the NBA. Jordan's story illustrates how resilience, born from perseverance, can turn failure into success.

Moreover, perseverance encourages individuals to learn from their mistakes. Each failure presents an opportunity to reflect, adapt, and grow. Thomas Edison, who faced numerous failures while inventing the electric light bulb, famously said, "I have not failed. I've just found 10,000 ways that won't work." Edison's persistence allowed him to learn from each unsuccessful attempt, ultimately leading to a groundbreaking invention that transformed society. His example underscores the importance of viewing failure as a steppingstone rather than a setback.

In addition to fostering resilience and learning, perseverance leads to long-term achievement by instilling a relentless work ethic. While talent is undoubtedly valuable, it is the dedication to continuous improvement that often sets successful individuals apart. For instance, J.K. Rowling faced multiple rejections before her Harry Potter series was finally published. Her unwavering commitment to her craft, despite repeated failures, resulted in one of the most successful literary franchises in history. Rowling's journey demonstrates that persistence is crucial for achieving lasting success.

In conclusion, Winston Churchill's assertion that "it is the courage to continue that counts" holds significant truth. Perseverance fosters resilience, encourages learning from mistakes, and drives long-term achievement. While talent is important, it is the persistent effort and dedication to one's goals that ultimately lead to success. Embracing this mindset can help individuals overcome challenges and realize their full potential.

Analysis

In this sample essay, the introduction starts with Winston Churchill's quote, setting the stage for the discussion on the importance of perseverance. The thesis statement clearly presents the author's position that persistence is more important than talent in achieving success.

Each body paragraph begins with a topic sentence that introduces the main idea. The paragraphs provide explanations, evidence, and analysis to support these points. For example, the first body paragraph discusses how perseverance fosters resilience, using Michael Jordan's story as a specific example. The analysis explains how this resilience can turn failure into success.

The essay also includes an example of learning from mistakes, highlighting Thomas Edison's persistence in inventing the light bulb. This supports the argument that perseverance leads to innovation and long-term achievement.

The conclusion restates the thesis in different words, summarizes the main points, and ends with a strong closing statement that reinforces the overall argument. This approach helps present a clear, concise argument, backed by specific examples, maintaining a strong, consistent voice throughout the essay.

Summary

We have shown you three sample essays in this chapter. They seem to follow the same formula, don't they? A formula for success, that is. The TSIA2 test is not the venue to invent or experiment with outlandishly original and daring essay structures. The test designers want to see you have a solid foundation to write and communicate effectively for your college career. So, follow the framework outlined here and demonstrate you do have what they are looking for.

By following this structured framework and practicing writing essays on various prompts, you can develop the skills needed to excel in the TSIA2 essay section. This approach will help you present a clear argument, backed by specific examples, and maintain a strong, consistent voice throughout your essay.

PART IV: TSIA2 MATHEMATICS

INTRODUCTION

The TSIA2 Mathematics suite assesses students' mathematical proficiency, ensuring that they possess the necessary skills to succeed in college. The TSIA2 Mathematics suite is composed of two primary components: the College Readiness Classification (CRC) Test and the Diagnostic Test. Together, these tests provide a comprehensive evaluation of a student's mathematical abilities, identifying areas of strength and pinpointing skills that may require further development.

College Readiness Classification (CRC) Test

The CRC Test is a multiple-choice assessment designed to measure a student's readiness for college-level mathematics. It evaluates a range of mathematical skills across four main content areas:

- **Quantitative Reasoning:** This area assesses the ability to work with rational and irrational numbers, solve problems involving ratios, proportions, and percentages, and apply quantitative reasoning to real-world scenarios.

- **Algebraic Reasoning:** This section evaluates the ability to solve linear equations, inequalities, and systems of equations, as well as manipulate quadratic, polynomial, exponential, rational, and radical expressions.

- **Geometric and Spatial Reasoning:** This component focuses on the understanding of geometric principles, including perimeter, area, surface area, and volume calculations, as well as transformations and trigonometric relationships.

- **Probabilistic and Statistical Reasoning:** This area tests the ability to compute probabilities, interpret statistical data, and draw conclusions from various data representations.

The CRC Test is adaptive, meaning it tailors the difficulty of questions based on the test taker's performance. This adaptive nature allows for a more accurate assessment of a student's capabilities, ensuring that students are neither overburdened with excessively difficult questions nor questions that are too easy.

Diagnostic Test

The Diagnostic Test serves as a complementary tool to the CRC Test, offering a deeper analysis of a student's mathematical strengths and weaknesses. It covers the same four content areas as the CRC Test but provides more detailed feedback on specific skills and competencies.

The decision to administer the Diagnostic Test is contingent upon the results of the CRC Test. If a student's performance on the CRC Test does not meet the established college readiness benchmark, they are routed to the Diagnostic Test. This seamless transition ensures that students who may not be ready for college-level mathematics receive targeted feedback and actionable insights into areas that require improvement.

The Diagnostic Test is also adaptive, allowing for a personalized assessment experience. It is designed to identify a student's current level of understanding, categorizing their performance into levels such as "Beginning Basic," "Low Intermediate," "Middle Intermediate," "High Intermediate," or "Adult Secondary." This classification helps educators and students develop tailored learning plans to address identified gaps in knowledge.

Number of Questions

The CRC Test consists of 20 multiple-choice questions distributed across the four content areas as follows:

- Quantitative Reasoning: 6 items
- Algebraic Reasoning: 7 items
- Geometric and Spatial Reasoning: 3 items
- probabilistic and Statistical Reasoning: 4 items

Students who do not meet the college readiness benchmark on the CRC Test are routed to the Diagnostic Test, which consists of 48 items. The Diagnostic Test provides a more in-depth evaluation of a student's skills, offering detailed feedback on their performance in each content area.

The results from the Diagnostic Test are categorized into levels of proficiency, which help educators and students identify specific areas for improvement and develop targeted instructional strategies to enhance mathematical competency.

How to Prepare and Score Well on the TSIA2 Math Section

If you are nervous about math assessments, you are not alone. Apprehension is often due to past struggles or a need for more confidence in one's mathematical abilities. However, with effective preparation and a strategic approach, you can overcome these anxieties and excel in the TSIA2 Mathematics assessment. Here are some essential tips to help you succeed.

Understand the Test Format and Content

The TSIA2 Mathematics assessment includes the College Readiness Classification (CRC) Test and, if necessary, the Diagnostic Test. The CRC Test consists of 20 multiple-choice questions across four content areas: Quantitative Reasoning, Algebraic Reasoning, Geometric and Spatial Reasoning, and Probabilistic and Statistical Reasoning. Understanding the format can help reduce anxiety by eliminating the element of surprise. This book will familiarize you with the types of questions in each area and hone your skills to tackle them.

Develop a Study Plan

Establish a consistent study routine, dedicating time to each content area. Regular practice is crucial for building confidence and mastering mathematical concepts. The study plan at the beginning of this book will help you review the content needed for the test three times before you take the test, which should reinforce your memory and enhance your confidence.

If needed, you can also reference other books and online resources. Studying the same information from various sources and formats will help you retain it better. Pay attention to strengthening your understanding of fundamental math concepts such as arithmetic operations, algebraic techniques, geometry, and statistics. Solidifying these basics will enhance your performance on more complex problems.

Utilize Test-Taking Strategies

- Pay close attention to the wording of each question to avoid errors.
- Eliminate clearly incorrect options to narrow down your choices and increase your chances of selecting the correct answer.
- Double-Check Your Work: Review your answers for errors if time permits, ensuring accuracy before submitting the test.

Following these simple tips and dedicating time to preparation can alleviate your apprehension and increase your readiness for the TSIA2 Mathematics assessment, ultimately improving your chances of achieving a college-ready score. Now, let's get busy studying!

§1: QUANTITATIVE REASONING

WHOLE NUMBER OPERATIONS

The TSIA2 Whole Number Operations knowledge assesses basic arithmetic skills, including addition, subtraction, multiplication, and division of whole numbers, order of operations, estimation, and rounding, and applying operations to real-life contexts, i.e., word problems.

Whole Number

Whole numbers are non-negative integers that include zero and all positive integers. They form the basic building blocks of arithmetic and are essential for mathematical operations. Whole numbers don't include fractions or decimals, making them suitable for simple arithmetic tasks. Examples of whole numbers include 0, 1, 2, 3, 56, 327, etc. They can be used in various contexts, such as counting objects, keeping track of scores, or measuring discrete quantities. For instance, if you have five apples, three friends, and two books, each of these counts can be expressed as whole numbers, making it easier to perform addition, subtraction, and other arithmetic operations.

Order of Operations (PEMDAS)

Order of Operations, commonly remembered by the acronym PEMDAS, dictates the order in which mathematical operations should be performed to ensure consistency and accuracy. PEMDAS stands for:

- Parentheses: Operations inside parentheses are performed first.
- Exponents: After parentheses, handle powers and roots.
- Multiplication and Division: Next, solve any multiplication or division from left to right.
- Addition and Subtraction: Finally, perform addition and subtraction from left to right.

Examples:

1. $3 + 2 \times 4$: According to PEMDAS, multiplication is done before addition. So, $2 \times 4 = 8$. Then, apply the addition: $3 + 8 = 11$.

2. $(2 + 3)^2$: Operations inside the parentheses come first. So, $2 + 3 = 5$. Then, apply the exponent: $5^2 = 25$.

3. $8 \div 2 \times 3$: Multiplication and division are handled from left to right. So, $8 \div 2 = 4$, and then $4 \times 3 = 12$.

Estimation

Estimation in mathematics is a method of roughly calculating an answer or checking the accuracy of a solution. It provides a way to arrive at a reasonable approximation quickly and efficiently.

Example 1: A tablet costs 244.99, but there is a 20% discount. Approximately how much does it cost now?

Solution: In this problem, the word "approximately" indicates that estimation is needed. The amount can be rounded to 250 or 240 for simplicity. However, rounding to 250 is straightforward, especially for percentage calculations.

Now, 20% of $250 is $50, allowing us to estimate the new cost: $250 - $50 = $200. This estimate is fairly close to the actual cost of $195.99, showing that rounding and approximate calculations can lead to reasonable results.

Example 2: Estimate a sensible answer to 54,893 x 29.

Solution: To approach this problem efficiently, we round 54,893 to the nearest ten thousand: 50,000. Similarly, 29 rounds to 30. The rounded values allow for quicker calculations: 50,000 x 30 = 1,500,000.

Rounding

Rounding to the Nearest Integer

Focus on the digit immediately following the decimal point:

If this digit is between 0 and 4, drop the decimal part, leaving the integer part as it is.

If this digit is between 5 and 9, drop the decimal part and add 1 to the integer.

Example 1: round 12.7 to the nearest integer

Solution: The digit immediately after the decimal point is 7, so the decimal part is dropped, and 1 is added to the integer part, making the number 13.

Rounding to the Nearest Ten

Focus on the ones digit:

If the digit is between 0 and 4, change it to 0, keeping the other digits the same.

If the digit is between 5 and 9, change it to 0 and add 1 to the tens digit.

Example 2: round 347 to the nearest ten

Solution: The ones digit is 7, so it changes to 0, and 1 is added to the tens digit, making the number 350.

Rounding to the Nearest Hundred

Focus on the tens digit:

If the digit is between 0 and 4, change it and the ones digit to 0.

If the digit is between 5 and 9, change it and the ones digit to 0 and add 1 to the hundreds digit.

Example 3: round 2836 to the nearest hundred

Solution: The tens digit is 3, which changes to 0, along with the ones digit, making the number 2800.

You must get the idea now! If you are asked to round to the nearest thousand, million, billion, trillion, and so on, just follow similar procedures as the above.

Inequalities

Inequalities provide a way to compare two values or expressions that are not necessarily equal. Common symbols used to express inequalities include:

< (less than): Indicates that the value on the left is smaller than the value on the right.

\> (greater than): Indicates that the value on the left is larger than the value on the right.

≤ (less than or equal to): Indicates that the value on the left is smaller than or equal to the value on the right.

≥ (greater than or equal to): Indicates that the value on the left is larger than or equal to the value on the right.

Below is a summary of inequalities symbols, their meanings, and how they appear on the number line.

Symbol	Meaning	On the Number Line
<	Less than	Open circle
>	Greater than	Open circle
≤	Less than or equal to	Closed circle
≥	Greater than or equal to	Closed circle

Example 1: Comparing Numbers Directly

Solution: Compare 45 and 38:

Since $45 > 38$, we write the inequality as: $45 > 38$.

Example 2: Inequality Expressions

For more complex scenarios, the TSIA2 test may require evaluating and simplifying expressions. Consider the expressions $2x + 10$ and $4x - 8$. Question: when the first expression is larger than the second? To find out, we write an inequality:

$$2x + 10 > 4x - 8.$$

Rearranging by subtracting 2x and adding 8 from both sides:

$$10 + 8 > 4x - 2x$$
$$18 > 2x.$$

Dividing both sides by 2:

$$9 > x.$$

This example shows how inequalities can help find ranges of values for variables.

Example 3: Inequalities in Real-Life Context

In practical applications, inequalities may compare numerical data. For example, a store offers a discount on products that cost at least $50. A customer has a coupon for 15% off any qualifying item. Question: should the customer qualify to use the coupon, how much will he/she save at a minimum?

We write an inequality to show how much the customer would save: $Savings \geq 0.15 * 50$.

This inequality shows that the customer would save at least $7.50 with the coupon.

This is illustrated on the following number line.

Below are more examples of inequalities illustrated on a number line.

Example 4: $-5 < X \leq 12$

Example 5: $X \leq -1$ or $X > 3$

Whole Number Operations | 81

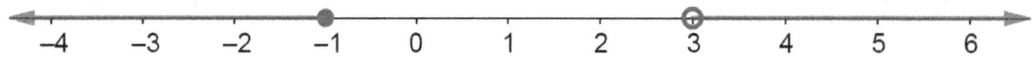

FRACTION OPERATIONS

In this section, we will review arithmetic operations with fractions, including addition, subtraction, multiplication, and division of fractions and mixed numbers, estimation and rounding.

Basic Fraction Concepts

Fraction: A way to represent parts of a whole, a fraction consists of a numerator and a denominator separated by a fraction bar. For example: In the fraction $\frac{3}{4}$, 3 parts of a whole that is divided into 4 equal parts are considered. The top part of a fraction is the **numerator**, indicating how many parts of the whole are being considered. The bottom part of a fraction is the **denominator**, indicating into how many parts the whole is divided. In the above example, 3 is the numerator, and 4 is the denominator. The numbers 3 and 4 are also called the **terms** of the fraction. The term on top of the fraction bar is the numerator, and the term on the bottom is the denominator.

Proper Fractions: Fractions where the numerator is less than the denominator. For example: $\frac{3}{5}$ is a proper fraction because the numerator, 3, is less than the denominator, 5.

Improper Fractions: Fractions where the numerator is greater than or equal to the denominator. For example: $\frac{7}{5}$ is a proper fraction because the numerator, 7, is bigger than the denominator, 5.

Reciprocals: Two numbers whose product is 1. Essentially, you flip the numerator and the denominator. For example: $\frac{7}{11}$ is the reciprocal $\frac{11}{7}$.

Zero as Numerator: Indicates that the fraction represents zero, as nothing is taken from the whole. For $\frac{0}{9} = 0$.

Zero as Denominator: This is undefined in mathematics because you cannot divide by zero.

Mixed Number: A whole number combined with a proper fraction. A mixed number is a way to express a number that includes both a whole part and a fraction part. It combines a whole number (like 1, 2, 3, and so on) with a proper fraction (where the top number, or numerator, is smaller than the bottom number, or denominator), e.g., $2\frac{1}{2}$.

Converting an Improper Fraction to a Mixed Number

Converting an improper fraction to a mixed number involves turning a fraction where the numerator (top number) is larger than the denominator (bottom number) into a number that shows how many whole parts there are, along with a proper fraction. Let's go through how to do this with an example.

Example: Convert $\frac{22}{7}$ to a Mixed Number.

Solution: This can be achieved by the following steps.

1. Divide the Numerator by the Denominator: Divide 22 by 7. When you divide 22 by 7, the quotient (the whole number part of the division) is 3, because 7 goes into 22 three times completely.

2. Calculate the Remainder: To find out how much is left over, multiply the whole number part (3) by the denominator (7), which equals 21. Subtract this product from the original numerator: 22 − 21 = 1.

3. The Whole Number: The quotient from your division (3) is the whole number part of the mixed number.
4. The Fraction Part: The remainder (1) is the new numerator, while the denominator remains the same (7), so the fraction part is $\frac{1}{7}$.
5. Write the Mixed Number: Combine the whole number and the fraction part to form the mixed number, which is $3\frac{1}{7}$.

This conversion demonstrates how an improper fraction can be expressed more intuitively as a mixed number, making it easier to visualize and understand.

Converting a Mixed Number to an Improper Fraction

Converting a mixed number to an improper fraction involves combining the whole number and the fractional parts into a single fraction, where the numerator is larger than the denominator.

Example: Convert $3\frac{2}{5}$ to an improper fraction.

Solution: This can be achieved by the following steps.

1. Multiply the Whole Number by the Denominator: Multiply the whole number part of the mixed number (3) by the denominator of the fraction part (5). This calculation represents the total number of fifths in the three whole parts: $3 \times 5 = 15$
2. Add the Numerator of the Fraction Part: Add the numerator of the fraction part (2) to the result from the first step. This step accounts for all the parts: $15 + 2 = 17$
3. Write the Improper Fraction: The sum from the second step (17) becomes the new numerator, and the original denominator (5) stays the same. So, the improper fraction is: $\frac{17}{5}$.

This improper fraction, $\frac{17}{5}$, represents the total number of fifths in $3\frac{2}{5}$. This method ensures that all parts of the mixed number are accounted for, translating it back into a single fraction format. This can be particularly useful in calculations involving multiple fractions or when needing a consistent format for mathematical operations.

Equivalent Fractions

Equivalent fractions are fractions that, although they have different numerators and denominators, actually represent the same value or portion of a whole. This concept is crucial for simplifying fractions, comparing them, and performing operations like addition and subtraction when the fractions involved have different denominators.

How to Find Equivalent Fractions: To find equivalent fractions, you multiply or divide the numerator and the denominator of a fraction by the same non-zero number. Here are the steps for each method.

Multiplication method

1. Choose a number (other than zero) to multiply both the numerator and the denominator.
2. This number is known as the 'scale factor'.

Example: Find two equivalent fractions for $\frac{1}{4}$.

Solution 1: Multiply both the numerator and the denominator by 2:

$$\frac{1 \times 2}{4 \times 2} = \frac{2}{8}$$

Solution 2: Multiply both the numerator and the denominator by 3:

$$\frac{1 \times 3}{4 \times 3} = \frac{3}{12}$$

Division method

If both the numerator and the denominator can be evenly divided by the same number (this number is known as the 'common divisor'), you can simplify the fraction by dividing the numerator and denominator with the common divisor.

Example: Find an equivalent fractions for $\frac{6}{9}$.

Solution: Since both 6 and 9 are divisible by 3, divide both by 3:

$$\frac{6 \div 3}{9 \div 3} = \frac{2}{3}$$

These examples illustrate how you can either increase or decrease the terms of a fraction while keeping its value unchanged.

The Fundamental Property of Fractions

The Fundamental Property of Fractions, also known as the Multiplicative Property of Equality, states that multiplying the numerator and the denominator of a fraction by the same non-zero number does not change the value of the fraction.

If a, b, and c are numbers, and $b \neq 0$ and $c \neq 0$, then: $\frac{a}{b} = \frac{a \cdot c}{b \cdot c}$

Both the multiplication method and the division method of finding equivalent fractions utilize the Fundamental Property of Fractions.

Greatest Common Divisor (GCD)

The Greatest Common Divisor (GCD), also known as the Greatest Common Factor (GCF), is the largest number that can evenly divide both the numerator and the denominator of a fraction without leaving a remainder. Finding the GCD is crucial for simplifying fractions to their lowest terms.

Steps to Find the GCD:

1. List the Factors of Each Number: Begin by listing all the factors (numbers that divide without leaving a remainder) for both the numerator and the denominator.

2. Identify the Common Factors: Compare the lists of factors for both the numerator and the denominator and identify the numbers that appear in both lists.

3. Select the Largest Common Factor: The largest number in the list of common factors is the GCD.

Example: Find the GCD of 18 and 24.

- **Explanation:**   Factors of 18: 1, 2, 3, 6, 9, 18
- Factors of 24: 1, 2, 3, 4, 6, 8, 12, 24

Common Factors: 1, 2, 3, 6

Greatest Common Factor: 6

Thus, the GCD of 18 and 24 is 6.

Cancellation and Lowest Terms

Cancellation and simplifying fractions to their lowest terms are are used to simplify calculations and make fractions easier to understand and compare.

Cancellation involves dividing both the numerator and the denominator of a fraction by the same non-zero number. This process reduces the fraction to a simpler form, often making it easier to work with in calculations. A fraction is in its **lowest terms** (or simplest form) when the numerator and the denominator have no common factors other than 1. This means the fraction cannot be simplified any further.

Steps for Simplifying Fractions:

1. **Identify a Common Factor**: Find a number that divides evenly into both the numerator and the denominator.
2. **Divide Both Terms**: Divide the numerator and the denominator by this common factor.
3. **Repeat if Necessary**: Continue this process with the new fraction until no further common factors can be found.

Example 1: Simplifying $\frac{18}{24}$.

Solution: First, identify the **greatest common divisor (GCD)** for 18 and 24, which is 6.

Then, divide both the numerator and the denominator by 6:

$$\frac{18 \div 6}{24 \div 6} = \frac{3}{4}$$

Now, $\frac{3}{4}$ is in its lowest terms because the only common factor between 3 and 4 is 1.

Example 2: Simplifying $\frac{40}{60}$.

Solution: The GCD for 40 and 60 is 20. Divide both the numerator and the denominator by 20:

$$\frac{40 \div 20}{60 \div 20} = \frac{2}{3}$$

$\frac{2}{3}$ is in its lowest terms, as 2 and 3 are coprime (they have no common factors other than 1).

These examples show how cancellation reduces fractions to their simplest form, facilitating easier manipulation and comparison of fractional values.

Multiplication of Fractions

Multiplying fractions is straightforward once you understand the basic rule: multiply the numerators together to get the new numerator, and multiply the denominators together to get the new denominator.

Steps for Multiplying Fractions:

1. Multiply the Numerators: Take the numerator of each fraction and multiply them together.
2. Multiply the Denominators: Take the denominator of each fraction and multiply them together.

3. **Simplify the Resulting Fraction**: If possible, simplify the new fraction by dividing both the numerator and the denominator by their greatest common divisor (GCD).

Example 1: Multiply $\frac{1}{4}$ and $\frac{3}{5}$.

Explanation: $\frac{1}{4} \times \frac{3}{5} = \frac{1 \times 3}{4 \times 5} = \frac{3}{20}$

Example 2: Multiply $\frac{7}{8}$ and $\frac{12}{15}$.

Explanation: $\frac{7}{8} \times \frac{12}{15} = \frac{7 \times 12}{8 \times 15} = \frac{84}{120}$

Simplify $\frac{84}{120}$ by finding the GCD of 84 and 120, which is 12. Divide both the numerator and the denominator by 12:

$$\frac{84 \div 12}{120 \div 12} = \frac{7}{10}$$

This example shows how multiplication of fractions can also involve simplification to reduce the fraction to its lowest terms.

Pre-cancelling when Multiplying Fractions

Pre-cancelling (also known as cross-cancelling) when multiplying fractions is a technique that simplifies the multiplication process by reducing the fractions before actually performing the multiplication. This method involves cancelling common factors between the numerators and denominators of the fractions involved in the multiplication. It makes calculations easier and helps to avoid dealing with unnecessarily large numbers.

Steps for Pre-cancelling:

1. **Identify Common Factors**: Look for any common factors that the numerator of one fraction has with the denominator of the other fraction.
2. **Cancel the Common Factors**: Divide the common factors out before multiplying.
3. **Multiply the Remaining Numbers**: Multiply the simplified numerators and denominators to get the final answer.

Example: Multiply $\frac{14}{45}$ by $\frac{27}{28}$.

Solution: Here's how you can pre-cancel. From the first fraction $\frac{14}{45}$, and the second fraction $\frac{27}{28}$:

- Notice that 14 in the numerator of the first fraction and 28 in the denominator of the second fraction share a common factor of 14.
- Notice that 27 in the numerator of the second fraction and 45 in the denominator of the first fraction share a common factor of 9.

Pre-cancel the common factors:

$\frac{14}{28}$ reduces to $\frac{1}{2}$ (14 divided by 14 is 1, 28 divided by 14 is 2).

$\frac{27}{45}$ reduces to $\frac{3}{5}$ (27 divided by 9 is 3, 45 divided by 9 is 5).

Now multiply the simplified fractions:

$$\frac{1}{2} \times \frac{3}{5} = \frac{1 \times 3}{2 \times 5} = \frac{3}{10}$$

The entire process of solving this problem can be written this way:

$$\frac{14}{45} \times \frac{27}{28} = \frac{14}{28} \times \frac{27}{45} = \frac{1}{2} \times \frac{9 \times 3}{9 \times 5} = \frac{1}{2} \times \frac{3}{5} = \frac{1 \times 3}{2 \times 5} = \frac{3}{10}$$

This example shows how pre-cancelling simplifies the process of multiplying fractions, making the multiplication straightforward and reducing the numbers involved.

Division of Fractions

Division of fractions involves reversing the process of multiplication by using the reciprocal of the divisor. The **reciprocal** of a fraction is obtained by swapping its numerator and denominator. This method, often summarized by the phrase "invert and multiply," simplifies the process of dividing fractions.

Steps for Dividing Fractions:

1. **Find the Reciprocal**: Take the reciprocal of the fraction that you are dividing by (the divisor).
2. **Multiply the Fractions**: Multiply the first fraction (the dividend) by the reciprocal of the second fraction.

Example 1: Divide $\frac{3}{7}$ by $\frac{6}{5}$

Explanation: $\frac{3}{7} \div \frac{6}{5} = \frac{3}{7} \times \frac{5}{6} = \frac{3 \times 5}{7 \times 6} = \frac{15}{42}$

As illustrated, the division of fractions is handled through the "invert and multiply" technique, transforming a division problem into a multiplication problem that is often simpler to solve.

Dividing fractions where one or both numbers are mixed fractions involves converting those mixed fractions to improper fractions first, and then following the "invert and multiply" method. Let's go through this with a detailed example.

Example 2: Divide $2\frac{1}{3}$ by $1\frac{1}{2}$

Solution: Convert Mixed Fractions to Improper Fractions first:

$$2\frac{1}{3} = \frac{2 \times 3 + 1}{3} = \frac{6 + 1}{3} = \frac{7}{3}$$

$$1\frac{1}{2} = \frac{1 \times 2 + 1}{2} = \frac{2 + 1}{2} = \frac{3}{2}$$

Invert the Divisor ($1\frac{1}{2}$) and Multiply:

$$\frac{7}{3} \div \frac{3}{2} = \frac{7}{3} \times \frac{2}{3} = \frac{7 \times 2}{3 \times 3} = \frac{14}{9}$$

Here the entire process:

$$2\frac{1}{3} \div 1\frac{1}{2} = \frac{7}{3} \div \frac{3}{2} = \frac{7}{3} \times \frac{2}{3} = \frac{7 \times 2}{3 \times 3} = \frac{14}{9}$$

Adding and Subtracting Fractions

The process of adding and subtracting fractions varies slightly depending on whether the fractions have the same denominator or different denominators.

Adding and Subtracting Fractions with the Same Denominator

When fractions have the same denominator (the bottom number of the fraction), the process is straightforward:

1. **Keep the Denominator**: The denominator remains the same.
2. **Add/Subtract the Numerators**: Simply add or subtract the numerators (the top numbers of the fractions) as indicated.

Example 1: Add $\frac{3}{7}$ and $\frac{2}{7}$

Explanation: $\frac{3}{7} + \frac{2}{7} = \frac{3+2}{7} = \frac{5}{7}$

Example 2: Subtracting $\frac{5}{7}$ from $\frac{6}{7}$

Explanation: $\frac{6}{7} - \frac{5}{7} = \frac{6-5}{7} = \frac{1}{7}$

Adding and Subtracting Fractions with Different Denominators

When fractions have different denominators, you must first find a common denominator before you can add or subtract them. This often involves finding the **Least Common Denominator** (LCD), which is the smallest number that both denominators can divide into without a remainder.

1. **Find the Least Common Denominator (LCD):** Determine the smallest common multiple of the denominators.
2. **Adjust the Fractions**: Convert each fraction to an equivalent fraction with the LCD as the new denominator.
3. **Add/Subtract the Adjusted Numerators**: With the same denominators, add or subtract the numerators.

Example 1: adding $\frac{1}{4}$ and $\frac{1}{6}$

Solution: Observe that the LCD of 4 and 6 is 12. Convert $\frac{1}{4}$ to $\frac{3}{12}$ and convert $\frac{1}{6}$ to $\frac{2}{12}$

Now, add the adjusted fractions:

$$\frac{1}{4} + \frac{1}{6} = \frac{3}{12} + \frac{2}{12} = \frac{3+2}{12} = \frac{5}{12}$$

Combined operations with fractions and mixed numbers

Combined operations with fractions and mixed numbers involve performing multiple arithmetic operations—such as addition, subtraction, multiplication, and division—on numbers in fractional and mixed number forms.

Steps for Combined Operations:

1. Convert Mixed Numbers: If the problem involves mixed numbers, convert them to improper fractions first. This simplifies the process of combining them with other fractions.
2. Find a Common Denominator: For addition and subtraction, ensure all fractions involved have a common denominator. This may involve converting each fraction to an equivalent form.
3. Perform Operations: Apply the relevant arithmetic operations. If the operation is addition or subtraction, combine the numerators as appropriate. For multiplication or division, follow the standard rules for fractions.

4. **Simplify**: Always simplify the resulting fraction to its lowest terms. This may involve finding the greatest common divisor (GCD) and reducing the fraction.

Example: Calculate $1\frac{2}{3} - \frac{3}{4} \times \frac{5}{6} + \frac{1}{2}$

Solution: Step 1: Convert Mixed Numbers

Convert $1\frac{2}{3}$ to an improper fraction:

$$1\frac{2}{3} = \frac{1 \cdot 3 + 2}{3} = \frac{5}{3}$$

Step 2: Perform Multiplication First by following PEMDAS rules.

Calculate $\frac{3}{4} \times \frac{5}{6}$:

$$\frac{3}{4} \times \frac{5}{6} = \frac{3 \cdot 5}{4 \cdot 6} = \frac{15}{24} = \frac{5}{8}$$

Step 3: Perform Subtraction

Subtract $\frac{5}{8}$ from $\frac{5}{3}$ (first find a common denominator, which is 24):

$$\frac{5}{3} = \frac{40}{24}, \quad \frac{5}{8} = \frac{15}{24}$$

$$\frac{40}{24} - \frac{15}{24} = \frac{25}{24}$$

Step 4: Add $\frac{1}{2}$ (convert $\frac{1}{2}$ to $\frac{12}{24}$):

$$\frac{25}{24} + \frac{12}{24} = \frac{37}{24}$$

Step 5: Simplify or Convert to Mixed Number

The result $\frac{37}{24}$ can be expressed as a mixed number:

$$\frac{37}{24} = 1\frac{13}{24}$$

Summary: When performing combined operations with fractions and mixed numbers, the key is to handle one operation at a time, simplify at each step, and always keep track of the order of operations to ensure accuracy.

DECIMAL OPERATIONS

Decimals are a way of expressing numbers that are not whole, using a base of ten. Here's an introduction to some fundamental concepts of decimals:

Decimal Point: The decimal point separates the whole number part from the fractional part of a number. It is denoted by a dot (.)

Writing Whole Numbers as Decimals: Any whole number can be written as a decimal by adding a decimal point and zeros. For example, the whole number 25 can be written as a decimal: 25=25.0. This shows that 25 is equivalent to 25 plus zero tenths.

Powers of Ten: Decimals are based on powers of ten. Each place to the right of the decimal point represents a negative power of ten. The first place to the right of the decimal point is the tenths place (10^{-1}), the next is the hundredths place (10^{-2}), and so on. Conversely, places to the left of the decimal point represent positive powers of ten, like tens (10^1), hundreds (10^2), etc.

Leading Zeros: In decimal fractions that fall strictly between -1 and 1, the leading zero digits between the decimal point and the first non-zero digit are essential for conveying the magnitude of a number and must not be omitted. For instance, for decimal 0.000357, the three zeros between decimal point and number 3 cannot be omitted.

The zero that appears immediately to the left of the decimal point, such as the 0 in 0.468, is sometimes dropped, although the decimal point must remain. Most of the time though, the zero to the left of the decimal point is not omitted. Keeping the zero to the left of the decimal point enhances clarity.

Trailing Zeros: Zeros after the last non-zero digit in a decimal number can affect the precision in a scientific or mathematical context but do not change the value of the number. For example: Compare 0.2500 and 0.25. The first number, 0.2500, suggests a precision measurement to the ten-thousandths place. This indicates a higher precision than 0.25, which suggests a precision measurement to the hundredths place. However, the two numbers are equal in value.

Decimal Place Values

Each position or place in a decimal number has a value based on powers of ten.

- Tenths (10^{-1}): This is the first place to the right of the decimal point. Each unit in this place is one-tenth of a whole.

- Hundredths (10^{-2}): The second place to the right of the decimal point, where each unit is one-hundredth of a whole.

- Thousandths (10^{-3}): The third place to the right of the decimal point, where each unit is one-thousandth of a whole.

- And so on, with ten-thousandths, hundred-thousandths, etc.

Example: Consider the decimal number 45.6789. Here's how each digit fits into the place value system:

- 4 is in the tens place (10^1),
- 5 is in the units or ones place (10^0),
- 6 is in the tenths place (10^{-1}),
- 7 is in the hundredths place (10^{-2}),
- 8 is in the thousandths place (10^{-3}),
- 9 is in the ten-thousandths place (10^{-4}).

Each position affects the value of the number. For instance, the 6 in 45.6789 contributes 6 tenths to the value, or 0.6. The 7 contributes 7 hundredths, or 0.07, and so on.

Multiplying and Dividing Decimals by Powers of 10

When you multiply a decimal by a power of 10, shift the decimal point to the right by as many places as there are zeros in the power of 10.

Example: Multiply 4.567 by 100 (which is 10^2): $4.567 \times 100 = 456.7$

The decimal point moves two places to the right.

When you divide by a power of 10, shift the decimal point to the left by as many places as there are zeros in the power of 10.

Example: Divide 3.25 by 1000 (which is 10^3): $3.25 \div 1000 = 0.00325$

The decimal point moves three places to the left.

If the number of zeros exceeds the number of digits before the decimal in the original number, you may need to add leading zeros. For example, multiplying 0.123 by 10^5 results in 12300, and dividing 0.00456 by 10^2 results in 0.0000456.

Rounding of Decimal Numbers

Rounding decimal numbers is used to make them easier to work with, particularly when precision is less critical. Rounding involves increasing or decreasing a number to a certain place value.

Steps for Rounding Decimals:

1. Identify the Place Value to round to: Determine the decimal place to which you want to round. This could be to the nearest tenth, hundredth, thousandth, etc.
2. Look at the Digit Immediately to the Right: This is the deciding digit.
3. If the deciding digit is 5 or higher, round up by adding one to the digit in the place you are rounding to and dropping all digits to the right.
4. If the deciding digit is less than 5, round down by keeping the digit in the place you are rounding to the same and dropping all digits to the right.

Example: Round 14.5379 to the nearest tenth, hundredth, and thousandth:

To the Nearest Tenth: The digit in the tenths place is 5. Look at the next digit (3). Since it's less than 5, the 5 stays the same. Hence, 14.5379≈14.5.

To the Nearest Hundredth: The digit in the hundredths place is 3. Look at the next digit (7). Since it's 5 or higher, round up the 3 to a 4. Hence, 14.5379≈14.54.

To the Nearest Thousandth: The digit in the thousandths place is 7. Look at the next digit (9). Since it's 5 or higher, round up the 7 to an 8. Hence, 14.5379≈14.538.

Adding and Subtracting Decimals

The key to successfully performing adding and subtracting decimals is ensuring the decimal points of all numbers involved are lined up correctly. Here's how to add and subtract decimals:

Steps for Adding Decimals

1. Align the Decimal Points: Write the numbers so that the decimal points are vertically aligned.
2. Fill in Missing Places: If the numbers have different numbers of digits after the decimal point, add zeros to the ends of the shorter decimals to make them equal in length.
3. Add as Whole Numbers: Ignore the decimal point and add the numbers as if they were whole numbers.
4. Place the Decimal Point: In the sum, place the decimal point directly below the other decimal points.

Example: Add 2.75 and 3.006

Solution: Write the numbers with aligned decimal points:

```
      2.75
  +   3.006
  ─────────
      5.756
```

Steps for Subtracting Decimals

1. Align the Decimal Points: As with addition, ensure the decimal points are vertically aligned.
2. Fill in Missing Places: Pad the number with fewer decimal places with zeros.
3. Subtract as Whole Numbers: Ignore the decimal point temporarily and subtract as if they were whole numbers.
4. Place the Decimal Point: Ensure the decimal point in the result lines up with the decimal points above.

Example: Subtract 7.82 from 10.5:

Solution: Write the numbers with aligned decimal points and pad with zeros if necessary:

$$\begin{array}{r} 10.50 \\ -7.82 \\ \hline 2.68 \end{array}$$

Key Points in this example are:

Alignment: When aligning decimals, it is crucial to be accurate with the placement of decimal points to ensure correct calculations.

Zero Padding: Adding zeros to the ends of shorter decimals does not change their value but helps make the addition and subtraction operations straightforward.

Carry/Borrow: In subtraction, remember to borrow as you would with whole numbers when subtracting one digit from another that is smaller. Similarly, remember to carry over in addition when sums of digits exceed 9.

Multiplying and Dividing Decimals

When multiplying decimals, it's crucial to handle the decimal points correctly to ensure the product has the correct number of decimal places.

Steps for Multiplying Decimals:

1. **Ignore the Decimal Points**: Multiply the numbers as if they were whole numbers.
2. **Count Decimal Places**: Add up the total number of decimal places in both factors.
3. **Place the Decimal Point**: In the product, position the decimal point so that it has the combined number of decimal places from the factors.

Example: Multiply 3.2 by 2.5

Solution: Multiply as whole numbers: 32×25=800

Count decimal places: 1+1=2

Position the decimal point: 3.2×2.5=8.00 or simply 8.

Steps for Dividing Decimals:

1. Make the Divisor a Whole Number: Shift the decimal point in the divisor right until it is a whole number, doing the same shift to the dividend.
2. Divide as Whole Numbers: Perform the division as you would with whole numbers.
3. Place the Decimal Point: Insert the decimal point in the quotient based on the initial shifts made.

Example: Divide 6.75 by 1.5

Solution: Steps for Dividing Decimals:

1. Make the Divisor a Whole Number: We'll adjust the divisor 1.5 to make it a whole number by shifting the decimal point to the right, so 1.5 becomes 15.
2. Adjust the Dividend Accordingly: Shift the decimal point in the dividend the same number of places as the divisor to maintain the balance. So, 6.75 becomes 67.5.
3. Divide as Whole Numbers: Perform the division on the adjusted numbers.
4. Position the Decimal Point: After the division, ensure the decimal point in the quotient is correctly placed based on the shifts made.
5. Now, perform the division:

$$\frac{67.5}{15} = 4.5$$

PERCENTAGE

Percents are a way to express a number as a fraction of 100. The word "percent" comes from the Latin phrase "per centum," which means "by the hundred." This makes percents very useful for describing proportions and comparisons.

For example, imagine you have a jar of 100 marbles, and 25 of them are red. You could say that 25% of the marbles are red. This percentage tells us how many marbles out of every 100 are red, making it easy to understand proportions even if the total number of marbles were to change.

Here's a simple mathematical example involving percents: Suppose you scored 45 out of 50 questions correct on a test. To find out the percentage of questions you got right, you divide the number of questions you answered correctly by the total number of questions, and then multiply by 100 to convert it to a percentage. The equation looks like this:

$$\text{Percentage} = \left(\frac{\text{Correct answers}}{\text{Total questions}}\right) \times 100$$

Plugging in the numbers:

$$\text{Percentage} = \left(\frac{45}{50}\right) \times 100$$

This calculation shows you got 90% of the questions correct.

Any problem involving percents can be expressed in the form "A is P percent of B." In this statement, one of the values A, B, or P is typically unknown. To handle such problems mathematically, we translate the statement into an equation:

$$A = \left(\frac{P}{100}\right) \times B$$

If we divide both sides of this equation by B, we derive the formula for P, the percentage:

$$\frac{A}{B} = \frac{P}{100}$$

This equation shows that the percentage P can be calculated by dividing A by B and then multiplying the result by 100. Let's explore this concept through three practical examples:

Example 1: Finding the Unknown Percent

Suppose you have savings of $500 and you learn that it is a part of your annual savings goal. If your total savings goal is $2000, what percent of your goal have you already saved?

Using the formula: $P = \left(\frac{A}{B}\right) \times 100$ to calculate the percent:

$$P = \left(\frac{500}{2000}\right) \times 100 = 25\%$$

So, you have saved 25% of your annual savings goal.

Example 2: Finding the Total (B)

Imagine you scored 92% on a test, and this percentage represents getting 46 questions correct. How many questions were on the test?

Rearrange the formula to solve for B: $B = \frac{A}{(P/100)}$, plug in the values:

$$B = \frac{46}{92\%} = \frac{46}{0.92} = 50$$

There were about 50 questions on the test.

Example 3: Finding the Part (A)

You want to buy a laptop that is on sale for 30% off its original price of $800. How much discount are you getting?

Apply the formula: $A = \left(\frac{P}{100}\right) \times B$

Calculate the discount: $A = 30\% \times 800 = 240$

You get a $240 discount on the laptop.

These examples demonstrate how versatile the percent formula is for solving various real-world problems involving percentages.

Percentage Increase and Decrease

Percentage increase and decrease are important concepts used to describe how much something grows or reduces in proportion over time.

Percentage increase is used to measure how much a quantity has grown relative to its original amount. It's calculated by finding the difference between the new value and the original value, dividing that difference by the original value, and then multiplying the result by 100 to convert it to a percentage. Here's the formula for calculating percentage increase:

$$\text{Percentage Increase} = \left(\frac{\text{New Value} - \text{Original Value}}{\text{Original Value}}\right) \times 100$$

Example: Suppose last year a store sold 150 units of a product, and this year the store sold 180 units. The percentage increase in sales is calculated as follows:

$$\text{Percentage Increase} = \left(\frac{180 - 150}{150}\right) \times 100 = 20\%$$

This means that sales increased by 20% from last year.

Percentage decrease is used to measure how much a quantity has reduced relative to its original amount. The formula is similar to that of percentage increase, but it starts with the original value being higher than the new value. Here's how to calculate percentage decrease:

$$\text{Percentage Decrease} = \left(\frac{\text{Original Value} - \text{New Value}}{\text{Original Value}}\right) \times 100$$

Example: If a car's value decreases from $20,000 to $15,000 over a year, the percentage decrease is:

$$\text{Percentage Decrease} = \left(\frac{20000 - 15000}{20000}\right) \times 100 = 25\%$$

This calculation shows that the car's value has decreased by 25%.

These calculations help us understand changes in terms of percentages, which are easier to compare than just absolute numbers. Percentage increases and decreases offer a clear and standardized method of measurement.

Convert between Percentages, Fractions, and Decimals

Converting between percentages, fractions, and decimals allows you to interpret and compare different forms of numerical expressions.

1. From Percentages to Fractions and Decimals

Converting Percentages to Fractions

To convert a percentage to a fraction, you simply place the percentage number over 100 and then simplify the fraction if possible.

Example: Convert 75% to a fraction.

Solution: First, write the percentage as a fraction: $\frac{75}{100}$. Then, simplify the fraction by dividing the numerator and the denominator by their greatest common divisor, which is 25 in this case:

$$\frac{75 \div 25}{100 \div 25} = \frac{3}{4}$$

Converting Percentages to Decimals

To convert a percentage to a decimal, divide the percentage by 100 or simply move the decimal point two places to the left.

Example: Convert 75% to a decimal.

Solution: Divide 75 by 100: $75 \div 100 = 0.75$

2. From Fractions and Decimals to Percentages

Converting Fractions to Percentages

To convert a fraction to a percentage, divide the numerator by the denominator to get a decimal, and then multiply by 100 to get the percentage.

Example: Convert 3/4 to a percentage.

Solution: First, divide the numerator by the denominator: $3 \div 4 = 0.75$

Then, multiply by 100 to convert to a percentage: $0.75 \times 100 = 75\%$

Converting Decimals to Percentages

To convert a decimal to a percentage, multiply the decimal by 100.

Example: Convert 0.75 to a percentage.

Solution: Multiply by 0.75 by 100: $0.75 \times 100 = 75\%$

3. Convert between Decimals and Fractions

Converting Decimals to Percentages

To convert a decimal to a percentage, multiply the decimal by 100. This shift of the decimal point two places to the right transforms the decimal into a percentage, as it essentially converts the decimal into a fraction with a denominator of 100.

Example: Convert 0.85 to a percentage.

Solution: Multiply the decimal by 100 to get the percentage: $0.85 \times 100 = 85\%$

This means 0.85 is equivalent to 85%.

Converting Decimals to Fractions

To convert a decimal to a fraction, the steps are as follows:

1. Write down the decimal divided by 1 (e.g., 0.85/1).

2. Multiply both the numerator (the top number) and the denominator (the bottom number) by 10 for every number after the decimal point. This step is necessary to eliminate the decimal point.

3. Simplify the resulting fraction by dividing both the numerator and the denominator by their greatest common divisor.

Example: Convert 0.85 to a fraction.

Solution: Express the decimal as a fraction: $\frac{0.85}{1}$. Since there are two digits after the decimal, multiply both the numerator and the denominator by 100 (10 raised to the power of 2):

$$\frac{0.85 \times 100}{1 \times 100} = \frac{85}{100}$$

Simplify the fraction:

$$\frac{85 \div 5}{100 \div 5} = \frac{17}{20}$$

Thus, the decimal 0.85 is equivalent to the fraction $\frac{17}{20}$.

NUMBER COMPARISONS AND EQUIVALENTS

One type of TSIA2 Arithmetic Test question is comparing values between fractions, decimals, and percentages.

Comparing Decimals

The key to comparing decimal values is understanding the place value of each digit. The digits to the left of the decimal point represent whole numbers, while the digits to the right represent fractions of a whole (tenths, hundredths, etc.).

Steps for Comparing Decimals:

1. Align Decimal Points: Make sure both numbers are written with their decimal points in the same position. If one number has fewer decimal places than the other, add zeros to make the numbers have the same number of decimal places.

2. Compare Whole Numbers: Look at the digits to the left of the decimal point. The number with the larger whole number is greater.

3. Compare Decimal Places: If the whole numbers are the same, compare each decimal place from left to right. The number with the larger digit in the first differing decimal place is greater.

Example: Find the largest among the following decimal numbers: 0.756, 0.765, 0.76, and 0.75.

Solution: Align the decimal points and pad with zeros if necessary to ensure that all have the same number of decimal places:

- 0.756
- 0.765
- 0.760 (added a zero)
- 0.750 (added a zero)

Compare from left to right: The whole number part is the same for all numbers: 0. The tenths place (first digit after the decimal point) is also the same: 7. The hundredths place is where differences appear:

- 0.756 has a 5
- 0.765 has a 6
- 0.760 has a 6
- 0.750 has a 5

The thousandths place further distinguishes the numbers with 0.765 having the largest value (5 compared to 0).

Hence, the answer is that 0.765 is the largest number among the group of numbers given.

Comparing Fractions

Comparing fractions with the same denominator is straightforward, so let's go directly to comparing Fractions with the different denominators. There are two methods: 1.) Cross Multiplication method, and 2.) Common Denominator Method.

Example 1: Compare $\frac{7}{9}$ and $\frac{8}{11}$ using Cross Multiplication Method.

Solution: Observe that $7 \times 11 = 77$, $8 \times 9 = 72$. Since $77 > 72$, we conclude that:

$$\frac{7}{9} > \frac{8}{11}$$

Example 2: Compare $\frac{7}{9}$ and $\frac{8}{11}$ using Common Denominator Method.

Solution: Convert $\frac{7}{9}$ and $\frac{8}{11}$ to fractions with a common denominator: the LCD of 9 and 11 is 99. So, convert $\frac{7}{9}$ to $\frac{77}{99}$ (by multiplying both numerator and denominator by 11). Convert $\frac{8}{11}$ to $\frac{72}{99}$ (by multiplying both numerator and denominator by 9).

Since $\frac{77}{99} > \frac{72}{99}$, we conclude that $\frac{7}{9} > \frac{8}{11}$.

Comparing Decimals, Fractions, and Percents

Some TSIA2 questions ask you to compare a mixture of Decimals, Fractions, and Percents. The two primary strategies are converting each value to a decimal or a fraction, depending on which method is easier. Let's explore both methods.

Convert All to Decimals

This method involves converting every value into a decimal, which allows for a direct comparison between the numbers.

Steps:

- Fractions to Decimals: Divide the numerator by the denominator.
- Percentages to Decimals: Divide the percentage by 100.

Example: Compare these values: $\frac{3}{4}$, 0.65, and 80%.

Solutions: Convert the fraction to a decimal: $\frac{3}{4}$=0.75.

Convert the percentage to a decimal: 80%=0.80

Now, compare all values as decimals: 0.75, 0.65, 0.80.

Conclusion: The correct order from smallest to largest is 0.65, 0.75, and 0.80. Hence, the original values can be order from smallest to largest as 0.65, $\frac{3}{4}$, 80%.

Convert All to Fractions

This method involves converting all values to fractions before making comparisons. This method is preferable if converting all values to decimals is cumbersome. Consider the following example.

Example: Rank the value of $\frac{5}{11}, \frac{7}{13}$, and 45%, from smallest to largest.

Solutions: It is obvious converting $\frac{5}{11}$ and $\frac{7}{13}$ into decimals is not the easiest task if you are doing long division manually. At the same time, it is obvious 45% can readily be converted into a fraction. Based on these observations, we can determine that the best step forward is probably to compare the three values as fractions using the cross multiplication method.

1. Convert 45% to a fraction: $45\% = \frac{45}{100} = \frac{9}{20}$. So, the three values to compare become: $\frac{5}{11}, \frac{7}{13}$, and $\frac{9}{20}$.
2. Compare $\frac{5}{11}$ and $\frac{7}{13}$. Cross-multiply to find: $5 \times 13 = 65$, $7 \times 11 = 77$.

Since $65 < 77$, we know $\frac{5}{11} < \frac{7}{13}$.

3. Compare $\frac{7}{13}$ and $\frac{9}{20}$. Cross-multiply to find: $7 \times 20 = 140$, $9 \times 13 = 117$.

   Since $140 > 117$, $\frac{7}{13} > \frac{9}{20}$.

4. Now that we know $\frac{7}{13}$ is the largest value, we still need to compare $\frac{5}{11}$ and $\frac{9}{20}$. Cross-multiply to find: $7 \times 20 = 140$, $9 \times 13 = 117$. Since $140 > 117$, $\frac{7}{13} > \frac{9}{20}$.

5. Hence, we conclude that: $\frac{9}{20} < \frac{5}{11} < \frac{7}{13}$.

An astute test-take may also be able to determine $\frac{7}{13}$ to be bigger than $\frac{5}{11}$ and 45% by noticing that $\frac{7}{13}$ is larger than 0.5, while the other two items are smaller than 0.5. This will help save two cross-multiplication comparisons.

In conclusion, when faced with TSIA2 comparisons questions between decimals, fractions, and percents, it is advisable to first assess quickly which method above is easier and then solve the problem accordingly.

Word Problems

The TSIA2 word problems, or math questions set in real-life contexts, challenge students to apply their mathematical knowledge practically. These questions test not only a student's math skills but also their ability to comprehend English, requiring careful interpretation of problem descriptions to determine how to approach the solution.

Basic steps when faced with word problems include:

- **Understand the Problem**: Carefully read and comprehend the problem to identify key instructions and requirements.
- **Identify Key Information**: Keep a mental note of relevant data, units, and mathematical operations required.
- **Plan and Solve**: Translate the word problem into mathematical expressions, equations, or series of calculations, then solve step by step.

Below are examples of the type of word problems you may run into in an TSIA2 test.

Addition/Subtraction Problem

Example 1: After her gym session, Sarah decided to do some shopping. She purchased new workout gear for $35.75 and bought two protein bars from the counter, each costing $1.25. Afterward, she treated herself to a smoothie, which was $6.50. What was the total amount that Sarah spent on these three purchases?

Solution:

Workout Gear: 35.75

Protein Bars: 2×1.25=2.50

Smoothie: 6.50

Total = 35.75 + 2.50 + 6.50 = 44.75.

Sarah spent a total of $44.75 on her shopping trip.

Example 2: Charlotte, a baker, starts Monday with an inventory of 5,275 cookies at her bakery. During the day, she sells 600 cookies to customers and bakes more batches to keep up with the demand. By the end of the day, her bakery's cookie count has reached 5,700. How many cookies did Charlotte's bakery bake on Monday?

Explanation: Initial Cookie Count (Monday Morning): 5,275

Cookies Sold During the Day: 600

Final Cookie Count (Monday Evening): 5,700

First, find out how many cookies should have been there if no new batches were baked:

Expected Count = 5275 − 600 = 4675

Now, calculate how many new cookies were baked to reach the final count of 5,700:

Cookies Baked = 5700 − 4675 = 1025

So, Charlotte's bakery baked 1,025 cookies on Monday to replenish the inventory after the sales.

Multiplication/Division Problem

Example 1: As part of a community outreach project, Carlos plans to distribute a 45-page brochure to each of the 20 organizations in his network. In addition, he wants to keep an extra 5% of the total number of brochures as a backup for any additional requests. How many pages will Carlos need to produce in total?

Explanation: Step 1: Calculate the total number of brochures required, including the backup:

$$\text{Total Brochures} = 20 \times 1.05 = 21$$

Step 2: Calculate the total number of pages required:

$$\text{Total Pages} = 45 \times 21 = 945.$$

Carlos will need to produce a total of 945 pages.

Example 2: A biologist needs to collect 528 leaf samples from various tree species in a forest research project. The project requires the biologist to divide the samples evenly among 24 research sites in the forest. How many leaf samples should be collected at each site?

Explanation: To determine how many leaf samples should be collected at each research site, divide the total number of samples by the number of sites:

$$\text{Samples per Site} = \frac{528}{24} = 22.$$

At each research site, one will need to collect 22 leaf samples.

Maximum/Minimum Problem

Example 1: A chemical storage tank can hold a maximum of 4,500 liters of liquid. Jordan needs to fill it with barrels of ethanol, each containing 320 liters. What is the maximum number of whole barrels that Jordan can fill the tank with?

Solution: To find out how many whole barrels can fit in the tank, divide the tank's capacity by the volume per barrel:

$$\text{Maximum Barrels} = \frac{4500}{320} \approx 14.06.$$

Since the tank can only hold whole barrels, round down to the nearest whole number: Maximum Barrels=14. Jordan can fill the tank with a maximum of 14 barrels of ethanol.

Example 2: As part of a new diet, Benjamin plans to drink at least 2,000 milliliters of water each day. He uses a reusable bottle that holds 350 milliliters. How many full bottles does Benjamin need to drink each day to reach his goal?

Solution: To find out how many full bottles Benjamin needs to drink, divide the daily water goal by the capacity of the bottle:

$$\text{Bottles Required} = \frac{2000}{350} \approx 5.71.$$

Since Benjamin can only drink whole bottles, round up to the nearest whole number: Bottles Required=6. Benjamin needs to drink at least 6 full bottles of water daily to meet his goal of 2,000 milliliters.

Parts of the Whole Problem

Example 1: In a local astronomy club, members voted on a new logo design. Design A received 36.2% of the votes, Design B garnered 29.4%, and Design C obtained 14.8%. The remaining votes were given to Design D. What percentage of the votes did Design D receive?

Solution: To find the percentage of votes that Design D received, first calculate the total percentage that Designs A, B, and C collectively obtained: 36.2+29.4+14.8=80.4.

To find the percentage of votes for Design D, subtract the total above from 100%: 100−80.4=19.6. Thus, Design D received 19.6% of the votes.

Example 2: A space research team is studying the different types of stars in a newly discovered star cluster. They determined that $\frac{1}{3}$ of the stars are red dwarfs and $\frac{1}{4}$ are white dwarfs. The remaining stars are either neutron stars or main-sequence stars. What fraction of the stars are neutron stars or main-sequence stars?

Solution: To find the fraction of neutron stars or main-sequence stars, first calculate the total fraction of stars that are either red dwarfs or white dwarfs.

Step 1: Find a common denominator to add the fractions $\frac{1}{3}$ and $\frac{1}{4}$. The least common denominator (LCD) is 12.

Step 2: Add the fractions:

$$\frac{1}{3} + \frac{1}{4} = \frac{4}{12} + \frac{3}{12} = \frac{7}{12}$$

This sum represents the fraction of stars that are either red dwarfs or white dwarfs.

Step 3: Subtract this from 1 to find the fraction of stars that are neutron stars or main-sequence stars.

$$1 - \frac{7}{12} = \frac{12}{12} - \frac{7}{12} = \frac{5}{12}$$

So, $\frac{5}{12}$ of the stars are neutron stars or main-sequence stars.

PRE-ALGEBRA CONCEPTS

Quantitative Reasoning in TSIA2 evaluates your ability to interpret numerical data and apply mathematical concepts in real-world situations. You'll handle rates, ratios, proportions, unit conversions, and so on, all crucial for practical problem-solving in daily life and non-STEM academic fields.

We will also cover the following Pre-Algebra concepts in this section: rational numbers, exponents, radicals, fractional exponents, and scientific notation.

Real Numbers

Real numbers form the comprehensive set of numbers used in mathematics, including rational and irrational ones. They represent all points on the number line and include various number types, from the simplest counting numbers to complex fractional and irrational forms.

Types of Real Numbers:

Natural Numbers: These are also known as counting numbers, which are the numbers used for counting objects. They start from 1 and continue infinitely: 1, 2, 3, 4, 5,...

Integers: This set includes all natural numbers, their negatives, and zero. Unlike natural numbers, integers cover both positive and negative values: ...,−3, −2, −1, 0, 1, 2, 3,...

Rational Numbers: Any number that can be expressed as a ratio (or fraction) of two integers is a rational number. This set includes all integers and fractions where the denominator is not zero. Examples include: $34, -2, -\frac{5}{7}, 0.75, \frac{49}{57}$ ...

Irrational Numbers: These are numbers that cannot be expressed as simple fractions. They have non-terminating, non-repeating decimal representations. Famous examples include:

- $\sqrt{2}$ (the square root of 2)
- π (the ratio of a circle's circumference to its diameter)

To recap, real numbers encompass all rational and irrational numbers. This vast collection allows for accurate representation and measurement of distances, quantities, and other numerical concepts.

Absolute Value

The absolute value of a number is its distance from zero on the number line, regardless of direction. It is always a non-negative value. The notation for absolute value is two vertical bars surrounding the number, like this: |x|.

Examples:

- |5| = 5 because 5 is 5 units away from zero.
- |-8| = 8 because -8 is 8 units away from zero.
- |0| = 0 because 0 is exactly at zero.

Absolute value is handled similarly to parentheses in the order of operations (PEMDAS):

- P: Parentheses (including absolute value bars)
- E: Exponents (including roots)
- MD: Multiplication and Division (left to right)
- AS: Addition and Subtraction (left to right)

This means that any operation inside the absolute value bars should be evaluated first, and the result's absolute value is taken afterward.

Examples:

- Simple Absolute Value: $|-4| = 4$
- Absolute Value with Expressions: $|5 - 8| = |-3| = 3$
- Combining Absolute Value with Other Operations:

$$3 \times |4 - 6| + 2 = 3 \times |-2| + 2 = 3 \times 2 + 2 = 6 + 2 = 8$$

- Absolute Value with Nested Operations: $|(2^3 - 10)| = |8 - 10| = |-2| = 2$

In all these cases, operations inside the absolute value bars are completed first, followed by taking the absolute value itself and then any other arithmetic operations outside the bars.

Rates

In arithmetic, a rate is a specific kind of ratio that compares two quantities with different units. It is a measure of one quantity relative to another, allowing us to understand how one variable changes with respect to another. Rates are commonly used to describe things like speed, price per unit, or productivity, etc.

Examples of Rates:

1. **Speed (Distance/Time):**
    - Speed is often expressed as a rate, such as miles per hour (mph) or kilometers per hour (km/h).

    Example: If a car travels 120 miles in 2 hours, its speed is: $\frac{120 \ miles}{2 \ hours} = 60 \ mph$

2. **Price (Cost/Unit):**
    - Prices are rates that indicate how much something costs per unit.

    Example: If a 10-pound bag of apples costs $20, the cost per pound is:

    $$\frac{20 \ dollars}{10 \ pounds} = 2 \ dollars \ per \ pound$$

3. **Productivity (Output/Time):**
    - Productivity rates describe the output or result produced within a given period.

    Example: If a worker assembles 300 items in 8 hours, the productivity rate is:

    $$\frac{300 \ items}{8 \ hours} = 37.5 \ items \ per \ hour$$

Unit Conversion

When you know the rate between two units, you can easily convert from one to the other. This is particularly useful when dealing with measurements like speed, currency, and volume.

Example: Suppose you have a speed of 60 miles per hour (mph) and want to convert it to kilometers per hour (km/h). The conversion rate is: 1 mile=1.60934 kilometers.

To convert 60 mph to km/h, multiply by the conversion factor:

$$60\, mph \times 1.60934\, km/mile = 96.56\, km/h$$

Therefore, 60 mph is equivalent to approximately 96.56 km/h.

Unit Rate

A unit rate is a rate where the denominator is reduced to 1. For example, if the speed of a vehicle is 60 mph, the rate is a unit rate—"miles per one hour," or simply "miles per hour". This contrasts with "miles per every two hours", or "miles per every 10 minutes", which are also rates, but not unit rates.

Ratios and Proportional Relationships

A **ratio** is a comparison of two or more numbers, often representing how many times one quantity is contained within another. Ratios can be written in different ways, including:

- Fraction Form: $\frac{a}{b}$
- Colon Form: a:b
- Word Form: "a to b"

Example: 3/5 or 3:5 or "3 to 5" are all ratios expressed differently but are equal in value.

In practice, you might encounter questions involving simplifying ratios, finding equivalent ratios, or comparing different ratios.

A **proportional relationship** occurs when two quantities always have the same ratio or are directly proportional. In other words, as one quantity increases or decreases, the other changes at a consistent rate.

These relationships can often be expressed as: $y = kx$, where y and x are the variables in the relationship, k is the constant of proportionality.

Example: If a recipe calls for 3 cups of flour to make 24 cookies, you can determine the cups of flour needed for 48 cookies through a proportion:

$$\frac{3}{24} = \frac{x}{48}$$

Cross-multiplying gives:

$$x = \frac{3 \times 48}{24} = 6$$

This shows that 6 cups of flour are needed to make 48 cookies.

You may get asked these types of questions on TSIA2:

- **Proportional Reasoning**: Questions may ask you to determine the missing value in a proportion or identify if two sets of values are proportional.
- **Rates and Unit Rates**: These could involve calculating unit prices, speeds, or other rates.
- **Scale Factors**: You might need to work with maps, diagrams, or blueprints involving scaling.

Exponents

Exponents represent repeated multiplication of a base number. Understanding different types of exponents and their applications is fundamental in algebra and scientific calculations. Here's an overview of various exponent concepts.

Positive Whole-Number Exponents

A positive whole-number exponent represents how many times a base number is multiplied by itself. It's a form of repeated multiplication that simplifies large calculations.

General Form: If a is the base and n is the exponent (a positive whole number), then:

$a^n = a \times a \times a \times \ldots (n \text{ times})$

Examples:

- $2^3 = 2 \times 2 \times 2 = 8$
- $5^4 = 5 \times 5 \times 5 \times 5 = 625$
- $10^2 = 10 \times 10 = 100$

Properties of Positive Whole-Number Exponents:

1. **Multiplying with the Same Base:** When multiplying two expressions with the same base, add their exponents: $a^m \times a^n = a^{m+n}$

   Example: $2^3 \times 2^2 = 2^{3+2} = 2^5 = 32$

2. **Dividing with the Same Base:** When dividing two expressions with the same base, subtract their exponents: $a^m \div a^n = a^{m-n}$

   Example: $7^5 \div 7^2 = 7^{5-2} = 7^3 = 343$

3. **Power of a Power:** When raising an expression with an exponent to another power, multiply the exponents: $(a^m)^n = a^{m \times n}$

   Example: $(3^2)^3 = 3^{2 \times 3} = 3^6 = 729$

Zero Exponents

Any nonzero base raised to the power of zero equals 1. This rule simplifies calculations involving expressions with zero exponents.

General Rule: $a^0 = 1$, where $a \neq 0$

Example: $(-5)^0 = 1$

This rule applies because, by definition, an expression like $a^n \div a^n$ equals 1.

Meanwhile, $a^n \div a^n = a^{(n-n)} = a^0$. Hence, $a^0 = 1$.

Negative Exponents

A negative exponent represents the reciprocal of a base raised to the corresponding positive exponent. This concept flips the base to its reciprocal and changes the sign of the exponent to positive. Sounds confusing? The example below will clarify it.

General Rule: For any nonzero number a and positive integer n:

$$a^{-n} = \frac{1}{a^n}$$

Examples:

- $4^{-2} = \frac{1}{4^2} = \frac{1}{16}$
- $10^{-3} = \frac{1}{10^3} = \frac{1}{1000} = 0.001$
- $(2x)^{-3} = \frac{1}{(2x)^3} = \frac{1}{8x^3}$

Properties of Negative Exponents:

1. **Multiplying with the Same Base:** When multiplying two expressions with the same base, add the exponents even if one or both are negative: $a^m \times a^{-n} = a^{m-n}$

   Example: $5^3 \times 5^{-2} = 5^{3-2} = 5^1 = 5$

2. **Dividing with the Same Base:** When dividing two expressions with the same base, subtract the exponents: $\frac{a^m}{a^{-n}} = a^{m+n}$

   Example: $\frac{2^4}{2^{-2}} = 2^{4+2} = 2^6 = 64$

3. **Power of a Power:** When raising a base with a negative exponent to another power, multiply the exponents: $(a^{-m})^n = a^{-m \times n}$

   Example: $(3^{-2})^4 = 3^{-8} = \frac{1}{3^8}$

Negative exponents allow for easy representation of reciprocals and small values. They are commonly used in scientific notation and simplify algebraic expressions involving division and reciprocal relationships.

Radicals

Radicals represent roots of numbers and provide a way to express roots in a simplified form. The most common type is the square root, but radicals can represent other roots like cube roots, fourth roots, etc.

Examples:

- **Square Root** ($\sqrt{x}$): The square root of a number x is a value y such that $y^2 = x$. Example: $\sqrt{16} = 4$ because $4^2 = 16$.

- **Cube Root** ($\sqrt[3]{x}$): The cube root of a number x is a value y such that $y^3 = x$.

    Example: $\sqrt[3]{27} = 3$ because $3^3 = 27$.

- **General Roots**: Other roots follow the same pattern, $\sqrt[n]{x}$ represents a radical where n is called the **root** of the radical.

    Example: $\sqrt[4]{81} = 3$

Properties of Radicals:

1. **Product Rule:** The product of two radicals can be combined into a single radical: $\sqrt[n]{a} \times \sqrt[n]{b} = \sqrt[n]{a \times b}$

   Example: $\sqrt{4} \times \sqrt{9} = \sqrt{36} = 6$

2. **Quotient Rule:** The quotient of two radicals can also be combined: $\sqrt[n]{\frac{a}{b}} = \frac{\sqrt[n]{a}}{\sqrt[n]{b}}$.

   Example: $\frac{\sqrt{25}}{\sqrt{4}} = \sqrt{\frac{25}{4}} = \frac{5}{2}$

Fractional Exponents

Fractional exponents are another way to represent roots or radicals. Instead of using the radical symbol, a root is expressed as an exponent in fractional form. This notation provides a concise way to represent both roots and powers.

General Form:

If a is the base and $\frac{m}{n}$ is the fractional exponent: $a^{\frac{m}{n}} = \sqrt[n]{a^m}$

where: n is the root (index), m is the power to which the base is raised before taking the root.

Examples:

- **Square Root** (Fractional Exponent as $\frac{1}{2}$): The square root of a number a is expressed using a fractional exponent as: $a^{\frac{1}{2}} = \sqrt{a}$.

  Example: $25^{\frac{1}{2}} = \sqrt{25} = 5$

- **Cube Root** (Fractional Exponent as $\frac{1}{3}$): The cube root of a number a is expressed using a fractional exponent as: $a^{\frac{1}{3}} = \sqrt[3]{a}$

  Example: $27^{\frac{1}{3}} = \sqrt[3]{27} = 3$.

- **Combining Roots and Powers:** A fractional exponent like $\frac{3}{4}$ indicates that the base should first be raised to the power of 3, and then the fourth root is taken: $a^{\frac{3}{4}} = \sqrt[4]{a^3}$.

  Example: $16^{\frac{3}{4}} = \sqrt[4]{16^3} = \sqrt[4]{4096} = 8$

Powers of 10

Powers of 10 refer to multiplying the base 10 by itself a certain number of times. They are especially important because our number system is based on powers of 10. This notation helps represent very large or very small numbers conveniently.

General Form:

If n is a positive integer, a power of 10 is expressed as: $10^n = 10 \times 10 \times 10 \times \ldots (n \text{ times})$

Examples: Positive Powers of 10

- $10^1 = 10$
- $10^3 = 10 \times 10 \times 10 = 1000$
- $10^6 = 1,000,000$ (one million)

A positive power of 10 shows how many zeros follow the number 1 in the standard form we write numbers, e.g., 1000, 1,000,000.

Examples: Negative Powers of 10

- $10^{-1} = \frac{1}{10} = 0.1$
- $10^{-2} = \frac{1}{10^2} = \frac{1}{100} = 0.01$
- $10^{-6} = 0.000001$ (one millionth)

A negative power of 10 shows how many decimal places the 1 is shifted to the left of the decimal point.

Scientific Notation

Powers of 10 are used extensively in scientific notation, a method to express very large or very small numbers. Scientific notation combines a coefficient and a power of 10: $a \times 10^n$, where a is a number between 1 and 10, n is an integer representing the power of 10.

Examples:

- The mass of Earth is approximately 5.97×10^{24} kilograms, a very large number.
- The mass of a hydrogen atom is about 1.67×10^{-27} kilograms, a very small number.

Calculations involving scientific notation follow the same rules as ordinary exponents. Here's a guide to handling scientific notation in various arithmetic operations:

Multiplication: To multiply numbers in scientific notation, multiply the coefficients and add the exponents of the powers of 10.

Example: $(2.5 \times 10^3) \times (4 \times 10^2)$

Solution:

1. Multiply the coefficients: $2.5 \times 4 = 10$
2. Add the exponents: $10^3 \times 10^2 = 10^{3+2} = 10^5$
3. Combine the results: $10 \times 10^5 = 1.0 \times 10^6$

Division: To divide numbers in scientific notation, divide the coefficients and subtract the exponents of the powers of 10.

Example: $\frac{4.8 \times 10^5}{2 \times 10^3}$

Solution:

1. Divide the coefficients: $\frac{4.8}{2} = 2.4$
2. Subtract the exponents: $10^5 \div 10^3 = 10^{5-3} = 10^2$
3. Combine the results: 2.4×10^2

Addition and Subtraction: When adding or subtracting numbers in scientific notation, make sure the exponents are the same before combining the coefficients.

Example: $(3.5 \times 10^4) + (2.3 \times 10^3)$

Solution:

1. Adjust the second term so the exponents match: $2.3 \times 10^3 = 0.23 \times 10^4$
2. Add the coefficients: $3.5 + 0.23 = 3.73$
3. Combine with the power of 10: 3.73×10^4

Summary of the Exponent Operation Rules

Now that we have spent so much time on exponents, let's summarize all the fundamental rules of exponent operations in one table.

Rule	Example
$x^n x^m = x^{n+m}$	$7^3 \cdot 7^2 = 7^5$
$\dfrac{x^n}{x^m} = x^{n-m}$	$\dfrac{5^5}{5^3} = 5^{5-3} = 5^2 = 25$
$x^0 = 1 \text{ provided } x \neq 0$	$39^0 = 1$
$(x \cdot y)^n = x^n \cdot y^n$	$(3 \cdot 4)^2 = 3^2 \cdot 4^2 = 9 \cdot 16 = 144$
$\left(\dfrac{x}{y}\right)^n = \dfrac{x^n}{y^n}$	$\left(\dfrac{1}{3}\right)^2 = \dfrac{1^2}{3^2} = \dfrac{1}{9}$
$(x^n)^m = x^{n \cdot m}$	$(2^3)^4 = 2^{3 \cdot 4} = 2^{12}$
$x^{-n} = \dfrac{1}{x^n} \text{ provided } X \neq 0$	$10^{-3} = \dfrac{1}{10^3}$

§2. Algebraic Reasoning

Algebra is a branch of mathematics that focuses on the manipulation of symbols and variables to represent and solve equations and expressions. It extends the basic principles of arithmetic by using letters (variables) to stand in for numbers. This allows for the generalization of mathematical concepts and relationships. Key concepts of Algebra include the following.

Variables: Symbols (typically letters) that represent unknown or general values. Examples include x and y.

Coefficients: Numerical values that multiply the variables. For instance, in the expression $3x$, 3 is the coefficient, meaning the variable x is multiplied by 3.

Terms: A term is a single mathematical expression involving a number (coefficient), a variable, or both, separated by addition or subtraction. Examples of terms include: $4x, -5y, 7$.

Expressions: Combinations of terms involving variables, numbers, and arithmetic operations (addition, subtraction, multiplication, and division). Example: $3x + 2y - 5$. This expression includes three terms: $3x, 2y, -5$. Notice that a minus sign is always included with the term that it immediately precedes. In this case, the third term is -5. To make it easier, the forgoing expression can be alternatively written as: $3x + 2y + (-5)$.

Equations: Statements that two expressions are equal, often containing one or more unknowns (variables). Example: $2x + 3 = 7$.

Inequalities: Statements that compare two expressions using inequality symbols such as greater than (>), less than (<), greater than or equal to (≥), or less than or equal to (≤). Example: $4x - 1 < 9$.

Functions: Relationships between two sets of variables, usually expressed as a rule or equation. Example: $f(x) = x^2 - 4$.

Evaluating Algebraic Expressions

Evaluating algebraic expressions means finding the value of an expression by substituting specific values for the variables involved and then performing the necessary calculations.

Steps for Evaluating Algebraic Expressions:

1. **Identify the Expression:** The expression is a combination of variables, coefficients, constants, and arithmetic operators like addition, subtraction, multiplication, and division.

2. **Substitute Values:** Replace the variables with specific numerical values provided in the problem.

3. **Perform the Calculations:** Follow the order of operations (PEMDAS): Parentheses, Exponents, Multiplication and Division (from left to right), Addition and Subtraction (from left to right).

Example: Given $x = 2$ and $y = 4$, evaluating $3x + 5y - 7$.

Solution: Substitute the values of x and y into the above expression:

$$3x + 5y - 7 = 3 \cdot 2 + 5 \cdot 4 - 7 = 6 + 20 - 7 = 19$$

OPERATIONS OF ALGEBRAIC EXPRESSIONS

In algebra, **like terms** are terms that contain the same variables raised to the same power. The coefficients (numbers in front of variables) can be different. For instance, in the expression:

$3x^2 + 4x - 5 + 7x^2 - 2x + 8$, like terms are as follows:

- $3x^2$ and $7x^2$ are like terms because both contain the variable x raised to the power of 2.
- $4x$ and $-2x$ are like terms because both contain the variable x raised to the power of 1.
- -5 and 8 are like terms because they are constants (terms without variables).

Addition and Subtraction

To add or subtract algebraic expressions, combine like terms.

Example: Simplify $3x^2 + 4x - 5 + 7x^2 - 2x + 8$

Steps:

1. Combine like terms involving x^2: $3x^2 + 7x^2 = 10x^2$
2. Combine like terms involving x: $4x - 2x = 2x$
3. Combine the constants: $-5 + 8 = 3$
4. Final Result: $10x^2 + 2x + 3$

Multiplication

To multiply algebraic expressions, apply the distributive property and combine like terms.

Example: Multiply the following: (x+3)(x−2)

Steps:

1. Distribute x over x−2: $x \cdot (x - 2) = x^2 - 2x$
2. Distribute 3 over $x - 2$: $3 \cdot (x - 2) = 3x - 6$
3. Add the results: $x^2 - 2x + 3x - 6 = x^2 + x - 6$

The above process is also called the **FOIL** method of multiplying two binomials. The acronym "FOIL" stands for: First, Outer, Inner, Last.

    First: Multiply the first terms of each binomial.

    Outer: Multiply the outer terms of each binomial.

    Inner: Multiply the inner terms of each binomial.

    Last: Multiply the last terms of each binomial.

In some cases, an algebraic expression is complicated by parentheses, and simplifying it requires removing the parentheses. To achieve this, distribute the term that directly precedes the parentheses by multiplying it with each term inside. Let's tackle an example where a polynomial is multiplied by a binomial:

Example: Multiply the following: $(2x^2 - 3x + 4)(3x + 5)$

Steps: Distribute each term in the polynomial $(2x^2 - 3x + 4)$ over the terms in the binomial $(3x + 5)$.

1. **First Term:** Distribute $2x^2$

   $2x^2 \cdot 3x + 2x^2 \cdot 5 = 6x^3 + 10x^2$

2. **Second Term:** Distribute $-3x$

   $-3x \cdot 3x + (-3x) \cdot 5 = -9x^2 - 15x$

3. **Third Term:** Distribute 4

   $4 \cdot 3x + 4 \cdot 5 = 12x + 20$

4. **Combine the Results:**

   $6x^3 + 10x^2 - 9x^2 - 15x + 12x + 20$

5. **Simplify by Combining Like Terms:**

   $6x^3 + (10x^2 - 9x^2) + (-15x + 12x) + 20 = 6x^3 + x^2 - 3x + 20$

Division

For division, expressions are often divided through factorization or by reducing fractions.

Example: Divide the following: $\frac{2x^2-8}{2x}$

1. Factor out 2 from the numerator: $2x^2 - 8 = 2(x^2 - 4)$
2. Recognize that $x^2 - 4$ is a difference of squares: $x^2 - 4 = (x + 2)(x - 2)$
3. Substitute back to rewrite the original expression: $\frac{2(x+2)(x-2)}{2x}$
4. Cancel out the common factor of 2 and reduce: $\frac{(x+2)(x-2)}{x}$

GCF Factoring

The greatest common factor (GCF) of a set of terms is the largest expression that divides each term evenly. Factoring out the GCF is the most basic type of polynomial factoring and simplifies expressions by grouping common factors.

Steps to Factor Out the GCF:

1. **Identify the GCF:** Determine the largest factor shared by all terms in the polynomial.
2. **Factor Out the GCF:** Divide each term by the GCF, leaving a simpler polynomial inside parentheses.
3. **Rewrite:** Multiply the GCF by the simplified polynomial inside the parentheses.

Example 1: Factor out the GCF from: $12x^3 - 18x^2 + 24x$

Solution:

1. Identify the GCF: The GCF of 12, 18, and 24 is 6. The common variable is x, and the smallest power among all terms is x. Thus, the GCF is $6x$.
2. Factor Out the GCF: Divide each term by $6x$:

   $12x^3 \div 6x = 2x^2, \quad 18x^2 \div 6x = 3x, \quad 24x \div 6x = 4$

3. Rewrite the Expression: $12x^3 - 18x^2 + 24x = 6x(2x^2 - 3x + 4)$

Example 2: GCF Factoring to Simplify Division: $\frac{15x^3+20x^2}{5x}$

1. **Explanation:** Factor Out the GCF (Numerator): The GCF of the numerator, $15x^3 + 20x^2$, is $5x^2$. Thus, factor it out: $15x^3 + 20x^2 = 5x^2(3x + 4)$
2. Rewrite the Expression: $\frac{15x^3+20x^2}{5x} = \frac{5x^2(3x+4)}{5x}$
3. Simplify the Division: Cancel out the common factor of 5x: $\frac{5x^2}{5x} = x$, leaving: $x(3x + 4) = 3x^2 + 4x$.

Hence, $\frac{15x^3+20x^2}{5x} = \frac{5x^2(3x+4)}{5x} = x(3x + 4) = 3x^2 + 4x$.

LINEAR EQUATIONS

A one-variable linear equation is an equation with a single unknown variable, typically denoted by x, and it forms a straight line when graphed on the coordinate plane. The standard form of a one-variable linear equation is: $ax + b = 0$ where: a and b are constants (with $a \neq 0$), and x is the unknown variable.

Solve One-Variable Linear Equations

To solve a linear equation means finding the value of the unknown variable that makes the equation true.

Steps to Solve:

1. **Isolate the Variable**: Rearrange the equation to express the unknown variable (x) on one side of the equation.
2. **Simplify**: Combine like terms or reduce fractions as needed.
3. **Solve for the Variable**: Perform arithmetic operations to obtain the value of the unknown variable.

Example 1—Simple Equation: Solve the equation: $2x + 5 = 13$

1. **Explanation:** Isolate $2x$: Subtract 5 from both sides.
$$2x + 5 - 5 = 13 - 5$$
$$2x = 8$$
2. Solve for x: Divide both sides by 2.
$$x = \frac{8}{2} = 4$$

Example 2—Fractional Coefficients: Solve the equation: $\frac{3x}{5} - 2 = 1$

1. **Explanation:** Isolate the Fractional Term: Add 2 to both sides.
$$\frac{3x}{5} - 2 + 2 = 1 + 2$$
$$\frac{3x}{5} = 3$$
2. Solve for x: Multiply both sides by 5 to clear the fraction.
$$3x = 3 \cdot 5$$
$$3x = 15$$
3. Divide both sides by 3.

$$x = \frac{15}{3} = 5$$

Example 3— Cross-Multiplication: Solve the equation: $\frac{2x-1}{3} = \frac{x+4}{5}$

1. **Explanation: Cross-Multiply:** Multiply the numerator on one side by the denominator on the other, and vice versa:

$$5 \cdot (2x - 1) = 3 \cdot (x + 4)$$

2. **Simplify Both Sides:** Perform the multiplication:

$$10x - 5 = 3x + 12$$

3. **Isolate the Variable:** To solve for x, get all the x-terms on one side of the equation by subtracting $3x$ from both sides:

$$10x - 3x - 5 = 12$$
$$7x - 5 = 12$$

4. **Solve for x:** Add 5 to both sides to isolate $7x$, and then divide by 7:

$$7x - 5 + 5 = 12 + 5$$
$$7x = 17$$
$$x = \frac{17}{7}$$

Example 4— Multiplying LCD: Solve the equation: $\frac{x}{4} + \frac{3}{2} = \frac{x-1}{3}$

1. **Explanation: Identify the LCD:** The denominators in the equation are 4, 2, and 3. The least common denominator (LCD) for these is 12.

2. **Multiply Each Term by the LCD:** Multiply both sides of the equation by 12 to clear the fractions.

$$12 \cdot \left(\frac{x}{4} + \frac{3}{2}\right) = 12 \cdot \frac{x-1}{3}$$
$$12 \cdot \frac{x}{4} + 12 \cdot \frac{3}{2} = 4(x-1)$$
$$3x + 18 = 4x - 4$$

3. **Solve for x:**

$$3x - 4x = -18 - 4$$
$$-x = -22$$
$$x = 22$$

Solving Equations in Terms of Other Variables

Sometimes, an equation involves multiple variables, and the goal is to solve for one variable in terms of the others. This allows us to express that variable as a function of the remaining variables. The steps to solve equations in terms of other variables are not any different from what we have already discussed above.

Example: Solve for x in terms of y in the equation: $2x + 3y = 12$

Explanation: $2x = 12 - 3y$

$$x = \frac{12 - 3y}{2}$$

Solving Inequalities

Linear inequalities are similar to linear equations, but instead of using an equal sign (=), they involve inequality signs like <, >, ≤, or ≥. The goal is to find the range of values that satisfy the given inequality.

Interval notation is a method used to represent the set of all solutions to an inequality. It describes the range of numbers that satisfy a condition or a series of conditions. The notation uses parentheses () and square brackets [] to show whether endpoints are included or excluded from the interval.

- **Parentheses** (): Used to exclude endpoints. For instance, (a, b) means all values between a and b, but not including a or b.

- **Square Brackets** []: Used to include endpoints. For example, $[a, b]$ includes both a and b in the range.

- **Infinity** (∞) and **Negative Infinity** ($-\infty$): Represent unbounded intervals. Infinity symbols are always used with parentheses because infinity itself isn't a specific number that can be included.

- **Examples**: Inequality solution and corresponding interval Explanation: $x > 3$ is equivalent to $(3, \infty)$

- $2 \leq x < 7$ is equivalent to $[2,7)$

- $x \leq -5$ is equivalent to $(-\infty, -5]$

Using interval notation provides a concise and standardized way to describe ranges of values that satisfy various conditions in inequalities.

Basic Steps for Solving Linear Inequalities

1. **Isolate the Variable**: Rearrange the inequality to isolate the unknown variable on one side, while keeping the other terms on the opposite side. This often involves addition, subtraction, multiplication, or division.

2. **Simplify if Needed**: Combine like terms or reduce fractions.

3. **Consider the Direction of the Inequality**: If you multiply or divide both sides of the inequality by a negative number, remember to reverse the direction of the inequality sign.

4. **Write the Solution**: Express the solution in interval notation or using inequality symbols.

Example 1—Simple Inequality: Solve the inequality: $3x - 7 < 5$

Explanation: $3x - 7 + 7 < 5 + 7$

$$3x < 12$$
$$x < \frac{12}{3} = 4$$
$$x < 4$$

The solution is all values of x less than 4. Interval Notation: $(-\infty, 4)$.

Here is how the solution looks like on a number line:

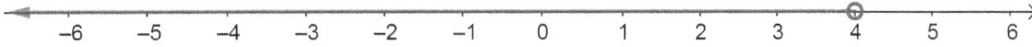

Example 2—Reversing the Inequality: Solve the inequality: $-2x + 8 \geq 4$

Explanation: $-2x + 8 - 8 \geq 4 - 8$
$$-2x \geq -4$$

Divide both sides by -2 to solve for x. Remember to reverse the direction of inequality because we are dividing both sides with a negative number.

$$x \leq \frac{-4}{-2} = 2$$
$$x \leq 2$$

The solution is all values of x less than or equal to 2. Interval Notation: $(-\infty, 2]$.

Here is how the solution looks like on a number line:

Solving Systems of Equations

A system of two equations consists of two equations with two variables, typically represented as x and y. The goal is to find a solution that satisfies both equations simultaneously.

Methods for Solving Systems of Equations

1. Substitution Method: This method involves solving one equation for one variable and substituting that expression into the other equation to find the second variable.

Example: Solve the following system:

$$x + 2y = 8 \quad (1)$$
$$3x - y = 1 \quad (2)$$

Steps:

1. Solve equation (1) for x:

$$x = 8 - 2y$$

2. Substitute $x = 8 - 2y$ into equation (2):

$$3(8 - 2y) - y = 1$$
$$24 - 6y - y = 1$$
$$24 - 7y = 1$$
$$-7y = -23$$
$$y = \frac{-23}{-7} = \frac{23}{7}$$

3. Substitute back to find x:

$$x = 8 - 2 \cdot \frac{23}{7}$$
$$x = 8 - \frac{46}{7} = \frac{56}{7} - \frac{46}{7} = \frac{10}{7}$$

So, the solution is: $\left(\frac{10}{7}, \frac{23}{7}\right)$.

2. Elimination Method: This method involves adding or subtracting the equations after multiplying one or both by suitable factors to cancel out one of the variables.

Example: Solve the following system:

$$2x + 3y = 11 \quad (1)$$
$$4x - y = 5 \quad (2)$$

Steps:

1. Multiply equation (2) by 3 to match the coefficients of y in equation (1):

$$3(4x - y) = 3(5)$$
$$12x - 3y = 15$$

2. Add equations (1) and the transformed (2) to eliminate y:

$$(2x + 3y) + (12x - 3y) = 11 + 15$$
$$14x = 26$$
$$x = \frac{26}{14} = \frac{13}{7}$$

3. Substitute $x = \frac{13}{7}$ into equation (1) to find y:

$$2 \cdot \frac{13}{7} + 3y = 11$$
$$\frac{26}{7} + 3y = 11$$
$$3y = 11 - \frac{26}{7} = \frac{77}{7} - \frac{26}{7} = \frac{51}{7}$$
$$y = \frac{\frac{51}{7}}{3} = \frac{51}{21} = \frac{17}{7}$$

So, the solution is: $\left(\frac{13}{7}, \frac{17}{7}\right)$.

SETTING UP ALGEBRA WORD PROBLEMS

TSIA2 algebra word problems require translating real-world situations into mathematical expressions and equations. Understanding how to identify key information and represent it mathematically is crucial to solving them effectively.

Steps to Set Up and Solve Algebra Word Problems

1. Read and Understand the Problem: Identify the important information given in the problem and determine the unknowns to be found.

2. Assign Variables to the Unknowns: Choose symbols, typically letters like x, y, etc., to represent unknown quantities.

3. Write an Equation or System of Equations: Translate the relationships and conditions described in the word problem into mathematical expressions or equations. Ensure that each equation accurately represents the conditions in the problem.

4. Solve the Equation(s): Use algebraic methods like substitution or elimination (for systems) to find the value(s) of the unknown variable(s).

5. Interpret and Verify: Interpret the solution back into the context of the problem to ensure it makes sense. Verify by substituting back into the original equations if necessary.

Translating English Sentences into Math Equations

Different phrases and words can hint at mathematical operations. Here are some common phrases and their mathematical equivalents:

- Addition: "Sum of," "more than," "increased by," "plus."

    Example: "Five more than x" translates to $x + 5$.

- Subtraction: "Difference," "less than," "decreased by," "minus."

    Example: "Ten less than x" translates to $x - 10$.

- Multiplication: "Product of," "times," "of."

    Example: "Twice x" translates to $2x$.

- Division: "Quotient of," "divided by," "per."

    Example: "Half of x" translates to $\frac{x}{2}$.

- Equals: "Is," "are," "will be," "gives."

    Example: "The result is ten" translates to $= 10$.

Example 1— Setting Up a Proportion Problem: A juice recipe requires 4 oranges to make 500 ml of juice. If you need to make 750 ml of juice, how many oranges do you need?

1. **Explanation:** Assign Variables: Let x represent the number of oranges needed to make 750 ml of juice.

2. Write the Proportion: Set up a ratio comparing oranges to juice in the original recipe: $\frac{4}{500}$

3. Set up a similar ratio for the desired quantity: $\frac{x}{750}$

4. Create an Equation: Establish the proportion by setting the two ratios equal:

$$\frac{4}{500} = \frac{x}{750}$$
$$4 \cdot 750 = 500 \cdot x$$
$$3000 = 500x$$
$$x = \frac{3000}{500} = 6$$

5. Interpret the Solution: You will need 6 oranges to make 750 ml of juice.

Example 2— Setting Up an Equation with One Unknown: In five years, John will be twice as old as he was three years ago. How old is John now?

1. **Explanation:** Assign Variables: Let x represent John's current age.

2. Write an Equation: In five years, John's age will be $x + 5$. Three years ago, John's age was $x - 3$.

3. The problem says that in five years, John will be twice as old as he was three years ago. Therefore, the equation becomes:

$$x + 5 = 2(x - 3)$$
$$x + 5 = 2x - 6$$
$$5 = 2x - x - 6$$
$$5 = x - 6$$
$$x = 5 + 6 = 11$$

4. **Interpret the Solution:** John is currently 11 years old.

Example 3— Setting Up Systems of Equations: Sarah is twice as old as Jane. Five years ago, Sarah was three times as old as Jane was. How old are Sarah and Jane now?

1. **Explanation:** Assign Variables: Let x represent Sarah's current age. Let y represent Jane's current age.

2. **Write Equations:** From "Sarah is twice as old as Jane," the equation becomes: $x = 2y$.

    From "Five years ago, Sarah was three times as old as Jane," the equation becomes:
    $$x - 5 = 3(y - 5)$$

3. **Solve the System:** Substitute $x = 2y$ into the second equation:
    $$2y - 5 = 3(y - 5)$$
    $$2y - 5 = 3y - 15$$
    $$2y - 3y = -15 + 5$$
    $$-y = -10$$
    $$y = 10$$

4. Find x by substituting back into the equation $x = 2y$:
    $$x = 2 \cdot 10 = 20$$

5. **Interpret the Solution:** Sarah is 20 years old, and Jane is 10 years old.

6. **Verify:** Five years ago, Sarah was $20 - 5 = 15$ and Jane was $10 - 5 = 5$. Thus, Sarah was three times as old as Jane five years ago, confirming the solution is correct.

LINEAR APPLICATIONS AND GRAPHS

Linear equations can be used to model relationships between two variables in many real-life situations. When graphed, these relationships form straight lines, and their general form is:
$y = mx + c$, where y is the dependent variable, x is the independent variable, m is the slope (rate of change), and c is the y-intercept (the value of y when $x = 0$).

Here, it's crucial to distinguish between the input variable (often represented as x) and the output variable (often represented as y). Here's a clear understanding of each:

Input Variable (x): The input variable is the independent variable in a function or equation. It represents the values you can freely choose or manipulate. For instance, in a business context, x might represent the number of products manufactured. In science, x could represent time.

In a function $y = f(x)$, x is the value provided to the function.

Output Variable (y): The output variable is the dependent variable in a function or equation. Its value depends on the input variable and the relationship defined by the function or equation. For instance, in business, y might represent the total revenue earned. In science, y could represent the distance traveled after a certain period.

In the function $y = f(x)$, y is the value calculated after plugging in the input x.

Example—Travel Distance and Speed: Suppose you're driving a car at a constant speed of 60 mph (miles per hour). The distance (y) traveled depends on the amount of time (x) spent driving. The relationship between distance and time can be expressed using the equation:
$y = 60x$.

Input (x): This represents the amount of time (in hours) spent driving.

Output (y): This represents the total distance traveled in miles.

For example: If you drive for 4 hours ($x = 4$), the distance traveled (y) is: $y = 60 \cdot 4 = 240$.

So, the output variable y (distance traveled) is 240 miles after driving for 4 hours at a speed of 60 mph. This example illustrates how the input (x representing time) directly influences the output (y representing distance traveled) based on a linear relationship.

Such a linear relationship between speed and travel distance can also be illustrated in a graph, as shown here.

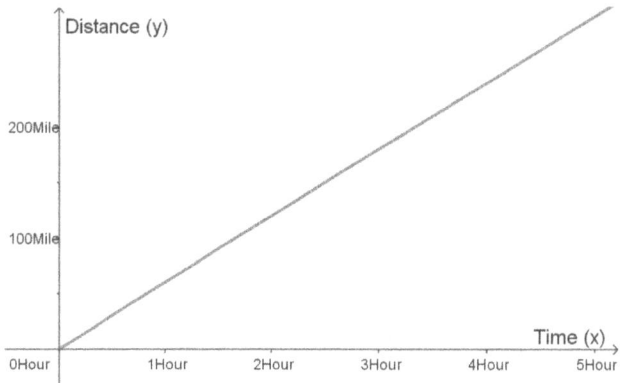

Linear Functions: Slope-Intercept Form ($y = mx + c$)

In linear equation $y = mx + c$, y is the output or dependent variable, x is the input or independent variable, m is the slope, which represents the rate of change, and c is the y-intercept, the value of y when $x = 0$. Let's examine the concept of slope and intercept further.

Slope (m): The slope is the ratio of the vertical change (rise) to the horizontal change (run) between two points on a line. A positive slope means the line is increasing, while a negative slope means the line is decreasing. If the slope is zero, the line is horizontal (constant function).

Intercept (c): The y-intercept is the point where the line crosses the y-axis, representing the value of y when $x = 0$.

Example—Continuing the Travel Example with an Intercept: In the previous travel example, we assumed that the starting point is zero miles (no intercept). However, let's consider that the car has already traveled 30 miles before starting to drive at a constant speed. The equation now changes to: $y = 60x + 30$, where $m = 60mph$ is the speed (slope), $c = 30$ miles is the initial distance already traveled (intercept).

In this case, if you drive for 4 hours ($x = 4$), the total distance traveled (y) is:

$$y = 60 \cdot 4 + 30 = 240 + 30 = 270$$

So, after driving for 4 hours, the total distance covered is 270 miles, including the 30 miles already covered. The relationship between time and distance can also been expressed graphically as follows.

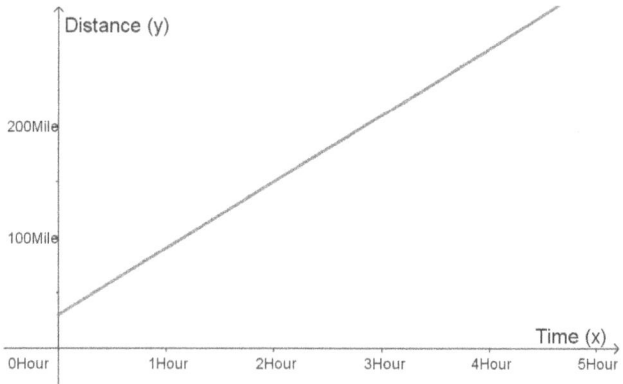

Compare the two figures and one will notice the second one has an intercept while the first one does not.

Graphing Linear Functions

Graphing linear functions involves plotting the relationship between an independent variable (x) and a dependent variable (y) on a two-dimensional plane.

Steps to Graph a Linear Equation

1. Identify the Slope and Intercept:

- The equation $y = mx + c$ provides the slope (m) and the y-intercept (c).
- The slope (m) measures the steepness of the line.
- The intercept (c) indicates the point where the line crosses the y-axis.

2. Plot the Y-Intercept: Mark the point on the y-axis where the line will pass. This is given by the y-intercept (c).

3. Use the Slope to Plot Another Point: The slope m is often written as a fraction $\Delta y/\Delta x$ (change in y over change in x). From the y-intercept, use the slope to find a second point on the graph:

- Move vertically by Δy (up if positive, down if negative).
- Move horizontally by Δx (right if positive, left if negative).

4. Draw the Line: Once you have two points, draw a straight line through them to complete the graph.

Example: Graphing the Equation $y = 2x + 3$

1. Identify Slope and Intercept: The slope (m) is 2, which means a vertical change of +2 for every horizontal change of +1. The y-intercept (c) is 3, meaning the line crosses the y-axis at $y = 3$.

2. Plot the Y-Intercept: Mark the point (0,3) on the y-axis.

3. Use the Slope to Find Another Point: Start at (0,3). Move up by 2 units (due to the slope's numerator) and right by 1 unit (due to the slope's denominator), reaching the point (1,5).

4. Draw the Line: Draw a line passing through the points (0,3) and (1,5).

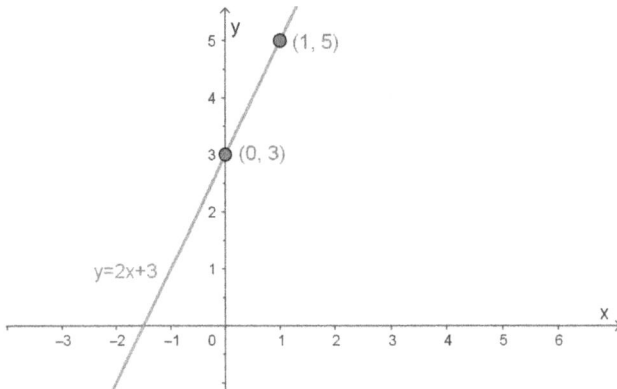

Note that the y-intercept marks the starting point of the line on the y-axis, and the slope controls the line's angle. Since the line will have a positive slope (2), it slants upward from left to right.

Writing Equations in Point-Slope Form

The point-slope form is particularly useful when you have a known point on the line and the slope. The equation in point-slope form is given by: $y - y_1 = m(x - x_1)$, where m is the slope of the line, (x_1, y_1) is a known point on the line.

Steps to Write an Equation in Point-Slope Form

1. Identify the Slope (m) and a Point (x_1, y_1): The slope indicates the rate of change or steepness of the line. A known point on the line helps anchor the line's position.

2. Substitute the Values into the Point-Slope Formula: Plug in the known slope (m) and the coordinates of the known point (x_1, y_1) into the formula.

3. Simplify or Leave in Point-Slope Form: You can either keep the equation in point-slope form or rearrange it to another form like slope-intercept ($y = mx + c$).

Example: Write the equation of a line with a slope of 3 passing through the point (2,−1).

Solution: Identify the Slope (m) and Point (x_1, y_1): $m = 3$, $(x_1, y_1) = (2, -1)$.

Substitute into the Formula:

$$y - (-1) = 3(x - 2)$$
$$y + 1 = 3(x - 2)$$

This is the equation of the line in point-slope form. If you prefer, you can convert this to slope-intercept form by expanding and simplifying.

Writing Equations from Two Known Points

When given two points, you can find the equation of the line that passes through them using the slope formula and the point-slope form. Here's a step-by-step process:

Steps to Write a Linear Equation from Two Known Points

1. Find the Slope (m): Use the slope formula to calculate the slope between the two points: $m = \frac{y_2 - y_1}{x_2 - x_1}$. This formula calculates the rate of change between the two given points, (x_1, y_1) and (x_2, y_2).

2. Substitute the Slope and One Point into Point-Slope Form: $y - y_1 = m(x - x_1)$

3. Simplify or Convert to Slope-Intercept Form: You can keep the equation in point-slope form or convert it to slope-intercept form ($y = mx + c$) by expanding and simplifying.

Example: Find the equation of the line that passes through the points (1,2) and (3,-4).

1. **Explanation:** Calculate the Slope: $m = \frac{-4-2}{3-1} = \frac{-6}{2} = -3$

2. Substitute into Point-Slope Form: Use the point-slope form formula $y - y_1 = m(x - x_1)$ with $m = -3$ and the point (1,2): $y - 2 = -3(x - 1)$

3. Simplify: Expand and simplify to convert to slope-intercept form:

$$y - 2 = -3x + 3$$
$$y = -3x + 5$$

This equation in slope-intercept form ($y = -3x + 5$) is the equation of the line that passes through the points (1,2) and (3,-4).

Parallel and Perpendicular Lines

In a two-dimensional coordinate system, lines can be parallel or perpendicular to each other based on the relationship of their slopes.

Parallel Lines

Parallel lines have the same slope but different y-intercepts. If two lines have the same slope (m), they are parallel and never intersect.

Example: Suppose the equation of an existing line is: $y = 4x + 2$. Any line parallel to this one will have the same slope, $m = 4$, but a different y-intercept (c).

Examples of a parallel lines include: $y = 4x - 3$, $y = 4x + 18$, $y = 4x - \frac{11}{17}$

Perpendicular Lines

Perpendicular lines intersect at right angles (90°). If the slope of one line is m, then the slope of any line perpendicular to it is the negative reciprocal, $-\frac{1}{m}$.

Example 1: Suppose the equation of an existing line is: $y = \frac{3}{4}x + 5$. The slope of this line is $m = \frac{3}{4}$. The slope of any line perpendicular to it will be the negative reciprocal: $m_\perp = -\frac{4}{3}$.

An example of a perpendicular line equation (using slope $m_\perp$ and an arbitrary y-intercept):

$$y = -\frac{4}{3}x + 1$$

By analyzing or adjusting the slopes of linear equations, you can quickly determine if lines are parallel or perpendicular to each other.

Example 2: Find a line that is perpendicular to the equation $y = 2x + 3$ and passes through the point (1, 5).

1. Identify the Slope of the Given Line: The given line is: $y = 2x + 3$. The slope (m) is 2.

2. Find the Perpendicular Slope: The slope of a line perpendicular to this one is the negative reciprocal. If the original slope is m=2, the perpendicular slope ($m_\perp$) is:
$$m_\perp = -0.5$$

3. Use the Point-Slope Formula: We'll use the point-slope formula to find the equation of the perpendicular line: $y - y_1 = m(x - x_1)$. Here, $(x_1, y_1) = (1,5)$ and $m = -0.5$.

    Substitute into the Point-Slope Formula: $y - 5 = -0.5(x - 1)$

4. Simplify the Equation:

$$y - 5 = -0.5x + 0.5$$
$$y = -0.5x + 5.5$$

Hence, the equation of the line perpendicular to the equation $y = 2x + 3$ and passes through the point (1, 5) is: $y = -0.5x + 5.5$.

Graphing Systems of Linear Equations

Graphing systems of linear equations involves plotting multiple lines on the same coordinate plane to identify where they intersect. The point of intersection (if it exists) represents the solution that satisfies all equations simultaneously.

Steps to Graph a System of Linear Equations

1. Plot Each Line using the method we have discussed before.

2. Identify the Point of Intersection: The point where the lines intersect is the solution to the system. If the lines are parallel, they have no intersection (no solution). If they coincide (same line), they have infinitely many solutions.

    Example—Graphing a System of Two Linear Equations: Problem: Graph the following system and find the Explanation: $y = 2x + 1$ (1)

$$y = -x + 4 \quad (2)$$

1. **Explanation:** Plot Equation 1 ($y = 2x + 1$): Slope (m) = 2. Y-Intercept (c) = 1. Plot the y-intercept
(0, 1). Use the slope $m = 2$ to find another point: go up 2 units and right 1 unit to reach (1, 3). Draw the line through these points.

2. Plot Equation 2 ($y = -x + 4$): Slope (m) = -1. Y-Intercept (c) = 4. Plot the y-intercept (0, 4). Use the slope $m = -1$ to find another point: go down 1 unit and right 1 unit to reach (1, 3). Draw the line through these points.

3. Find the Intersection Point: Solve the systems of equations, and one will find that both lines intersect at the point (1, 3).

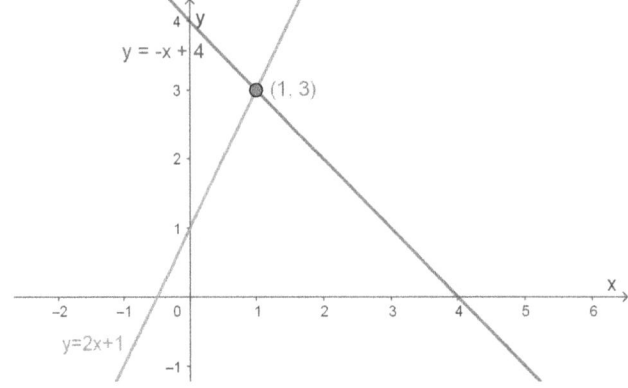

Graphing Linear Inequalities

Graphing linear inequalities involves plotting a region of the coordinate plane that satisfies a given inequality. The boundary of this region is defined by a line, and the region itself is shaded to represent all the points that meet the inequality's condition.

Steps to Graph Linear Inequalities

1. Write the Inequality in Slope-Intercept Form ($y = mx + c$): This form helps identify the slope (m) and the y-intercept (c) of the boundary line.
2. Graph the Boundary Line: Treat the inequality as an equation to draw the boundary line.

- If the inequality symbol is > or <, use a dashed line to represent that points on the line aren't included.
- If the inequality symbol is ≥ or ≤, use a solid line to represent that points on the line are included.

3. Shade the Appropriate Half-Plane:

- Choose a test point not on the boundary line (often (0,0) if it isn't on the line). Substitute the test point into the inequality: If the test point satisfies the inequality, shade the region that contains the test point. Otherwise, shade the opposite region.
- An alternative method to choose which region to shade: When a linear inequality is expressed in slope-intercept form, shade the region lies below the line for inequalities with < and ≤, and shade the region above the line for inequalities with > and ≥.

Example: Graphing the Inequality $y \leq 2x + 3$

1. Write in Slope-Intercept Form: The inequality is already given in slope-intercept form.
2. Graph the Boundary Line: $y = 2x + 3$. Draw a solid line because the inequality includes ≤.
3. Shade the Appropriate Region: Choose a test point not on the boundary line, such as (0,0). Substitute (0,0) into the inequality: $0 \leq 2 \cdot 0 + 3$. The result is $0 \leq 3$, which is true. Therefore, the region containing (0,0) is shaded, representing all points satisfying $y \leq 2x + 3$. Alternatively, we can also determine we should shade the region underneath the line due to the inequality sign of ≤.

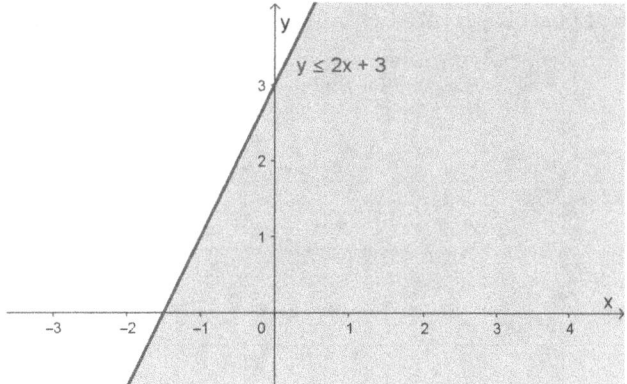

Summary:

Dashed Line is used for inequalities with < or >. **Solid Line** is used for inequalities with ≤ or ≥. **Shaded Region** represents the solution set that satisfies the inequality.

Graphing Systems of Inequalities

Now that we're already familiar with graphing a single inequality, the process of graphing systems of inequalities involves finding the overlapping region that satisfies all inequalities. Here's how to do it:

Steps to Graph Systems of Inequalities

1. Graph Each Inequality Separately: Draw the boundary line for each inequality.
- Use a solid line for inequalities with ≤ or ≥ to include the boundary.
- Use a dashed line for inequalities with < or > to exclude the boundary.
2. Shade the region that satisfies each inequality:
- If the inequality is ≥ or >, shade above the line.
- If the inequality is ≤ or <, shade below the line.
3. Find the Overlapping Region: The solution set is the area where all shaded regions overlap, meaning it satisfies all inequalities in the system.
4. Check a Test Point in the Overlapping Region: Choose a point inside the overlapping region and substitute it into each inequality to confirm that it satisfies all conditions.

Example—Graphing a System of Two Inequalities

$$y \geq 2x - 1 \quad (1)$$
$$y < -x + 4 \quad (2)$$

1. **Explanation:** Graph Inequality (1) and (2).
2. Find the Overlapping Region: The solution region is the area where both shaded regions overlap. This is the region that satisfies both inequalities.
3. Check a Test Point: Choose a point in the overlapping region, such as (0,0). Substitute this point into both inequalities to confirm it satisfies both.

- For inequality (1): $y \geq 2x - 1$: $\quad 0 \geq 2 \cdot 0 - 1 \Rightarrow 0 \geq -1$
- For inequality (2): $y < -x + 4$: $\quad 0 < -0 + 4 \Rightarrow 0 < 4$

Since the test point (0,0) satisfies both inequalities, it's within the solution region.

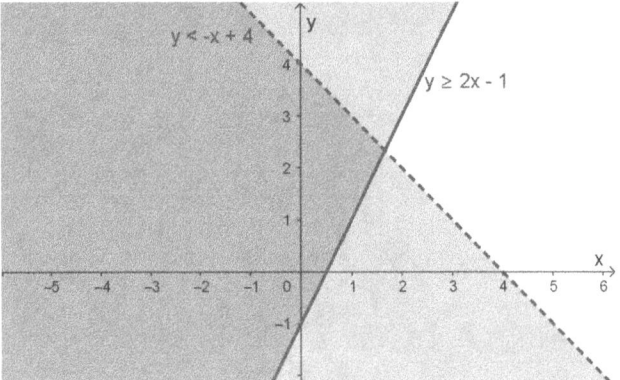

§3 Geometric and Spatial Reasoning

In the TSIA2 Mathematics Test, you won't need to tackle geometric proofs, and the exam only covers a well-defined list of practical geometry topics, which we will cover below.

Perimeter and Circumference

The perimeter and circumference formula of common geometric shapes is summarized in the following table. The TSIA2 test will usually give you the needed formula except the simplest.

Shape	Formula	Description
Rectangle	Perimeter of a rectangle $P = 2(l + w)$	l and w are length and width
Square	Perimeter of a square $P = 4s$	s is the length of one side
Triangle	Perimeter of a triangle $P = a + b + c$	a, b, c are the length of the three sides
Circle	Circumference of a circle $C = 2\pi r$ (or $C = \pi d$)	r is the radius, d is the diameter

Area

Here's a table summarizing the formulas for calculating the area of common geometric shapes.

Shape	Formula	Description
Triangle	$A = \frac{1}{2}bh$	b is the base, h is the height
Square	$A = s^2$	s is the length of one side
Rectangle	$A = lw$	l and w are the length and width
Parallelogram	$A = bh$	b is the base, h is the height
Trapezoid	$A = \frac{1}{2}(a + b)h$	a and b are the bases, h is the height
Circle	$A = \pi r^2$	r is the radius

Volume

Shape	Formula	Description
Rectangular Prism	$V = lwh$	$l, w,$ and h are the length, width, and height of the prism
Right Cylinder	$V = \pi r^2 h$	r is the radius of the base, h is the height of the cylinder
Sphere	$V = \frac{4}{3}\pi r^3$	r is the radius of the sphere

Pythagorean Theorem

The Pythagorean Theorem is a fundamental principle in geometry that relates the lengths of the sides of a right triangle.

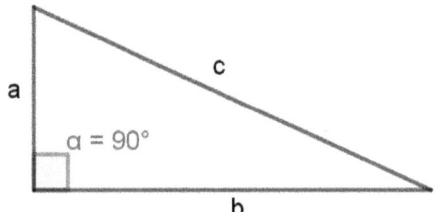

According to the theorem, the square of the length of the hypotenuse (the side opposite the right angle) is equal to the sum of the squares of the lengths of the other two sides. This relationship is usually expressed with the formula:

$$c^2 = a^2 + b^2$$

Here, c represents the length of the hypotenuse, and a and b represent the lengths of the other two sides. The Pythagorean Theorem is frequently used in trigonometry to solve problems involving right triangles. Let's go through a couple of examples where we apply the Pythagorean Theorem.

Example 1—Finding the Hypotenuse: Suppose you have a right triangle with legs of lengths 3 cm and 4 cm. You want to find the length of the hypotenuse.

According to the Pythagorean Theorem: $c^2 = a^2 + b^2$

Plugging in the values:

$$c^2 = 3^2 + 4^2$$
$$c^2 = 9 + 16$$
$$c^2 = 25$$
$$c = \sqrt{25}$$
$$c = 5\ cm$$

So, the hypotenuse is 5 cm long.

Example 2—Finding a Leg of the Triangle: Imagine you know the hypotenuse of a right triangle is 10 cm and one of the legs is 8 cm. You need to find the length of the other leg.

Using the Pythagorean Theorem: $c^2 = a^2 + b^2$

Let b be the unknown side, and rearrange the equation: $b^2 = c^2 - a^2$

Substitute the known values:

$$b^2 = 10^2 - 8^2$$
$$b^2 = 100 - 64$$
$$b^2 = 36$$
$$b = 6\ cm$$

The unknown leg measures 6 cm.

DISTANCE FORMULA

The distance formula is used to calculate the distance between two points in a coordinate system. It is derived from the Pythagorean Theorem, which we just discussed. The formula provides the distance between two points (x_1, y_1) and (x_2, y_2) in a 2-dimensional Cartesian plane. The distance d between two points (x_1, y_1) and (x_2, y_2) is given by:

$$d = \sqrt{(x_2 - x_1)^2 + (y_2 - y_1)^2}$$

The expression $(x_2 - x_1)^2 + (y_2 - y_1)^2$ calculates the sum of the squares of the differences in the x and y coordinates. This is analogous to finding the square of the lengths of the two legs in a right triangle, where the line segment between the two points forms the hypotenuse.

Example: Calculating Distance Between Two Points

Let's calculate the distance between two points, $A(1,2)$ and $B(4,6)$.

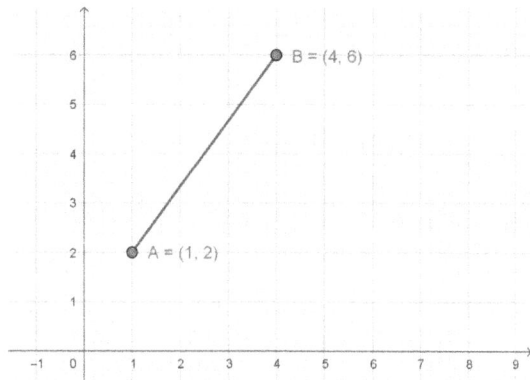

Using the distance formula:

$$d = \sqrt{(x_2 - x_1)^2 + (y_2 - y_1)^2}$$

Plugging in the coordinates:

$$d = \sqrt{(4 - 1)^2 + (6 - 2)^2}$$
$$d = \sqrt{3^2 + 4^2}$$
$$d = \sqrt{9 + 16}$$
$$d = \sqrt{25}$$
$$d = 5 \text{ units}$$

Thus, the distance between points A and B is 5 units.

§4 Probabilistic and Statistical Reasoning

Probability is a measure of how likely an event is to occur. It's a value between 0 and 1, where 0 means the event will not happen, and 1 means it will definitely happen. For example, if you toss a coin, the probability of it landing on heads is 0.5, meaning there's a 50% chance of it happening.

Key Probability Terms

- **Experiment:** A procedure that results in one or more outcomes. Tossing a coin is an example of an experiment.

- **Outcome:** A possible result of an experiment. For example, "heads" is an outcome of tossing a coin.

- **Sample Space:** The set of all possible outcomes. For example, for a coin toss, the sample space is {Heads,Tails}.

- **Event:** A subset of the sample space, representing one or more outcomes that we're interested in. If we're only interested in getting "heads," that outcome is an event.

Calculating Probability

Simple Probability: Simple probability refers to the likelihood of a single event occurring.

Formula: The probability of an event E is:

$$P(E) = \frac{Number\ of\ favorable\ outcomes}{Total\ number\ of\ possible\ outcomes}$$

Example: If you roll a six-sided die, the probability of rolling a 4 is:

$$P(Rolling\ a\ 4) = \frac{1}{6}$$

Compound Probability: Compound probability involves finding the likelihood of two or more events occurring together. For independent events (events that don't affect each other), multiply their probabilities to get Compound Probability.

Example: If you roll a die and flip a coin, the probability of rolling a 3 <u>and</u> flipping heads is:

$$P(Rolling\ a\ 3) \cdot P(Flipping\ Heads) = \frac{1}{6} \cdot \frac{1}{2} = \frac{1}{12}$$

Conditional Probability: Conditional probability is the likelihood of an event occurring given that another event has already happened.

Example: If 80% of students in a class pass math and 60% of those who pass also pass science, the probability of a student passing science given that they passed math is:

$$P(Pass\ Science\ |\ Pass\ Math) = \frac{0.6}{0.8} = 0.75$$

Table-Based Probability Questions

On TSIA2, probability questions are sometimes based on facts presented in a table. So, let's use the following example to review the three types of probabilities.

Example: Let's consider a table summarizing the distribution of animals in a nature reserve based on two traits: whether they are mammals or reptiles and whether they are nocturnal or diurnal.

Table of Animal Distribution

	Nocturnal	Diurnal	Total
Mammal	15	30	45
Reptile	10	25	35
Total	**25**	**55**	**80**

Simple Probability: Find the probability that a randomly chosen animal is nocturnal.

From the table, 25 animals are nocturnal out of a total of 80.

$$P(Nocturnal) = \frac{25}{80} = 0.3125$$

Compound Probability: Find the probability that a randomly chosen animal is both a mammal and nocturnal.

From the table, 15 animals are both mammals and nocturnal.

$$P(Mammal\ and\ Nocturnal) = \frac{15}{80} = 0.1875$$

Conditional Probability: Find the probability that an animal is a reptile given that it is diurnal.

From the table, 25 out of the 55 diurnal animals are reptiles.

$$P(Reptile\ |\ Diurnal) = \frac{25}{55} \approx 0.455$$

DESCRIPTIVE STATISTICS

Descriptive statistics involve methods for summarizing and organizing data, providing simple insights into the patterns and characteristics of a dataset. Instead of analyzing every individual data point, descriptive statistics condense information into meaningful measures to help understand trends, variability, and distribution.

Measures of Central Tendency

Mean, median, and mode are measures of central tendency, used to describe the central point or typical value within a dataset. Each measure provides different insights into the nature of the data.

Mean (Average):

The mean is the sum of all data values divided by the total number of values. It is influenced by every value in the dataset.

$$\text{mean} = \frac{x_1 + x_2 + \cdots + x_n}{n}$$

where:

- $x_1, x_2, \ldots, x_n$ are the data values,
- n is the number of data points.

Example: Given the dataset {3,5,7,8,10}, what is the mean?

Explanation: mean $= \frac{3+5+7+8+10}{5} = \frac{33}{5} = 6.6$

Median

The median is the middle value when all data values are arranged in ascending or descending order. If the number of data points is even, the median is the average of the two middle values.

Example: Given the dataset {3,5,7,8,10}, the median value is 7 because it is the third value in a dataset with five numbers.

If the dataset were {3,5,7,8}, the median would be: $\frac{5+7}{2} = \frac{12}{2} = 6$.

Mode

The mode is the most frequently occurring value(s) in a dataset. There can be one mode (unimodal), more than one mode (bimodal or multimodal), or no mode if no value repeats.

Example: Given the dataset {3,5,5,8,10}, the mode is 5 because it occurs most frequently (twice). If the dataset were {3,3,5,5,8,10}, the mode would be both 3 and 5, making the dataset bimodal.

Measures of Dispersion (Spread)

The range of data helps describe the spread of values within a dataset. Here are some basic concepts:

Maximum (Max):

The maximum is the largest value in a dataset.

Example: In the dataset {2,4,6,8,10}, the maximum value is: Max = 10.

Minimum (Min):

The minimum is the smallest value in a dataset.

Example: In the dataset {2,4,6,8,10}, the minimum value is: Min = 2.

Range:

The range is the difference between the maximum and minimum values in a dataset.

Range = Max − Min

Example: In the dataset {2,4,6,8,10}: Range = 10 − 2 = 8

Quantile:

A quantile divides the data into intervals containing an equal number of data points.

Common quantiles:

- Quartile: Divides data into four equal parts.
- Percentile: Divides data into 100 equal parts.

Example: Given the dataset {3,5,7,9,11,13,15}, let's find the first quartile (Q_1) and the third quartile (Q_3).

Solution: The following table illustrates how we analyze the data.

3	5	7	9	11	13	15
Minimum	First Quartile		Median		Third Quartile	Maximum

◄─── Lower half ───►◄─── Upper half ───►

Hence, $Q_1 = 5$, $Q_3 = 13$.

In this example, the first quartile (Q_1) marks the value below which 25% of the data falls, and the third quartile (Q_3) marks the value below which 75% of the data falls. Together, these measures provide insight into the data's spread and distribution, helping identify potential outliers and the overall range of values.

Visual Representations

Graphical displays offer a visual way to analyze and interpret data. They reveal trends, patterns, and outliers that might not be evident through raw numbers alone. Here are three common types of data visualization tools appear on TSIA2: histograms, box plots, and scatterplots.

Histogram

A histogram is a bar graph that displays the distribution of a dataset. The data is grouped into intervals (bins), and each bar represents the frequency (or count) of values within that interval.

Interpretation:

- **Height of Bars:** Indicates how many data points fall within each interval.
- **Shape:** The shape of the histogram provides insight into the data distribution (e.g., skewed, symmetric).
- **Outliers:** Bars that are separate from the main distribution can indicate outliers.

Example: A histogram depicting the scores of students on a test might show that most scores fall between 70 and 95, with an outlier below 50.

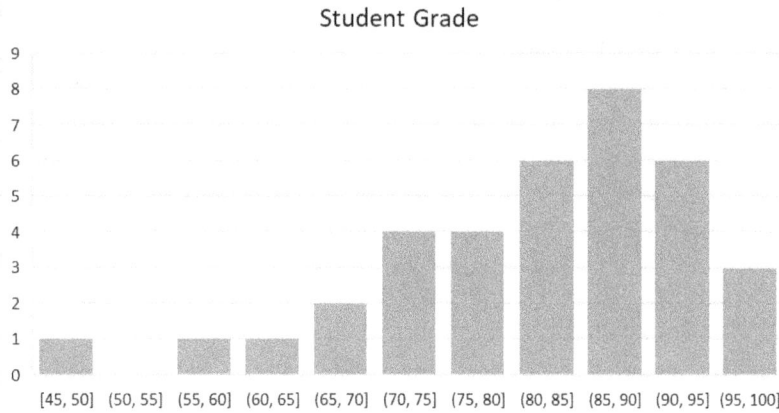

Box Plot (Box-and-Whisker Plot)

Definition: A box plot shows the data distribution by dividing it into quartiles and highlighting the median. It also displays potential outliers using whiskers.

Interpretation:

- **Box:** Represents the interquartile range (IQR) between the first quartile (Q_1) and third quartile (Q_3), which contains the middle 50% of the data.

- **Median Line:** Divides the box into two halves, showing the median of the data.
- **Whiskers:** In the usual convention, they extend from the box to the minimum and maximum values within a specified range.

Example: A box plot showing employee salaries might reveal that the median salary is near $82,000, while outliers earning above $100,000 form a distinct tail.

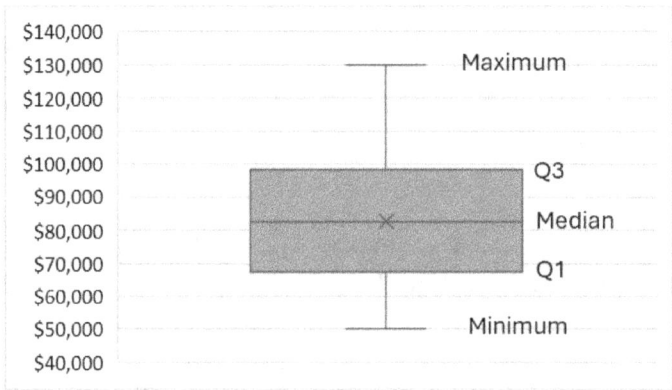

Scatter Plot

Definition: A scatter plot displays data points on a Cartesian plane to illustrate the relationship between two variables.

Interpretation:

- **Trend:** Points that form an upward or downward pattern indicate positive or negative correlations, respectively.
- **Clusters:** Groups of points in different areas may suggest different categories or clusters of data.
- **Outliers:** Points that lie far from the main cluster may represent outliers.

Example: A scatter plot comparing advertising expenditure and sales revenue might reveal that higher ad spending correlates with higher revenue.

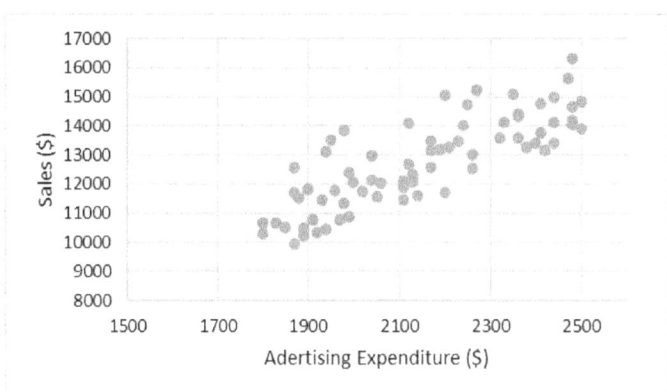

§5 Algebra & Geometry Fundamentals

To help prepare you for more advanced algebra and geometry concepts, in this section we will cover the following: factoring, quadratics, functions, radical and rational equations, polynomial equations, exponential and logarithmic equations, geometry concepts for algebra, and trigonometry.

Factoring

Factoring is a fundamental algebraic process used to simplify expressions, solve equations, and understand polynomial functions. Factoring involves breaking down a complex expression into simpler, multiplied components known as factors. These factors, when multiplied together, reconstruct the original expression. Factoring can simplify calculations and reveal useful properties and relationships within algebraic expressions.

Greatest Common Factor (GCF) and Factoring by Grouping

Mastering the techniques of finding the greatest common factor (GCF) and factoring by grouping are essential for simplifying and solving algebraic expressions. This section will guide you through both processes, helping you break down more complex polynomial expressions.

Finding the Greatest Common Factor (GCF)

The GCF of two or more expressions is the largest expression that divides each of the original expressions without leaving a remainder. Finding the GCF is often the first step in factoring polynomials effectively.

Steps to Find the GCF:

1. **List Factors**: List all factors (or use prime factorization) of each term in the expression.
2. **Identify Common Factors**: Identify the largest factor that is common to all terms.

Example: Finding the GCF of $12x^2$ and $18x$

1. Prime Factorization:

$$12x^2 = 2 \times 2 \times 3 \times x \times x$$

$$18x = 2 \times 3 \times 3 \times x$$

2. Common Factors: The common prime factors are 2, 3, and x.
3. Greatest Common Factor: The GCF is $6x$ (since $2 \times 3 \times x = 6x$).

Factoring by Grouping

Factoring by grouping involves rearranging and grouping terms in a polynomial to simplify factoring, especially useful for polynomials with four or more terms.

Steps to Factor by Grouping:

1. **Group the Terms**: Arrange the polynomial into groups that have a common factor.
2. **Factor Out the GCF from Each Group**: Apply the GCF method within each group.
3. **Factor Out the Common Binomial Factor**: Look for and factor out the common binomial factor from the grouped terms.

Example: Factoring $x^3 + 3x^2 + 2x + 6$ by Grouping

1. Group the Terms: $x^3 + 3x^2$ and $2x + 6$
2. Factor Out the GCF from Each Group:
   - From $x^3 + 3x^2$, factor out x^2, resulting in $x^2(x + 3)$
   - From $2x + 6$, factor out 2, resulting in $2(x + 3)$
3. Factor Out the Common Binomial Factor: The common factor is $x + 3$, hence:

$$x^3 + 3x^2 + 2x + 6 = x^2(x + 3) + 2(x + 3)$$
$$= (x^2 + 2)(x + 3)$$

By understanding and applying these methods, you can efficiently simplify and solve a variety of polynomial expressions.

Factoring Quadratics $x^2 + bx + c$

Quadratic expressions in the standard form $x^2 + bx + c$ are a common sight in algebra. These are polynomials where the highest exponent is 2, and they do not have a coefficient in front of x^2. The goal of factoring such quadratics is to express them as the product of two binomials. This section will guide you through the process of factoring these types of quadratics using a straightforward method that involves finding two numbers.

The key to factoring a quadratic expression of the form $x^2 + bx + c$ is to find two numbers that multiply to c (the constant term) and add up to b (the coefficient of x). These numbers will be used to create the binomials.

Steps to Factor $x^2 + bx + c$:

1. **Identify the Numbers**: Find two numbers that multiply to give the constant term c, and at the same time, add up to the coefficient b.
2. **Write the Binomials**: Use these numbers to write two binomials. The binomials will have the form $(x + m)(x + n)$, where m and n are the numbers identified in the first step.

Example: Factor $x^2 + 5x + 6$

1. Identify the Numbers: We need two numbers that multiply to 6 (the constant term) and add to 5 (the coefficient of x). After checking possible pairs, we find that 2 and 3 fit the requirements because $2 \times 3 = 6$ and $2 + 3 = 5$.
2. Write the Binomials: Using the numbers 2 and 3, we can write the quadratic as $(x + 2)(x + 3)$.

Check the Factorization: To verify, expand $(x + 2)(x + 3)$ using the distributive property (also known as the FOIL method for binomials):

$$(x + 2)(x + 3) = x^2 + 3x + 2x + 6 = x^2 + 5x + 6$$

The expansion matches the original expression, confirming our factorization is correct.

Factoring Quadratics $ax^2 + bx + c$

Factoring quadratic expressions where the leading coefficient (a) is not 1, such as in the general form $ax^2 + bx + c$, can be more challenging than factoring when $a = 1$. This section will introduce a method known as the "ac method" or "splitting the middle term," which is effective for tackling these more complex quadratics.

The ac method involves manipulating the middle term of the quadratic by finding two numbers that multiply to ac (the product of the coefficients of x^2 and the constant term) and add up to b (the coefficient of x). These numbers are then used to split the middle term, allowing the expression to be factored by grouping.

Steps to Factor $ax^2 + bx + c$:

1. **Multiply and Find**: Calculate ac and find two numbers that multiply to ac and add up to b.
2. **Split the Middle Term**: Use these numbers to split the middle term into two terms.
$$ax^2 + bx + c = ax^2 + nx + mx + c$$
3. **Group and Factor**: Group the terms in pairs and factor out the greatest common factor from each group: $(ax^2 + nx) + (mx + c)$
4. **Factor Out the Common Binomial Factor**: Extract the common binomial factor from the grouped terms to complete the factorization.

Example: Factor $6x^2 + 11x + 4$

1. Multiply and Find: Calculate $ac = 6 \times 4 = 24$.
2. Find two numbers that multiply to 24 and add to 11. These numbers are 8 and 3.
3. Split the Middle Term: Rewrite the middle term using 8 and 3: $6x^2 + 8x + 3x + 4$.
4. Group and Factor: Group the terms: $(6x^2 + 8x) + (3x + 4)$.
5. Factor out the GCF from each group: $2x(3x + 4) + 1(3x + 4)$.
6. Factor Out the Common Binomial Factor: The common factor is $(3x + 4)$, so the expression factors as $(2x + 1)(3x + 4)$.

$$6x^2 + 11x + 4 = 2x(3x + 4) + 1(3x + 4)$$
$$= (2x + 1)(3x + 4)$$

By following these steps, you can successfully factor quadratic expressions with a leading coefficient greater than one.

Factoring Perfect Square Trinomials

Perfect square trinomials are a special form of quadratic expressions that result from squaring a binomial. These trinomials are always in the form of $ax^2 + 2abx + b^2$ or $ax^2 - 2abx + b^2$ where the square of the first term and the square of the last term are perfect squares, and the middle term is twice the product of the square roots of these squares. Factoring perfect square trinomials is straightforward once you recognize the pattern.

Steps to Factor $ax^2 + 2abx + b^2$ or $ax^2 - 2abx + b^2$

To factor a perfect square trinomial, you need to identify whether it can be written as the square of a binomial. Here are the steps to follow:

1. **Identify the Squares**: Ensure that the first and last terms are perfect squares.
2. **Check the Middle Term**: Verify that the middle term is twice the product of the roots of the first and last terms.
3. **Write the Binomial**: Express the trinomial as the square of a binomial.

Example: Factor $x^2 + 6x + 9$

1. Identify the Squares: The first term x^2 is the square of x, and the last term 9 is the square of 3.

2. Check the Middle Term: The middle term $6x$ should be twice the product of x and 3, which it is: $2 \cdot 3 \cdot x = 6x$.
3. Write the Binomial: Since all conditions are satisfied, the trinomial can be written as the square of a binomial: $(x + 3)^2$.

$$x^2 + 6x + 9 = (x + 3)^2$$

Factoring Differences of Squares $a^2 - b^2$

The difference of squares is a common algebraic pattern that is simple to factor once recognized. This pattern applies to expressions where two terms are squared and subtracted from each other, taking the general form $a^2 - b^2$. Factoring differences of squares relies on a fundamental algebraic identity, making it a quick and effective process.

Steps to Factor $a^2 - b^2$

To factor a difference of squares, you utilize the identity $a^2 - b^2 = (a - b)(a + b)$. Here are the steps to factor such expressions:

1. **Identify the Squares**: Ensure both terms are perfect squares.
2. **Apply the Difference of Squares Formula**: Write the expression as the product of two binomials, one representing the sum of the square roots and the other the difference of the square roots.

Example: Factor $x^2 - 16$

1. Identify the Squares: The first term, x^2, is the square of x, and the last term, 16, is the square of 4.
2. Apply the Difference of Squares Formula: Since x^2 and 16 are perfect squares, apply the formula $a^2 - b^2 = (a - b)(a + b)$ with $a = x$ and $b = 4$.

$$x^2 - 16 = (x - 4)(x + 4)$$

This straightforward factorization shows how the difference of squares identity simplifies the process, quickly breaking down the expression into a product of binomials.

Factoring the Sum or Difference of Cubes

Factoring the sum or difference of cubes involves breaking down expressions that are either the sum or the subtraction of two cubed terms. These expressions take the forms $a^3 + b^3$ and $a^3 - b^3$, respectively. The factoring of these forms is based on specific algebraic identities, which allow for simplification into products of binomials and trinomials.

Factoring $a^3 + b^3$ and $a^3 - b^3$

To factor the sum or difference of cubes, you use the following identities:

- For the sum of cubes: $a^3 + b^3 = (a + b)(a^2 - ab + b^2)$
- For the difference of cubes: $a^3 - b^3 = (a - b)(a^2 + ab + b^2)$

The mnemonic "SOAP" is a helpful way to remember the signs used in the formulas for factoring the sum or difference of cubes. There are a total of three plus or minus signs to the right of the equal sign in the above two formulas. Here's how each letter in the mnemonic corresponds to these three plus or minus signs in the formulas:

1. **S - Same**: This stands for the first sign in the binomial part of the factorization formula, which is the same as the sign in the original cubic expression. For instance:

- In $a^3 + b^3$, the sign between a and b in the binomial $(a + b)$ is positive.
- In $a^3 - b^3$, the sign between a and b in the binomial $(a - b)$ is negative.

  2. **O - Opposite**: This represents the first sign in the trinomial part of the factorization formula, which is the opposite of the sign in the binomial. For example:

- In $a^3 + b^3 = (a + b)(a^2 - ab + b^2)$, the sign after a^2 is negative, which is the opposite of the positive sign in $(a + b)$.
- In $a^3 - b^3 = (a - b)(a^2 + ab + b^2)$, the sign after a^2 is positive, opposite the negative sign in $(a - b)$.

  3. **AP - Always Positive**: This refers to the last sign in the trinomial part of the factorization formula, which is always positive, regardless of whether the expression is a sum or a difference of cubes. This means:

- Both $a^2 - ab + b^2$ in the sum of cubes and $a^2 + ab + b^2$ in the difference of cubes end with a positive term $(+b^2)$.

Example: Factor $x^3 - 27$

1. Identify the Cubes: The term x^3 is the cube of x, and 27 is the cube of 3.
2. Apply the Difference of Cubes Formula: Since the expression involves subtraction, use the difference of cubes formula: $a^3 - b^3 = (a - b)(a^2 + ab + b^2)$ with $a = x$ and $b = 3$.

$$x^3 - 27 = (x - 3)(x^2 + 3x + 9)$$

General Strategy of Factoring Polynomials

Factoring polynomials efficiently requires a systematic approach, ensuring each polynomial is broken down into its simplest form. Below is a structured method to guide you through the factoring process:

Step 1—Identify the Greatest Common Factor (GCF): Check if there is a GCF in all terms of the polynomial. If one exists, factor it out first. This simplifies the polynomial, reducing the complexity of further factoring steps.

Step 2—Analyze the Structure of the Polynomial: Determine the type of polynomial and apply the appropriate factoring technique:

Binomial Factors:

Sum of Squares: Note that sums of squares generally do not factor over the real numbers.

Sum of Cubes: Apply the sum of cubes formula: $a^3 + b^3 = (a + b)(a^2 - ab + b^2)$

Difference of Squares: Factor as the product of conjugates using $a^2 - b^2 = (a - b)(a + b)$

Difference of Cubes: Use the difference of cubes formula: $a^3 - b^3 = (a - b)(a^2 + ab + b^2)$

Trinomial Factors:

Simple Form $(x^2 + bx + c)$: Undo the FOIL process by finding two numbers that multiply to c and add to b.

Complex Form $(ax^2 + bx + c)$: Check if a and c are perfect squares and fit the trinomial square pattern where the first term, ax^2, and the last term, c, must both be perfect squares, and the middle term, bx, must be twice the product of the square roots of ax^2 and c.

Otherwise, use trial and error or the "ac" method, finding two numbers that multiply to ac and add to b, then group and factor.

Polynomials with More than Three Terms:

Grouping Method: Group terms to create factorable chunks, typically aiming for common factors or binomial factors within the groups.

Step 3—Verification: Check if the polynomial is factored completely. Ensure that no further factorization is possible. Multiply the factors to verify that they combine to form the original polynomial.

The following table summarizes the factoring methods we have covered, and the general strategy of factoring polynomials.

Table: General Strategy of Factoring Polynomials

Category	Type	Formula/Method
GCF		Always check for and factor out the GCF first.
Binomial	Difference of Squares	$a^2 - b^2 = (a - b)(a + b)$
	Sum of Squares	Sums of squares do not factor (over real numbers)
	Sum of Cubes	$a^3 + b^3 = (a + b)(a^2 - ab + b^2)$
	Difference of Cubes	$a^3 - b^3 = (a - b)(a^2 + ab + b^2)$
Trinomial	Simple: $x^2 + bx + c$	Look for two numbers that multiply to c and add to b
	Complex: $ax^2 + bx + c$	Use the 'ac' method
More than 3 terms	Grouping	Group terms to factor by common factors

FUNCTIONS

A function is a relation that uniquely associates each element of a given set, called the domain, with an element in another set, known as the range. In simpler terms, a function takes an input, applies a specific rule to it, and then produces <u>exactly one output</u>. Below are a couple of examples:

- Numerical Example: Consider the function $f(x) = x + 3$. If the input x is 2, then the output $f(2)$ is $2 + 3 = 5$.

- Real-life Example: Consider the relationship between the distance traveled and the amount of fuel used by a vehicle. This function, often referred to as the fuel efficiency function, calculates the fuel consumption based on the distance traveled.

Function Notation

Function notation is a concise way to represent functions. The notation $f(x)$ denotes a function named f evaluated at an input x. Here, f represents the function itself, and x is the variable or input to the function. The expression $f(x)$ represents the output of the function.

Example: In the function $f(x) = x^2 - 4x + 4$,

- $f(0) = 0^2 - 4 \times 0 + 4 = 4$

- $f(2) = 2^2 - 4 \times 2 + 4 = 0$

Different Representations of Functions

Functions can be represented in various forms, each providing different insights:

1. **Verbal Descriptions**: Describing the relationship in words, such as "add three to any number."
2. **Equations**: A mathematical statement like $f(x) = 2x + 1$ that defines the output for each input.
3. **Tables**: Listing input values alongside their corresponding output values.
4. **Graphs**: Visual representations, where the input values are plotted on the x-axis, and the output values are plotted on the y-axis.

Evaluating Linear and Quadratic Functions

Linear Functions

Linear functions are functions of the form $f(x) = mx + b$, where m is the slope and b is the y-intercept. Evaluating a linear function means substituting a value for x and calculating the corresponding y value.

Example: For the function $f(x) = 3x + 2$

To find f(4), substitute x=4: $f(4) = 3(4) + 2 = 14$

Quadratic Functions

Quadratic functions are expressed as $f(x) = ax^2 + bx + c$, with a, b, and c being constants. Evaluating a quadratic function involves substituting the x value into the equation and calculating the result.

Example: For $f(x) = x2 - 5x + 6$, find $f(3)$.

To evaluate $f(3)$, substitute $x = 3$: $f(3) = 3^2 - 5 \cdot 3 + 6 = 0$

Evaluating Combined Functions

Combined functions involve the arithmetic combination of two distinct functions. These combinations can include addition, subtraction, multiplication, and division. To evaluate combined functions, you perform the indicated operation using the outputs of the individual functions.

Forms of Combined Functions

1. **Addition** $(f + g)(x)$: The output is the sum of the outputs of $f(x)$ and $g(x)$.
2. **Subtraction** $(f - g)(x)$: The output is the difference between the outputs of $f(x)$ and $g(x)$.
3. **Multiplication** $(fg)(x)$: The output is the product of the outputs of $f(x)$ and $g(x)$.
4. **Division** $\left(\frac{f}{g}\right)(x)$ The output is the quotient of the outputs of $f(x)$ over $g(x)$, assuming $g(x) \neq 0$.

Evaluating Combined Functions Step-by-Step

1. **Identify and understand each function**: Determine what $f(x)$ and $g(x)$ represent and ensure you understand the form of each function.
2. **Evaluate each function independently**: Before combining, find the values of $f(x)$ and $g(x)$ for a specific input.
3. **Apply the arithmetic operation**: Use the results of $f(x)$ and $g(x)$ to compute the combined function according to the operation defined (addition, subtraction, multiplication, or division).

Example: Consider the functions $f(x) = 2x + 3$ and $g(x) = x^2 - 1$. Evaluate $(f + g)(x)$, $(f - g)(x)$, $(fg)(x)$, and $\left(\frac{f}{g}\right)(x)$ at $x = 2$.

- Evaluating $f(x)$ and $g(x)$ at $x = 2$:

$$f(2) = 2(2) + 3 = 7$$
$$g(2) = 2^2 - 1 = 3$$

- Addition $(f + g)(2)$: $(f + g)(2) = f(2) + g(2) = 7 + 3 = 10$
- Subtraction $(f - g)(2)$: $(f - g)(2) = f(2) - g(2) = 7 - 3 = 4$
- Multiplication $(fg)(2)$: $(fg)(2) = f(2) \cdot g(2) = 7 \cdot 3 = 21$
- Division $\left(\frac{f}{g}\right)(2)$ (assuming $g(2) \neq 0$): $\left(\frac{f}{g}\right)(2) = \frac{f(2)}{g(2)} = \frac{7}{3}$

Evaluating Composite Functions

Composite functions, denoted as $(f \circ g)(x)$, involve applying one function to the result of another function. This operation is often described as "f of g of x." The somewhat confusing $(f \circ g)(x)$ notation simply means $f(g(x))$. Evaluating a composite function means you first apply the inner function and then use its output as the input for the outer function.

It's important to note that the order of function application matters significantly. The inner function is always applied first, followed by the outer function.

Steps to Evaluate Composite Functions

1. **Identify the inner and outer functions**: Determine which function is $g(x)$ (the inner function) and which is $f(x)$ (the outer function).
2. **Evaluate the inner function**: Substitute the given input into the inner function $g(x)$ to find its output.
3. **Apply the outer function**: Use the output from $g(x)$ as the input for the outer function $f(x)$.

Example: Consider the functions $f(x) = 3x - 1$ and $g(x) = x^2 + 2$. Evaluate $(f \circ g)(x)$ and $(g \circ f)(x)$ at $x = 2$.

- Evaluating $g(x)$ at $x = 2$: $g(2) = 2^2 + 2 = 6$
- Applying f to $g(2)$:

$$(f \circ g)(2) = f(g(2)) = f(6) = 3(6) - 1 = 17$$

- Evaluating $f(x)$ at $x = 2$:

$$f(2) = 3(2) - 1 = 5$$

- Applying g to $f(2)$:

$$(g \circ f)(2) = g(f(2)) = g(5) = 5^2 + 2 = 27$$

Common Errors to Avoid

- **Reversing the order of application**: It's a common mistake to reverse the order and compute $g(f(x))$ instead of $f(g(x))$ when given $(f \circ g)(x)$.
- **Incorrectly substituting**: Ensure that each function is evaluated entirely before its output is used as the input for the next function.

Graphing Functions

Graphing functions is a fundamental skill in mathematics that helps visualize relationships between variables, understand the behavior of functions, and identify their properties such as intercepts, and slopes. Since we have covered graphing linear functions earlier, we will go directly to graph quadratic functions here and extend the skills to more complex functions.

Graphing Quadratic Functions

Quadratic functions form parabolas and are typically written as $y = ax^2 + bx + c$. The shape of the parabola (opening upwards or downwards) is determined by the coefficient a.

Steps to Graph a Quadratic Function:

1. **Identify the vertex**: The vertex form of a quadratic is $y = a(x - h)^2 + k$, where (h, k) is the vertex. Use the formula $h = -\frac{b}{2a}$ and $k = f(h)$ to find the vertex.
2. **Plot the vertex**: Mark the vertex on the graph.
3. **Find additional points**: Substitute other x-values into the equation to find corresponding y-values. Plot at least two points on each side of the vertex.
4. **Draw the parabola**: Connect the points with a smooth curve, ensuring it is symmetrical about the vertex.

Example: Graph the function $y = x^2 - 4x + 3$

- Vertex $x = -\frac{-4}{2(1)} = 2$. Substitute $x = 2$ in $y = x^2 - 4x + 3$ to find $y = 3 - 8 + 3 = -1$. Vertex is (2, -1).
- Plot additional points like (1, 0), (3, 0), (0, 3), and (4, 3).
- Connect these points to form a symmetrical parabola around (2, -1).

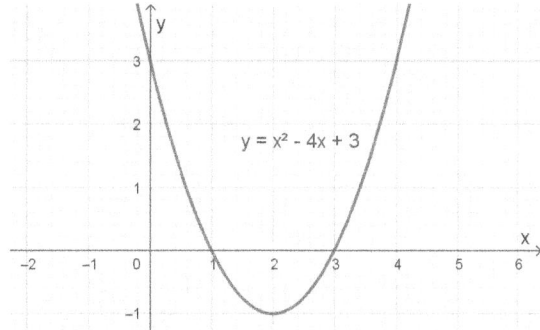

Interpreting Functions within a Context

Interpreting functions within a context involves understanding how the characteristics of functions relate to real-world situations. This skill is crucial for applying mathematical models to solve practical problems in various fields such as science, engineering, economics, and social sciences.

Contextual Analysis of Linear Functions

Linear functions, represented by the equation $y = mx + b$, are straightforward to interpret due to their constant rate of change, represented by the slope mm. The y-intercept b provides the starting value or initial condition of the function.

Steps to Interpret Linear Functions:

1. **Identify the slope and y-intercept**: Understand the slope as the rate of change or growth, and the y-intercept as the starting point.
2. **Apply to real-world scenarios**: For example, if $y = 14.95x + 4$ represents the cost y in dollars of buying x books, where each book costs $14.95 and there's a fixed cost of $4, the slope tells us the cost per book and the y-intercept represents the fixed cost—possibly due to shipping.

Contextual Analysis of Quadratic Functions

Quadratic functions, which form parabolas, are characterized by their vertex and direction of opening (upward or downward). They often model scenarios with maximum or minimum values, such as projectile motion or profit maximization.

Steps to Interpret Quadratic Functions:

1. **Vertex and direction of the parabola**: Identify the vertex as the maximum or minimum point. The direction indicates whether it is a maximum (opens downward) or a minimum (opens upward).
2. **Real-world application**: For instance, a function $y = -x^2 + 125x + 3$ might model the height y (measured in meters) of a projectile x seconds after it is launched. The vertex gives the maximum height reached. In this example, y is meaningful only in the range where it is bigger than 0. Hence, we have the following graph describing the relationship between x and y.

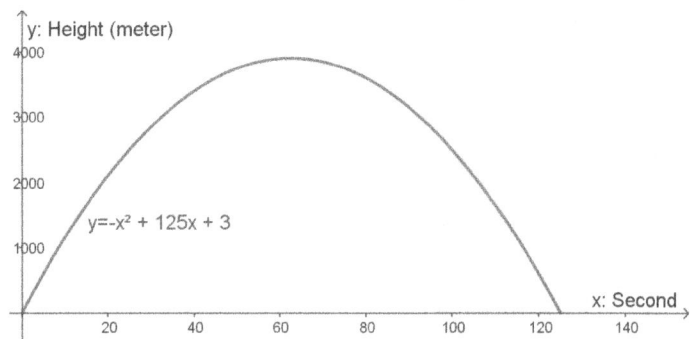

Interpreting Graphs

Graphs provide a visual representation of functions and are invaluable for interpreting the relationship between variables.

1. **Intercepts**: Points where the function crosses the axes. These often represent important baseline conditions in context.
2. **Slope**: For linear functions, the slope indicates the rate of change. For non-linear functions, slopes at different points can indicate acceleration or deceleration.
3. **Asymptotes**: In rational or logarithmic functions, asymptotes represent boundaries or limitations in real-world contexts.

Example—Function Interpretation in a Business Context

Consider a function $P(x) = -2x^2 + 12x - 20$ representing the profit P, in thousands of dollars, from producing x hundred units of a product. Interpreting this function involves:

- **Finding the vertex**: To determine the maximum profit and the corresponding production level.
- **Analyzing the intercepts**: To understand the break-even points where profit equals zero.
- **Evaluating the parabola's shape**: It opens downwards, indicating that there is a maximum profit level.

QUADRATIC EQUATIONS AND INEQUALITIES

Quadratic equations are characterized by their standard form $ax^2 + bx + c = 0$, where a, b, and c are coefficients and $a \neq 0$. These equations often appear in various scientific, engineering, and mathematical contexts, representing parabolic shapes when graphed. This section introduces methods to solve quadratic equations, including factoring, using the quadratic formula, and completing the square.

Solving Quadratic Equations

Method 1: Factoring

Factoring involves expressing the quadratic equation in a product form $(px + q)(rx + s) = 0$, where $p, q, r,$ and s are numbers that satisfy the equation. This method works best when the quadratic can be easily decomposed into factors.

Steps:

1. **Write the equation in standard form**: Ensure the equation is in the form $ax^2 + bx + c = 0$.

2. **Factor the quadratic**: Look for two numbers that multiply to ac (the product of the coefficient of x^2 and the constant term) and add up to b (the coefficient of x). Break down the middle term using the identified pairs and factor by grouping.

3. **Set each factor to zero**: Solve $px + q = 0$ and $rx + s = 0$ for x.

Example: Solve $x^2 - 5x + 6 = 0$ by factoring.

Solution:

1. Factor pairs of 6 that add up to -5 are -2 and -3.

2. Factor the quadratic: $(x - 2)(x - 3) = 0$.

3. Set each factor to zero: $x - 2 = 0$ or $x - 3 = 0$, so $x = 2$ or $x = 3$.

Method 2: Quadratic Formula

The quadratic formula is a universal method that can solve any quadratic equation, regardless of its coefficients. The formula is derived from the process of completing the square.

Formula:

$$x = \frac{-b \pm \sqrt{b^2 - 4ac}}{2a}$$

Steps:

1. **Identify coefficients a, b, and c.**

2. **Substitute into the quadratic formula**: Plug the values of a, b, and c into the formula.

3. **Calculate the discriminant**: $b2 - 4ac$. The nature of the roots depends on the discriminant (real and distinct, real and equal, or complex).

4. **Solve for x**: Compute the values using plus and minus versions of the formula.

Example: Solve $2x^2 - 4x - 6 = 0$ using the quadratic formula.

Solution:

1. Substitute $a = 2, b = -4, c = -6$ into the formula.
2. Compute the discriminant: $(-4)^2 - 4 \times 2 \times (-6) = 16 + 48 = 64$.
3. Solve for x: $x = \frac{-(-4) \pm \sqrt{64}}{2 \times 2} = \frac{4 \pm 8}{4}$. So, $x = 3$ or $x = -1$.

Method 3: Completing the Square

Completing the square involves rewriting the quadratic equation in a way that it forms a perfect square trinomial $(dx + e)^2 + f = 0$, which can then be solved by taking square roots.

Steps:

1. **Isolate the quadratic and linear terms**: Move the constant term to the other side of the equation.
2. **Divide through by** a if $a \neq 1$.
3. **Complete the square**: Add and subtract the square of half the coefficient of x inside the equation.
4. **Factor and solve for** x.

Example: Solve $x^2 - 6x + 5 = 0$ by completing the square.

Solution:

1. Move the constant term: $x^2 - 6x = -5$.
2. Half the coefficient of x is -3, square it to get 9, add and subtract 9: $x^2 - 6x + 9 = 4$.
3. Factor and solve: $(x - 3)^2 = 4$, so $x - 3 = \pm 2$, thus $x = 5$ or $x = 1$.

Which Method to Choose

Choosing the right method to solve a quadratic equation—whether to factor, complete the square, or use the quadratic formula—depends largely on the equation's complexity and the specific coefficients involved.

Factoring is the fastest and most straightforward for equations with simple, small integer coefficients and obvious roots. However, not all quadratics neatly factor, especially those with large or complex coefficients. In these cases, completing the square can be useful for deriving the vertex form and understanding the equation's geometric properties, although it can be algebraically demanding.

The quadratic formula is the most universally applicable method, capable of solving any quadratic equation, but it can be computationally intensive.

Simplifying complex quadratic equations is always a good idea before attempting to solve it. Steps such as factoring out the greatest common divisor, rationalizing fractions, or methodically testing factor combinations can make solving the equation easier regardless of the chosen method.

POLYNOMIAL FUNCTIONS AND EQUATIONS

Polynomial functions are a class of mathematical functions that play a crucial role in numerical analysis, theoretical studies, and practical applications. A **polynomial function** is a function that can be written as:

$$f(x) = a_n x^n + a_{n-1} x^{n-1} + \cdots + a_2 x^2 + a_1 x + a_0$$

where:

- x is the variable or the input of the function.
- $a_n, a_{n-1}, \ldots, a_1, a_0$ are coefficients (where $a_n \neq 0$ for the highest non-zero term).
- n is a non-negative integer that represents the degree of the polynomial, indicating the highest power of x in the polynomial.

Key Concepts

Degree: The degree of a polynomial is the highest power of the variable x that appears in the polynomial. It determines many properties of the polynomial, such as the number of roots (including multiplicity) and the behavior of the polynomial as x approaches infinity or negative infinity.

Coefficients: These are the numbers multiplying the powers of x. They can be real or complex numbers and significantly affect the shape and location of the polynomial graph.

Roots or Zeros: The values of x for which the polynomial equals zero are called roots or zeros. The fundamental theorem of algebra states that a polynomial of degree n has exactly n roots in the complex number system, counting multiplicities.

End Behavior: The end behavior of a polynomial function depends on the leading term (the term with the highest power of x). As x approaches positive or negative infinity, the behavior of the polynomial is dominated by this term.

Turning Points: A polynomial of degree n can have up to $n - 1$ turning points. These are points where the function changes from increasing to decreasing or decreasing to increasing.

Intercepts: The y-intercept of the polynomial is the value of the function when $x = 0$, which is a_0. The x-intercepts (or roots) are found by solving the equation $f(x) = 0$.

Graphs of Polynomial Functions

The graph of a polynomial function is always a smooth and continuous curve. There are no breaks, holes, or sharp corners in a polynomial graph. Depending on the degree of the polynomial, the graph will exhibit different numbers of turning points and intercepts.

Examples

1. **Linear Polynomial**: $f(x) = 2x + 1$ is a polynomial of degree 1 (linear polynomial), forming a straight line.
2. **Quadratic Polynomial**: $f(x) = x^2 - 4x + 4$ is a polynomial of degree 2, forming a parabola.
3. **Cubic Polynomial**: $f(x) = x^3 - 3x^2 + 3x - 1$ is a polynomial of degree 3, which can have up to two turning points.

Even and Odd Polynomials

Even and odd polynomials are categories of polynomial functions that exhibit specific symmetrical properties related to their behavior with respect to the y-axis or the origin in the coordinate system.

Even Polynomials

A polynomial is **even** if all the powers of x in its expression are even numbers. Mathematically, a polynomial $p(x)$ is even if:

$$p(-x) = p(x)$$

This means that replacing x with $-x$ in the polynomial yields the same polynomial. The graph of an even polynomial is symmetric with respect to the y-axis. For example, the polynomial $p(x) = x^2 - 4x^4 + 6$ is even because:

$$p(-x) = (-x)^2 - 4(-x)^4 + 6 = x^2 - 4x^4 + 6 = p(x)$$

Odd Polynomials

A polynomial is odd if all the powers of x in its expression are odd numbers. Mathematically, a polynomial $p(x)$ is odd if:

$$p(-x) = -p(x)$$

This property implies that the graph of an odd polynomial is symmetric with respect to the origin. For example, the polynomial $p(x) = x^3 - 3x$ is odd because:

$$p(-x) = (-x)^3 - 3(-x) = -x^3 + 3x = -p(x)$$

Non-Symmetric Polynomials

It should be noted that while every integer is classified as either even or odd, a polynomial can be neither even nor odd.

Example: consider the polynomial $p(x) = x^2 + x$, it is neither even nor odd because:

$$p(-x) = (-x)^2 + (-x) = x^2 - x \neq p(x)$$
$$p(-x) = x^2 - x \neq -p(x) = -x^2 - x$$

These calculations show that $p(x) = x^2 + x$ doesn't satisfy the conditions for being even or odd, illustrating a polynomial that is neither.

A polynomial that is not even or odd will not exhibit the symmetrical properties associated with even and odd polynomials.

On the other hand, the symmetrical properties of even and odd polynomials can often make them simpler to analyze, especially when considering their behavior over the entire set of real numbers. They play a crucial role in various applications.

Power Functions

Power functions are a type of mathematical function defined by an expression of the form $f(x) = kx^n$, where k and n are constants, and x can be any real number. The constant k is known as the coefficient, and n is the exponent, which determines the degree and the basic behavior of the function.

Characteristics of Power Functions

- **Exponent n:** This can be any real number—positive, negative, integer, or fractional. The value and type of n significantly affect the shape and properties of the graph of the function.

- **Coefficient k:** This determines the scaling and direction (if negative) of the function. A positive k results in a graph that maintains the direction of the basic shape dictated by n, while a negative k reflects it across the x-axis.

Common Power Functions

Here are some common power functions and their graphs.

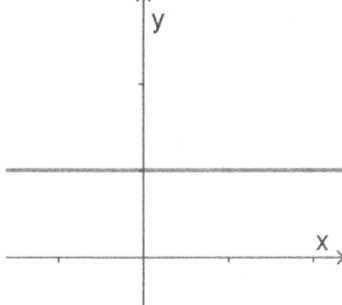
Constant function: $f(x) = 1$

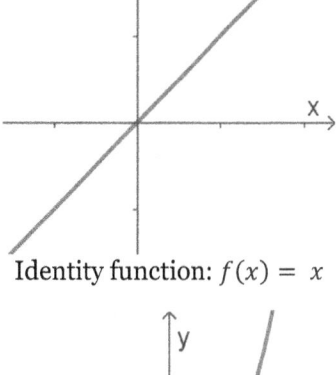
Identity function: $f(x) = x$

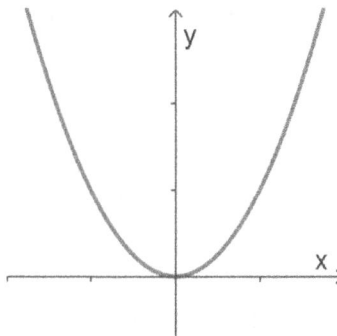
Quadratic function: $f(x) = x^2$

Cubic function: $f(x) = x^3$

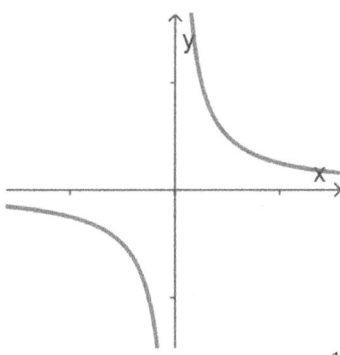
Reciprocal function: $f(x) = \frac{1}{x}$

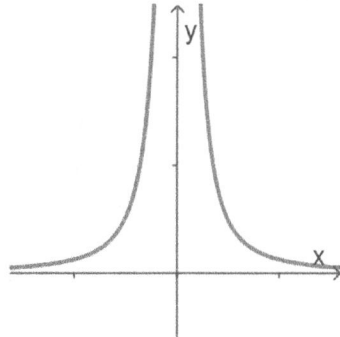
Reciprocal squared function: $f(x) = \frac{1}{x^2}$

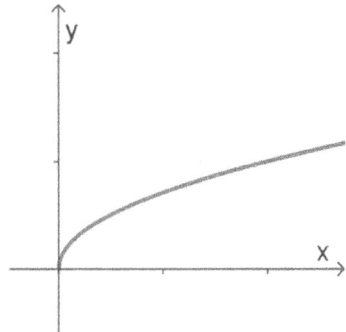
Square root function: $f(x) = \sqrt{x}$

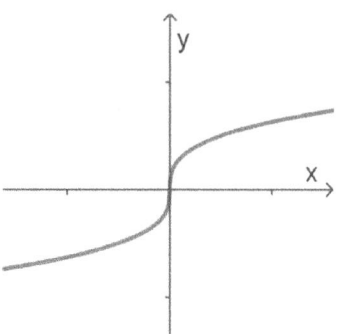
Cubic root function: $f(x) = \sqrt[3]{x}$

Types of Power Functions

1. **Positive Integer Exponents** ($n > 0$): These functions are polynomial functions of x. For example, $f(x) = x^3$ is a cubic function, which is symmetric about the origin and increases on both sides as $|x|$ increases.

2. **Negative Integer Exponents** ($n < 0$): These functions are hyperbolas. For example, $f(x) = \frac{1}{x}$ (or $x^{(-1)}$) has a vertical and horizontal asymptote, reflecting its values approaching zero as x approaches infinity and negative infinity.

3. **Fractional Exponents**: When n is a fraction, the function involves roots of x. For example, $f(x) = x^{\frac{1}{2}}$ represents the square root of x, defined only for $x \geq 0$ in the real number system.

End Behavior of Power Functions

The end behavior of power functions, given by $f(x) = kx^n$, where n is a non-negative integer and k is a constant, depends on the values of n and k. These parameters influence how the function behaves as x approaches infinity ($x \to \infty$) and negative infinity ($x \to -\infty$).

Influence of the Exponent n

1. **Even n**: When n is even, the function $f(x) = kx^n$ will have the same behavior at both $x \to \infty$ and $x \to -\infty$. Regardless of the sign of x, x^n will always be positive because an even power of a negative number is positive.

2. **Odd n**: When n is odd, the function $f(x) = kx^n$ will behave differently as x approaches ∞ compared to when x approaches $-\infty$. Since an odd power of a negative number is negative, the function will inherit the sign of x.

Influence of the Coefficient k

1. **Positive k**: A positive k does not change the fundamental end behavior dictated by n but affects the magnitude. For example, if n is even, $f(x)$ approaches ∞ as x approaches both ∞ and $-\infty$. If n is odd, $f(x)$ approaches ∞ as $x \to \infty$ and $-\infty$ as $x \to -\infty$.

2. **Negative k**: A negative k reverses the directions of the end behavior. For an even n, f(x) approaches $-\infty$ as x approaches both ∞ and $-\infty$. For an odd n, $f(x)$ approaches $-\infty$ as $x \to \infty$ and ∞ as $x \to -\infty$.

The graphs of the common power functions above provide some examples of how n and k influence the end behavior of power functions.

Visualizing the Behavior

The graphs of these common power functions provide a visual confirmation of these behaviors. Even functions exhibit U-shaped or inverted U-shaped curves symmetric about the y-axis, while odd functions have origin-symmetric curves that pass through the origin, reflecting their respective behaviors as x moves towards infinity or negative infinity.

The following figure shows the end behavior of power functions in the form $f(x) = kx^n$ where n is a non-negative integer depending on the power n and the constant k.

Table: Power Function End Behavior

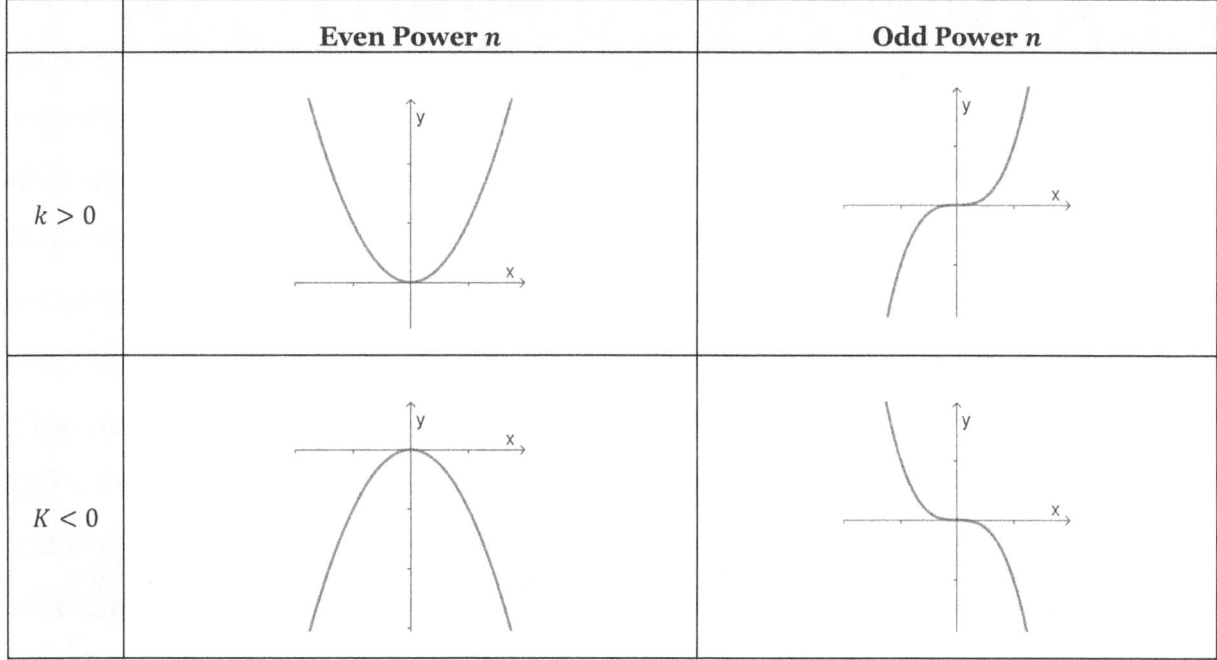

Solving Polynomial Equations

Solving polynomial equations allows us to find the values of the variable that make the equation true, typically referred to as the roots or zeros of the polynomial. Polynomial equations can range from simple linear equations to complex higher-degree equations. Here's a general guide on how to approach solving them:

1. Simplify the Equation: Ensure the polynomial equation is set to zero, $f(x) = 0$. This standard form makes it easier to apply various algebraic techniques. Simplify the polynomial by combining like terms and reducing the equation to its simplest form if necessary.

2. Factorization: Factorizing the polynomial is often the first approach:

- **Common Factor**: Start by extracting any common factors from all terms.

- **Grouping**: For higher-degree polynomials, grouping terms to factor by grouping may be effective.

- **Special Products**: Look for patterns like difference of squares, perfect square trinomials, and sum/difference of cubes.

- **Splitting the Middle Term**: Useful for quadratic polynomials, where the middle term is split into two terms that can easily be grouped and factored.

Once the polynomial is factored, set each factor equal to zero and solve for x.

3. Quadratic Formula: For quadratic equations $ax^2 + bx + c = 0$, if factorization is not straightforward, use the quadratic formula, which provides the roots directly and works for any quadratic equation, regardless of whether it is factorable.

Example: Solve the polynomial equation: $x^3 - 3x^2 - 4x + 12 = 0$

1. **Explanation:** Factor by Grouping: To factor this polynomial, we can use the method of grouping. First, group the terms in pairs and factor out the greatest common factor from each group:

  - From the first two terms $x^3 - 3x^2$, factor out x^2: $x^2(x - 3)$
  - From the last two terms $-4x + 12$, factor out -4: $-4(x - 3)$
  - Now, put the factored groups together: $x^2(x - 3) - 4(x - 3) = 0$

2. **Factor Out the Common Binomial Factor:** Notice that $x - 3$ is a common factor in both groups, we do the following: $(x - 3)(x^2 - 4) = 0$

3. **Factor Further if Possible:** $(x - 3)(x^2 - 4) = (x - 3)(x + 2)(x - 2) = 0$

  Set each factor equal to zero and solve for x:

- $x - 3 = 0 \implies x = 3$
- $x + 2 = 0 \implies x = -2$
- $x - 2 = 0 \implies x = 2$

Conclusion: The solutions are $x = 3$, $x = -2$, and $x = 2$. Thus, the polynomial factors completely into $(x - 3)(x + 2)(x - 2) = 0$, and the roots of the equation are $x = 3, -2$, and 2. This example illustrates the power of factoring by grouping and recognizing patterns such as the difference of squares in simplifying polynomial equations.

Let's take this opportunity to introduce **Zeros of a Polynomial**: they are the values of the variable that make the polynomial equal to zero. In other words, if $P(x)$ is a polynomial, then the zeros are the solutions to the equation $P(x) = 0$. In the example above, zeros of polynomial $x^3 - 3x^2 - 4x + 12$ are $x = 3$, $x = -2$, and $x = 2$. Hence, to find the zeros of a polynomial, one just needs to set the polynomial to zero, and then solve for the solutions.

Identifying Polynomial Function's x- and y-Intercept

Identifying y-Intercept

Identifying the y-intercept of a polynomial function is a step in drawing the function in a coordinate system. The y-intercept is the point where the graph of the polynomial crosses the y-axis. In mathematical terms, this occurs when $x = 0$. The steps to find the y-intercept of a polynomial function are thus straightforward:

Steps to Find the y-Intercept

1. **Substitute $x = 0$ in the Polynomial**: Given a polynomial function $f(x) = a_n x^n + a_{n-1} x^{n-1} + \cdots + a_1 x + a_0$, replace every x in the equation with 0.

2. **Simplify the Expression**:
   After substituting $x = 0$, all terms containing x will equal zero because any number raised to a positive power multiplied by zero equals zero. The only term that remains is the constant term a_0.

3. **Result is the y-Intercept**:
   The value obtained from the substitution is the y-coordinate of the y-intercept, thus the y-intercept of the polynomial $f(x)$ is at $(0, a_0)$.

Example: Find the y-intercept for the polynomial function $f(x) = 3x^3 - 5x^2 + 6x - 4$.

Solution: Substitute $x = 0$ into the polynomial: $f(0) = 3(0)^3 - 5(0)^2 + 6(0) - 4 = -4$.

Therefore, the y-intercept is therefore at $(0, -4)$.

Identifying x-Intercept

The x-intercept(s) of a polynomial function are the points where the graph crosses the x-axis, meaning these are the values of x for which the function $f(x) = 0$. Hence, one only needs to solve the equation $f(x) = 0$ to identify all the x-intercept(s).

Example: Let's consider the polynomial $f(x) = x^3 - 4x^2 + 5x - 2$.

Step 1: Set the Polynomial to Zero: $x^3 - 4x^2 + 5x - 2 = 0$

Step 2: Factor the Polynomial

$$\begin{aligned} x^3 - 4x^2 + 5x - 2 &= 0 \\ (x^3 - 1) - (4x^2 - 5x + 1) &= 0 \\ (x-1)(x^2 + x + 1) - (x-1)(4x - 1) &= 0 \\ (x-1)(x^2 + x + 1 - 4x + 1) &= 0 \\ (x-1)(x^2 - 3x + 2) &= 0 \\ (x-1)(x-1)(x-2) &= 0 \end{aligned}$$

Step 3: Solve for x: It is obvious the solutions are $x = 1$ and $x = 2$. Thus, the x-intercepts are: $x = 1$ and $x = 2$.

Graphing Polynomial Functions

Graphing polynomial equations involves several key steps to accurately depict the function's behavior on a coordinate plane. Here's a concise guide:

Step 1: Determine Degree and Leading Coefficient: Identify the highest power of x (degree) and its coefficient to predict the end behavior of the graph:

- Odd Degree: Ends in opposite directions.
- Even Degree: Ends in the same direction.
- Leading coefficient positive: Right end upwards.
- Leading coefficient negative: Right end downwards.

Step 2: Find Y-Intercept: Set $x = 0$ and calculate $f(0)$. This gives the y-intercept, the point where the graph crosses the y-axis.

Step 3: Solve for X-Intercepts: Set the polynomial equal to zero, $f(x) = 0$, and solve for x. These roots are the x-intercepts, where the graph crosses the x-axis.

Step 4: Identify Turning Points: Look at the sign changes between consecutive test points and the degree of the polynomial to estimate local maxima and minima. This helps in sketching the curvature of the graph.

Step 5: Plot and Connect Points: Using the identified intercepts and estimated turning points, plot these on a graph. Connect these points smoothly, respecting the end behavior and curvature dictated by the polynomial's degree and coefficients.

TSIA2 Test requires understanding the steps and principles to graph polynomial functions. However, you won't be tested on drawing a graph during the test. Instead, you will be facing multiple-choice questions like the following.

Example 1: The graph of $y = g(x)$ is shown in the xy-plane below.

Which of the following equations could define $g(x)$?

A. $g(x) = x^2 - 3x + 2$

B. $g(x) = -x^2 + 3x - 2$

C. $g(x) = (x + 1)(x - 3)$

D. $g(x) = -(x + 1)^2 + 4$

C.

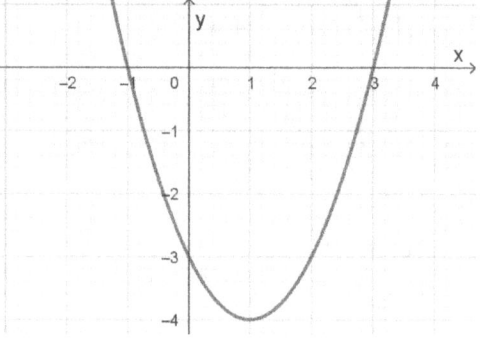

Explanation: Function g(x) intersects with x-axis at $(-1, 0)$ and $(3, 0)$, indicating the equation $g(x) = 0$ must have two solutions of $x = -1, x = 3$. Function $g(x) = (x + 1)(x - 3)$ is the only function that such two solutions.

Example 2: Which of the following could be an equation of the function matching this graph?

A. $f(x) = x^2 - 6x + 9$

B. $f(x) = (x - 2)^2$

C. $f(x) = -x^2 + 6x - 5$

D. $f(x) = -(x + 2)(x - 4)$

B.

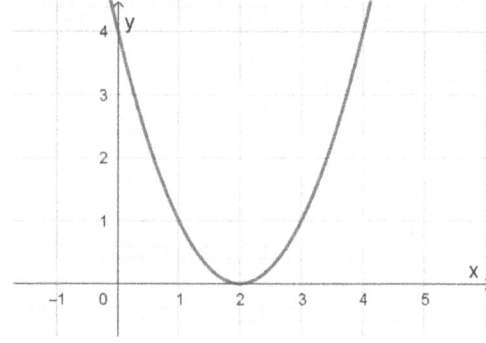

Explanation: Since the parabola points upwards, we know that the coefficient before x^2 must be positive. Hence, only A or B are valid choices. Since the vertex of the graph is at $(2, 0)$, we know when $x = 2, f(x)$ must be 0. Only B satisfies this condition.

RADICAL FUNCTIONS

Radical functions are functions that involve a variable within a radical symbol, most commonly a square root. These functions are characterized by the presence of roots, such as square roots, cube roots, or higher-order roots. The general form of a radical function is: $f(x) = \sqrt[n]{x}$, where n is the degree of the root.

Domain of Radical Functions

The domain of a radical function includes all the values of x for which the expression under the radical is defined. This depends on the type of radical:

1. **Square Root Functions**: For a function of the form $f(x) = x$ or $f(x) = \sqrt{g(x)}$ the expression under the square root must be non-negative. Therefore, the domain is found by solving: $g(x) \geq 0$. For example, for $f(x) = \sqrt{x - 2}$, the domain is determined by $x - 2 \geq 0$, so $x \geq 2$.

2. **Higher-Order Root Functions**: For functions involving even roots (such as fourth roots), the domain also requires the expression under the radical to be non-negative. For odd roots (such as cube roots), the expression under the radical can be any real number, so the domain is all real numbers.

Range of Radical Functions

The range of a radical function depends on the values that the function can output:

1. **Square Root Functions**: Since the square root function $\sqrt{x}$ produces non-negative values, the range of $f(x) = \sqrt{x}$ is $y \geq 0$. For $f(x) = \sqrt{g(x)}$, the range is determined by evaluating the function over its domain.

2. **Higher-Order Root Functions**: The range of functions involving even roots is also non-negative. For odd roots, the range is all real numbers because these functions can produce both positive and negative values.

Examples

1. Square Root Function: $f(x) = \sqrt{x-1}$

- Domain: $x - 1 \geq 0 \Rightarrow x \geq 1$
- Range: $y \geq 0$

2. Cube Root Function: $f(x) = \sqrt[3]{x+2}$

- Domain: All real numbers (since cube roots are defined for all real numbers)
- Range: All real numbers

Determining the domain and range helps in graphing the function accurately and understanding its behavior within the specified intervals.

Simplifying Radical Expressions

Simplifying radical expressions involves rewriting them in their simplest form. This process includes reducing the radicand (the expression under the radical) and rationalizing the denominator if necessary.

Steps to Simplify Radical Expressions

1. **Factor the Radicand**: Break down the expression inside the radical into its prime factors or simpler expressions.

- For example, $\sqrt{50}$ can be factored as $\sqrt{25 \cdot 2}$

2. **Simplify the Radical**: Apply the property $\sqrt{a \cdot b} = \sqrt{a} \cdot \sqrt{b}$ to separate the factors.

- Simplify each part: $\sqrt{25 \cdot 2} = \sqrt{25} \cdot \sqrt{2} = 5\sqrt{2}$.

3. **Combine Like Terms**: If you have multiple radical terms, combine like terms by ensuring they have the same radicand.

- For example, $3\sqrt{2} + 5\sqrt{2} = 8\sqrt{2}$

4. **Rationalize the Denominator**: If a radical expression is in the denominator, multiply the numerator and the denominator by a term that will eliminate the radical in the denominator.

- For example, to simplify $\frac{1}{\sqrt{3}}$ multiply by $\frac{\sqrt{3}}{\sqrt{3}}$ to get $\frac{\sqrt{3}}{3}$.

Examples:

1. Simplifying a Single Radical: Simplify $\sqrt{72}$

- Factor 72: $72 = 36 \times 2$
- Simplify: $\sqrt{72} = \sqrt{36 \times 2} = \sqrt{36} \cdot \sqrt{2} = 6\sqrt{2}$.

2. Combining Like Radicals: Simplify $2\sqrt{3} + 4\sqrt{3}$
   - Combine like terms: $2\sqrt{3} + 4\sqrt{3} = (2 + 4)\sqrt{3} = 6\sqrt{3}$.

3. Rationalizing the Denominator: Simplify $\frac{5}{\sqrt{7}}$
   - Multiply by $\frac{\sqrt{7}}{\sqrt{7}}$: $\frac{5}{\sqrt{7}} \cdot \frac{\sqrt{7}}{\sqrt{7}} = \frac{5\sqrt{7}}{7}$.

4. Simplifying a Radical with a Variable: Simplify $\sqrt{18x^3}$
   - Factor: $18x^3 = 9 \times 2 \times x^2 \times x$
   - Simplify: $\sqrt{18x^3} = \sqrt{9 \times 2 \times x^2 \times x} = \sqrt{9} \cdot \sqrt{2} \cdot \sqrt{x^2} \cdot \sqrt{x} = 3x\sqrt{2x}$

Tips for Simplifying Radical Expressions
- **Perfect Squares**: Look for perfect squares within the radicand to simplify.
- **Prime Factorization**: Use prime factorization to break down complex radicands.
- **Rationalization**: Always rationalize the denominator if a radical is present.

Graphing Radical Functions

Below are the two most common radical functions along with their corresponding graphs. Although there are countless variations of radical functions, understanding the principles of function transformations allows us to determine their approximate shapes and locations based on these two graphs below. Radical functions with even roots all resemble a transformed (translated, dilated, or flipped) graph of $f(x) = \sqrt{x}$, while those with odd roots resemble a transformed graph of $y = \sqrt[3]{x}$.

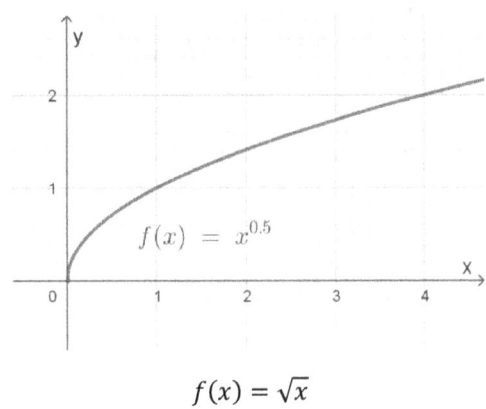

$f(x) = \sqrt{x}$

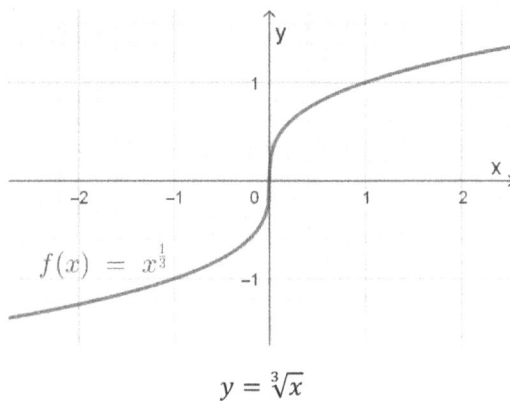

$y = \sqrt[3]{x}$

RATIONAL FUNCTIONS

Rational functions are functions that can be expressed as the ratio of two polynomials. The general form of a rational function is: $f(x) = \frac{P(x)}{Q(x)}$, where $P(x)$ and $Q(x)$ are polynomials, and $Q(x) \neq 0$. Rational functions are defined for all values of x except where the denominator $Q(x)$ is zero, as division by zero is undefined. These functions exhibit a wide range of behaviors and are particularly notable for their asymptotic properties.

Domain of Rational Functions

The domain of a rational function includes all real numbers except where the denominator is zero. To find the domain:

1. **Identify the Denominator**: Determine the polynomial in the denominator of the rational function.
2. **Set the Denominator Equal to Zero**: Solve for x where the denominator is zero to find the values that are not in the domain.
3. **Exclude These Values from the Domain**: The domain consists of all real numbers except these excluded values.

Example: For $f(x) = \frac{P(x)}{Q(x)}$, where $P(x) = x^2 - 4$ and $Q(x) = x^2 - 1$:

1. Denominator: $x^2 - 1$
2. Set the denominator to zero: $x^2 - 1 = 0$
3. Solve for x: $x = \pm 1$
4. Domain: All real numbers except $x = 1$ and $x = -1$

Hence: Domain: $x \in R, x \neq 1, x \neq -1$

Range of Rational Functions

The range of a rational function is the set of all possible output values. Finding the range is often more complex than finding the domain and may require analyzing the function's behavior. Here are the steps:

1. **Identify Horizontal Asymptotes**: Determine the behavior of the function as x approaches infinity or negative infinity. Compare the degrees of the numerator and the denominator:

- If the degree of $P(x)$ is less than the degree of $Q(x)$, the horizontal asymptote is $y = 0$

- If the degrees are equal, the horizontal asymptote is $y = \frac{\text{leading coefficient of } P(x)}{\text{leading coefficient of } Q(x)}$

- If the degree of $P(x)$ is greater than the degree of $Q(x)$, there is no horizontal asymptote (but there may be an oblique asymptote).

2. **Vertical Asymptotes and Holes**:

- Determine vertical asymptotes where the denominator is zero and not canceled by the numerator.
- Identify any holes where factors cancel out between the numerator and the denominator.

3. **Analyze the Function's Behavior**: Check for any other values that y cannot take by analyzing the function's graph or solving for y.

Example: Let's analyze the domain and range of the rational function $f(x) = \frac{1}{x}$

Domain: The domain of a rational function includes all real numbers except where the denominator is zero. For $f(x) = \frac{1}{x}$ the denominator is x. So, the domain is all real numbers except $x = 0$. Using mathematical notation: Domain: $x \in R, x \neq 0$.

Range: To determine the range, we analyze the function's behavior.

1. Behavior as x Approaches Zero:

- As x approaches 0 from the positive side ($x \to 0^+$), $f(x)$ approaches $+\infty$.
- As x approaches 0 from the negative side ($x \to 0^-$), $f(x)$ approaches $-\infty$.

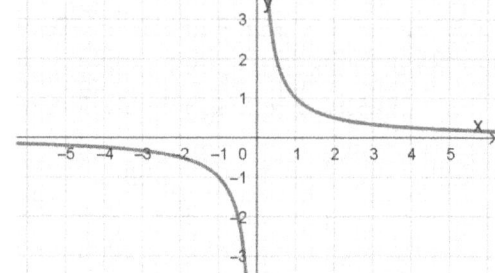

2. Behavior as x Approaches $\pm\infty$:

- As $x \to +\infty, f(x) \to 0^+$
- As $x \to -\infty, f(x) \to 0^-$

3. Horizontal Asymptote:

- The function $f(x) = \frac{1}{x}$ has a horizontal asymptote at $y = 0$ but $y = 0$ is never actually reached.

4. Range:

- The function $f(x) = \frac{1}{x}$ can take any real value except $y = 0$ Hence, its range is: $y \in R, y \neq 0$.

These characteristics highlight the fundamental properties of the rational function $f(x) = \frac{1}{x}$ The function is undefined at $x = 0$ leading to a vertical asymptote there, and it can approach but never reach $y = 0$ giving it a horizontal asymptote at $y = 0$

EXPONENTIAL FUNCTIONS AND EQUATIONS

Exponential functions are mathematical expressions where the variable appears in the exponent. They are of the form:

$$f(x) = a \cdot b^x$$

where a is a constant, b is the base (a positive real number not equal to 1), and x is the exponent. Exponential functions are characterized by rapid growth or decay, depending on whether the base b is greater than 1 (growth) or between 0 and 1 (decay).

Exponential equations involve solving for the variable in the exponent. Understanding exponential functions and equations is essential for analyzing situations involving exponential growth or decay.

Simplifying Fractional Exponents

Fractional exponents provide a convenient way to express roots using exponents. The general form of a fractional exponent is:

$$a^{\frac{m}{n}} = \sqrt[n]{a^m} = \left(\sqrt[n]{a}\right)^m$$

This means that $a^{\frac{m}{n}}$ can be interpreted as the n-th root of a raised to the m-th power, or equivalently, the m-th power of the n-th root of a. Below are some examples using this formula.

Square Roots: $-a^{\frac{1}{2}} = \sqrt{a}$

- Examples: $9^{\frac{1}{2}} = \sqrt{9} = 3$, $16^{\frac{1}{2}} = \sqrt{16} = 4$

Cube Roots: $a^{\frac{1}{3}} = \sqrt[3]{a}$

- Examples: $8^{\frac{1}{3}} = \sqrt[3]{8} = 2, \quad 27^{\frac{1}{3}} = \sqrt[3]{27} = 3$

Higher-Order Roots: $a^{\frac{1}{4}} = \sqrt[4]{a}$

- Examples: $16^{\frac{1}{4}} = \sqrt[4]{16} = 2, \quad 81^{\frac{1}{4}} = \sqrt[4]{81} = 3$

Combining Roots and Powers: $a^{\frac{m}{n}} = \sqrt[n]{a^m}$

- Examples: $27^{\frac{2}{3}} = \sqrt[3]{27^2} = \sqrt[3]{729} = 9, \quad 16^{\frac{3}{4}} = \sqrt[4]{16^3} = \sqrt[4]{4096} = 8$

Rewriting Expressions:

- Example: $x^{\frac{3}{2}}$
- $x^{\frac{3}{2}} = \left(\sqrt{x}\right)^3 = \left(\sqrt{x}\right)\left(\sqrt{x}\right)\left(\sqrt{x}\right)$
- $x^{\frac{3}{2}} = \sqrt{x^3} = \sqrt{x \cdot x \cdot x}$
- Example: $y^{\frac{5}{2}}$
- $y^{\frac{5}{2}} = \left(\sqrt{y}\right)^5 = \left(\sqrt{y}\right)\left(\sqrt{y}\right)\left(\sqrt{y}\right)\left(\sqrt{y}\right)\left(\sqrt{y}\right)$
- $y^{\frac{5}{2}} = \sqrt{y^5} = \sqrt{y \cdot y \cdot y \cdot y \cdot y}$

Simplifying Expressions:

Example: Simplify $32^{\frac{3}{5}}$

- First, find the fifth root: $\sqrt[5]{32} = 2$
- Then, raise it to the third power: $2^3 = 8$

Example: Simplify $125^{\frac{4}{3}}$

- First, find the cube root: $\sqrt[3]{125} = 5$
- Then, raise it to the fourth power: $5^4 = 625$

Solving Exponential Equations

Solving exponential equations often involves rewriting the expressions so that they have a common base. This allows us to set the exponents equal to each other and solve for the unknown variable. Here's a step-by-step guide on how to do this:

1. **Express Both Sides with a Common Base**: Rewrite both sides of the equation as powers of the same base.
2. **Set the Exponents Equal to Each Other**: Once both sides have the same base, set the exponents equal to each other because if $a^m = a^n$ then $m = n$
3. **Solve for the Variable**: Solve the resulting equation for the unknown variable.

Example 1—Simple Exponential Equation: $2^x = 16$

- Rewrite 16 as a power of 2: $16 = 2^4$
- Now the equation is: $2^x = 2^4$

- Set the exponents equal: $x = 4$

Example 2—More Complex Bases: $3^{2x} = 27$

- Rewrite 27 as a power of 3: $27 = 3^3 \Rightarrow 3^{2x} = 3^3$
- Set the exponents equal: $2x = 3$
- Solve for x: $x = \frac{3}{2}$

Example 3—Fractional Base: $4^{x-1} = \frac{1}{16}$

- Rewrite $\frac{1}{16}$ as a power of 4: $\frac{1}{16} = 4^{-2}$
- Now the equation is: $4^{x-1} = 4^{-2}$
- Set the exponents equal: $x - 1 = -2$
- Solve for x: $x = -1$

Example 4—Different Bases Requiring Conversion: $2^{x+1} = 8^{2x}$

- Rewrite 8 as a power of 2: $8 = 2^3$. So, $8^{2x} = (2^3)^{2x} = 2^{6x}$
- Now the equation is: $2^{x+1} = 2^{6x}$
- Set the exponents equal: $x + 1 = 6x$
- Solve for x: $x = \frac{1}{5}$

Exponential Growth and Decay Functions

Exponential growth and decay functions model scenarios where quantities increase or decrease at rates proportional to their current values. In TSIA2, they often appear as word problems. The approach to distinguishing exponential growth from decay are as follows.

Exponential Growth: $y = ab^x$, where $b > 1$. The function increases as x increases.

Exponential Decay: $y = ab^x$, with $0 < b < 1$. This function decreases as x increases.

Example 1—Exponential Growth: $y = 2 \cdot 3^x$

With this function, initial value (a) is 2. Base (b) is 3, which is greater than 1. As x increases, y grows rapidly.

Example 2—Exponential Growth: A population of bacteria doubles every hour, starting with 100 bacteria. The population y after x hours can be modeled by $y = 100 \cdot 2^x$

Example 3—Exponential Decay: $y = 5 \cdot 2^{-x}$

With this function, initial value (a) is 5. Base (b) is 2, and since the exponent is negative, this represents decay. As x increases, y decreases.

Example 4—Exponential Decay: The amount of a radioactive substance halves every year. Starting with 1000 grams, the amount y remaining after x years can be modeled by $y = 1000 \cdot \left(\frac{1}{2}\right)^x$, or $y = 1000 \cdot 2^{-x}$.

Example 5—A town's population is growing at an annual rate of 2%. If the current population is 50,000, what will the population be in 5 years?

1. **Explanation:** Identify the Variables: Initial population (P_0): 50,000, Growth rate (r): 2%, Time (t): 5 years.
2. Exponential Growth Formula: $P(t) = P_0(1+r)^t$
3. Substitute the Values: $P(5) = 50000(1+0.02)^5$
4. Calculate: $P(5) = 50000(1.02)^5 \approx 50000 \cdot 1.10408 \approx 55204$

Hence, the population will be approximately 55,204 in 5 years.

Example 6—A car depreciates in value by 10% per year. If the initial value of the car is $30,000, what will be its value after 5 years?

Solution:

1. Identify the Variables: Initial value (V_0): $30,000, Decay rate ($r$): 10% or 0.1, Time ($t$): 5 years.

2. Exponential Decay Formula: $V(t) = V_0(1-r)^t$

3. Substitute the Values: $V(5) = 30000(1-0.1)^5$

4. Calculate: $V(5) = 30000(0.9)^5 \approx 30000 \cdot 0.59049 \approx 17714.7$

Hence, the car's value will be approximately $17,714.70 after 5 years.

Graphing Exponential Functions

The following graph plots two exponential functions in the form of $y = ab^x$, with $b > 1$ and $0 < b < 1$, respectively. As one can readily see, when $b > 1$, a function exponentially increases; when $0 < b < 1$, a function exponentially decreases.

Although there are countless variations of exponential functions, with the principles of function transformations we have covered earlier, one can determine their approximate shapes and locations based on these two graphs below.

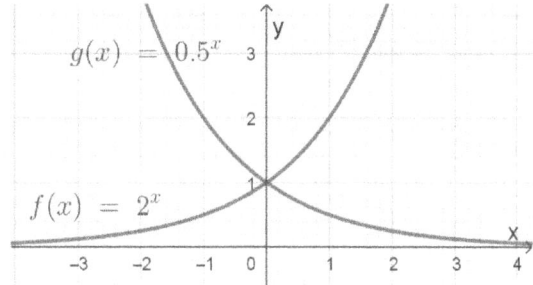

LOGARITHMIC FUNCTIONS AND EQUATIONS

Logarithmic functions are the inverse of exponential functions. They are used to solve equations where the variable is in the exponent and to model phenomena that change multiplicatively. A logarithmic function is defined as: $y = \log_b(x)$, where b is the base of the logarithm ($b > 0$ and $b \neq 1$), x is the argument of the logarithm ($x > 0$), y is the exponent to which the base b must be raised to obtain x.

Properties of Logarithms

- Inverse Property: $b^{\log_b(x)} = x$, $\log_b(b^y) = y$

- Product Property: $\log_b(xy) = \log_b(x) + \log_b(y)$
- Quotient Property: $\log_b\left(\frac{x}{y}\right) = \log_b(x) - \log_b(y)$
- Power Property: $\log_b(x^k) = k \cdot \log_b(x)$
- Change of Base Formula: $\log_b(x) = \frac{\log_k(x)}{\log_k(b)}$

Solving Logarithmic Equations

To solve logarithmic equations, we often use the properties of logarithms and their inverse relationship with exponential functions.

Examples 1—Simple Logarithmic Equation: $\log_2(x) = 3$
- Rewrite as: $x = 2^3$
- Solution: $x = 8$

Examples 2—Equation with Addition: $\log_5(x) + \log_5(2) = 1$
- Use the product property: $\log_5(2x) = 1$
- Rewrite as: $2x = 5^1$
- Solution: $2x = 5 \Rightarrow x = \frac{5}{2}$

Examples 3—Natural Logarithm Equation: $\ln(x) = 4$
- Rewrite as: $x = e^4$
- Solution: $x \approx 54.598$

Examples 4—Change of Base: $\log_2(x) = \log_3(27)$
- Simplify using change of base formula: $\log_3(27) = \frac{\log(27)}{\log(3)}$
- Since $27 = 3^3$ $\log_3(27) = 3$. So, $\log_2(x) = 3$.
- Rewrite as: $x = 2^3 \Rightarrow x = 8$

Logarithmic functions can be confusing, but the difficulty level in the TSIA2 test is usually not more than what we have reviewed here.

Below is how a common logarithmic function, f(x) = $\log_{10}(x)$, looks in a graph.

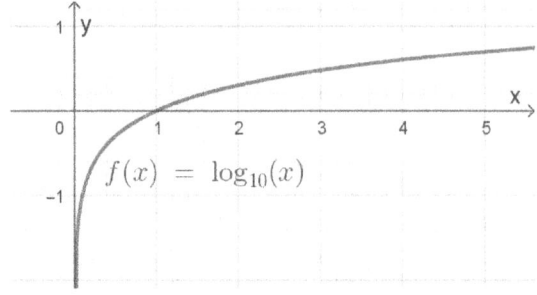

GEOMETRY CONCEPTS FOR ALGEBRA

Volume of Non-Prism Objects

Calculating the volume of non-prism objects, such as spheres, cylinders, cones, and pyramids, involves using specific geometric formulas for each shape. Unlike prisms, these objects have curved surfaces or varying cross-sectional areas. Here's how to find the volume of these non-prism objects.

Volume of a Cylinder

A cylinder has two parallel circular bases connected by a curved surface. The formula for the volume of a cylinder is derived from the area of the base and the height.

Formula: $V = \pi r^2 h$, where r is the radius of the base, h is the height of the cylinder.

Example: If a cylinder has a radius of 3 units and a height of 5 units:

$$V = \pi(3)^2(5) = 45\pi \text{ cubic units}$$

Volume of a Sphere

A sphere is a perfectly round object in three-dimensional space, like a ball. The volume of a sphere is proportional to the cube of its radius.

Formula: $V = \frac{4}{3}\pi r^3$, where r is the radius of the sphere.

Example: If a sphere has a radius of 4 units:

$$V = \frac{4}{3}\pi(4)^3 = \frac{4}{3}\pi(64) = \frac{256}{3}\pi \text{ cubic units}$$

Volume of a Cone

A cone has a circular base and a single vertex. The volume of a cone is one-third the volume of a cylinder with the same base and height.

Formula: $V = \frac{1}{3}\pi r^2 h$, where r is the radius of the base, h is the height of the cone.

Example: If a cone has a radius of 2 units and a height of 9 units:

$$V = \frac{1}{3}\pi(2)^2(9) = \frac{1}{3}\pi(4)(9) = 12\pi \text{ cubic units}$$

Volume of a Pyramid

A pyramid has a polygonal base and triangular faces that meet at a single point (the apex). The volume of a pyramid is one-third the volume of a prism with the same base area and height.

Formula: $V = \frac{1}{3}Bh$, where B is the area of the base, h is the height of the pyramid (perpendicular distance from the base to the apex).

Example: If a pyramid has a rectangular base with length 6 units and width 4 units, and a height of 10 units:

$$B = \text{length} \times \text{width} = 6 \times 4 = 24 \text{ square units}$$

$$V = \frac{1}{3}(24)(10) = 80 \text{ cubic units}$$

Intersecting Line Theorems

Intersecting lines create a variety of angles and geometric relationships that are governed by several theorems. Here's an overview:

Vertical Angles Theorem

If two lines intersect, then the vertical angles are congruent.

Example:

Given lines AB and CD intersecting at point E:

$$\angle AEC = \angle BED$$
$$\angle AED = \angle BEC$$

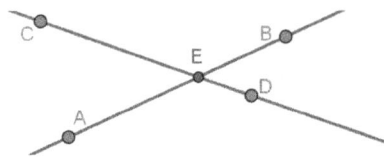

Linear Pair Theorem

If two angles form a linear pair, then they are supplementary (their measures add up to 180°).

Example:

Given lines AB and CD intersecting at point E:

$$\angle AEC + \angle CEB = 180°$$
$$\angle AED + \angle DEB = 180°$$

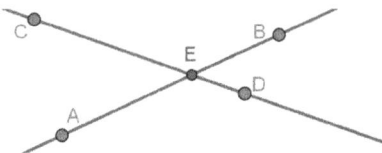

Corresponding Angles Postulate (with Parallel Lines)

If a transversal intersects two parallel lines, then each pair of corresponding angles is congruent.

Example:

Given parallel lines AB and CD intersected by transversal EF:

$$\angle AEF \cong \angle CDF$$

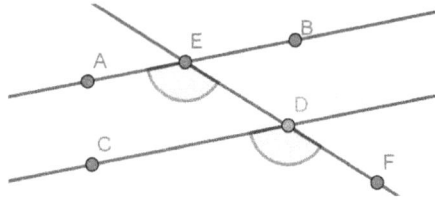

Alternate Interior Angles Theorem (with Parallel Lines)

If a transversal intersects two parallel lines, then each pair of alternate interior angles is congruent.

Example:

Given parallel lines AB and CD intersected by transversal EF:

$$\angle BED \cong \angle CDE$$

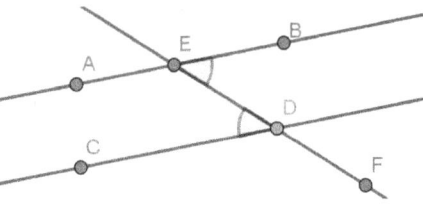

Same-Side Interior Angles Theorem (with Parallel Lines)

If a transversal intersects two parallel lines, then each pair of same-side interior angles is supplementary.

Example:

Given parallel lines AB and CD intersected by transversal EF :

$$\angle AEF + \angle CDE = 180°$$

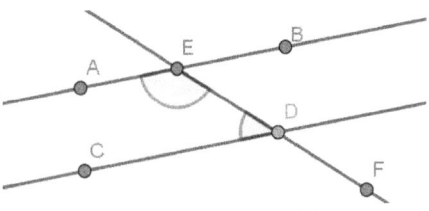

Alternate Exterior Angles Theorem (with Parallel Lines)

If a transversal intersects two parallel lines, then each pair of alternate exterior angles is congruent.

Example:

Given parallel lines AB and CD intersected by transversal EF :

$$\angle ABE \cong \angle DCF$$

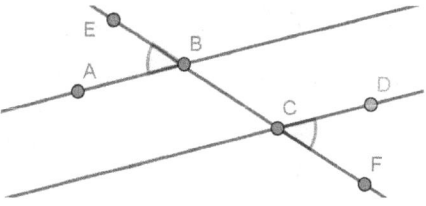

Now, let's put to these theorems to use in the following example.

Example: Given MN and ST are parallel lines, and $\angle a = 30°$, find all the rest of the angles.

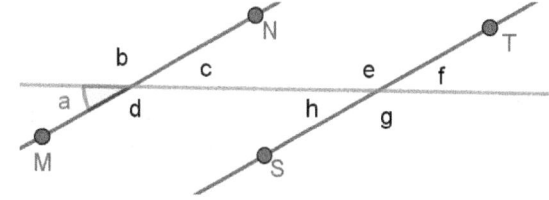

Solution:

Step 1: Identify the Vertical Angles

The vertical angle opposite $\angle a$ is $\angle c$ Hence, $\angle c = \angle a = 30°$.

Step 2: Identify the Linear Pairs

Angles a and d form a linear pair, so they add up to 180°.

$$\angle d = 180° - \angle a = 180° - 30° = 150°$$

Since b and d are vertical angles: $\angle b = \angle d = 150°$

Step 3: Identify the Corresponding Angles

Since MN and ST are parallel, $\angle a$ corresponds to $\angle h$. Hence, $\angle h = \angle a = 30°$.

Similarly, $\angle d$ *corresponds to* $\angle g$. Hence, $\angle g = \angle d = 150°$.
$\angle e$ *corresponds to* $\angle b$ Hence, $\angle e = \angle b = 150°$.
$\angle f$ *corresponds to* $\angle c$ Hence, $\angle f = \angle c = 30°$.

Example: Given angle $\angle a = 36°$, find $\angle \theta$

Solution:

From the diagram:

1. Identify Angles in Triangle $\triangle ABC$: $\alpha = 36°, \beta = 90°$.

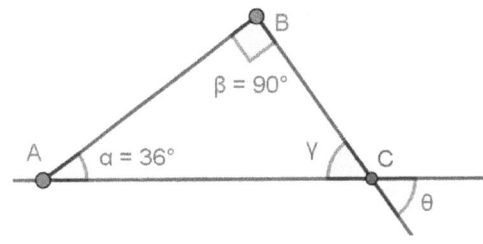

Geometry Concepts for Algebra | 165

2. Triangle Sum Theorem: The sum of the angles in a triangle is $180°$.

$$\alpha + \beta + \gamma = 180°$$
$$36° + 90° + \gamma = 180°$$
$$\gamma = 180° - 36° - 90°$$
$$\gamma = 54°$$

3. Find $\angle\theta$: since $\angle\theta$ and $\angle\gamma$ are vertical angles. $\angle\theta = \angle\gamma = 54°$.

$$\frac{AB}{DE} = \frac{AC}{DF} \quad \text{and} \quad \angle A = \angle D$$

Triangle Congruency Theorems

Triangle congruency describes a condition where two triangles are exactly identical in shape and size. Two triangles are congruent if all their corresponding sides are equal in length and all their corresponding angles are equal in measure. When two triangles are congruent, they can be perfectly overlaid on each other, with every corresponding side and angle matching precisely.

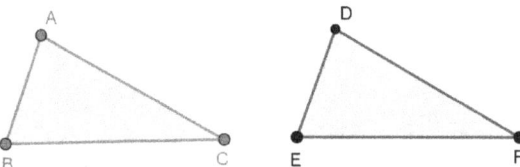

If two triangles $\triangle ABC$ and $\triangle DEF$ are congruent, this relationship is denoted as: $\triangle ABC \cong \triangle DEF$. This means that $AB = DE$, $BC = EF$, $CA = FD$ and $\angle A = \angle D, \angle B = \angle E, \angle C = \angle F$.

SSS (Side-Side-Side) Congruency

Two triangles are congruent if all three sides of one triangle are equal to all three sides of another triangle. This is known as the SSS congruency criterion.

If $AB = DE$, $BC = EF$, $CA = FD$, then $\triangle ABC \cong \triangle DEF$.

SAS (Side-Angle-Side) Congruency

Two triangles are congruent if two sides and the included angle of one triangle are equal to two sides and the included angle of another triangle. This is known as the SAS congruency criterion.

If $AB = DE$, $AC = DF$, $\angle A = \angle D$, then $\triangle ABC \cong \triangle DEF$.

ASA (Angle-Side-Angle) Congruency

Two triangles are congruent if two angles and the included side of one triangle are equal to two angles and the included side of another triangle. This is known as the ASA congruency criterion.

If $\angle A = \angle D$, $\angle B = \angle E$, $AB = DE$, then $\triangle ABC \cong \triangle DEF$.

AAS (Angle-Angle-Side) Congruency

Two triangles are congruent if two angles and a non-included side of one triangle are equal to two angles and the corresponding non-included side of another triangle. This is known as the AAS congruency criterion.

If $\angle A = \angle D$, $\angle B = \angle E$, $BC = EF$, then $\triangle ABC \cong \triangle DEF$.

HL (Hypotenuse-Leg) Congruency (Right Triangles Only)

Two right triangles are congruent if the hypotenuse and one leg of one triangle are equal to the hypotenuse and one leg of another triangle. This is known as the HL congruency criterion.

If $AC = DF$, $BC = EF$, and $\angle C = \angle F = 90°$, then $\triangle ABC \cong \triangle DEF$.

SSA (Side-Side-Angle) ≠ Congruency

There is one side and angle combination that does not prove triangle congruency: SSA. The SSA (Side-Side-Angle) condition fails to prove that a pair of triangles are congruent due to the possibility of multiple non-congruent triangles satisfying this condition. To understand why, let's look at the following scenario:

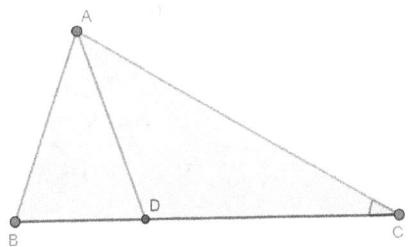

Consider triangles $\triangle ABC$ and $\triangle ACD$ as shown in the figure. Clearly, triangles $\triangle ABC$ and $\triangle ACD$ are not congruent. In fact, $\triangle ABC$ includes all of $\triangle ACD$ and then some. However, the two triangles share the same angle $\angle C$ and the same side AC. Also, they have one side where the length is equal: $AB = AD$.

The key here is the two sides that $\triangle ABC$ and $\triangle BCD$ have the same length ($AB = AD$, $AC = AC$) don't inscribe their shared angle, $\angle C$, leading to a SSA situation. If the two congruent sides inscribe the angle of equal value, leading to a SAS situation, then the two triangles will be congruent without any ambiguity.

AAA (Angle-Angle-Angle) ≠ Congruency

This should be self-evident. Two triangles with all three angles being equal can differ greatly in size. So, AAA does not necessarily guarantee two triangles are congruent.

Here is a tip on how to remember these theorems and exceptions: ALL combinations of three elements of A and S, be it AAS, ASA, SSA, SSS, will prove congruency, except AAA, and SSA. It is easy to remember AAA does not prove congruency—again, it is self-evident.

As for remembering SSA, the author has always remembered it as ASS instead. Should you associate it with anything other than a donkey though, it is on you, not me. The author's innocence is proven by a poem he wrote for this situation:

> Two asses live on a farm,
>
> Both tan and both tame.
>
> One is healthy and one is lame,
>
> Two asses are NOT always the same!

Triangle Similarity Theorems

Triangle similarity describes a condition where two triangles have the same shape but not necessarily the same size. Two triangles are similar if their corresponding angles are equal, and their corresponding sides are proportional. This means that one triangle can be obtained from the other by scaling (enlarging or reducing), possibly followed by a translation, rotation, or reflection.

If two triangles $\triangle ABC$ and $\triangle DEF$ are similar, this relationship is denoted as: $\triangle ABC \sim \triangle DEF$, which means that $\angle A = \angle D$, $\angle B = \angle E$, $\angle C = \angle F$ and $\frac{AB}{DE} = \frac{BC}{EF} = \frac{CA}{FD}$.

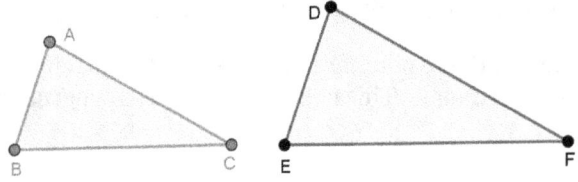

AA (Angle-Angle) Similarity

Two triangles are similar if two angles of one triangle are congruent to two angles of the other triangle. This is known as the AA similarity criterion. When two triangles are similar, their corresponding sides are proportional, and their corresponding angles are equal.

If $\angle A = \angle D$ and $\angle B = \angle E$, then $\triangle ABC \sim \triangle DEF$.

SSS (Side-Side-Side) Similarity

Two triangles are similar if the corresponding sides of one triangle are proportional to the corresponding sides of the other triangle. This is known as the SSS similarity criterion.

If $\frac{AB}{DE} = \frac{BC}{EF} = \frac{CA}{FD}$, then $\triangle ABC \sim \triangle DEF$.

SAS (Side-Angle-Side) Similarity

Two triangles are similar if one angle of one triangle is congruent to one angle of the other triangle, and the lengths of the sides inscribing these angles are proportional. This is known as the SAS similarity criterion.

If $\frac{AB}{DE} = \frac{AC}{DF}$ and $\angle A = \angle D$, then $\triangle ABC \sim \triangle DEF$.

Triangle Congruency and Similarity Questions

On the TSIA2 AAF Test, some questions may ask you to prove that a pair of triangles are congruent. These questions typically require you to be familiar with the four congruency theorems and apply them to the question to establish triangle congruency.

Example 1: For triangle ABC and triangle DEF, if $\angle A$ is congruent to $\angle D$, which of the following must be true in order to prove that triangles ABC and DEF are congruent?

A. $\angle B = \angle E$ and $AC = DF$

B. $BC = EF$ and $DF = AC$

C. $AB = DE$ and $BC = EF$

D. $\angle C = \angle F$ and $\angle B = \angle E$

A

Explanation: Triangles are congruent if they meet the SSS, SAS, AAS, or ASA criterion. Here, choice A will satisfy AAS, so it is correct. Choice B and C constitute SSA situation, choice D constitutes AAA situation. Hence, B, C, and D are not correct answers.

Other TSIA2 questions give you some choices and may ask you to identify a pair of similar triangles. This type of question often involves some calculation, such as creating and solving a proportion, before you can decide.

Example 2: Triangle ABC and triangle DEF are shown below. If $\angle A$ is congruent to $\angle D$ and $AC = 4, DE = 3, DF = 6$, which of the following must be true for triangles ABC and DEF to be similar?

A. $AB = 1.5$

B. $AB = 2$

C. $AB = 2.5$

D. $AB = 3$

B

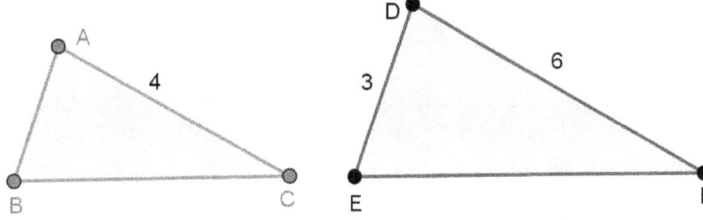

Explanation: Two triangles are similar if one angle of one triangle is congruent to one angle of the other triangle, and the lengths of the sides inscribing these angles are proportional. This is known as the SAS similarity criterion. So, to have $\triangle ABC \sim \triangle DEF$, it must be true that:
$\frac{AB}{DE} = \frac{AC}{DF}$. Thus, $\frac{AB}{3} = \frac{4}{6} \Rightarrow AB = \frac{3 \times 4}{6} = 2$. Hence, B is the right choice.

TRIGONOMETRY

Section 1: Arc Length and Radian Measures

Understanding the concepts of arc length and radian measure is fundamental in trigonometry. These concepts provide the basis for defining angles and their relationships within the unit circle, which is crucial for understanding trigonometric functions.

Arc Length

The arc length s of a circle is the distance along the curved path of the circle between two points. It is related to the radius r of the circle and the central angle θ subtended by the arc.

The formula for the arc length is given by: $s = r\theta$, where s is the arc length, r is the radius of the circle, θ is the central angle in radians.

Example: Consider a circle with a radius of 5 units and a central angle of $\frac{\pi}{3}$ radians. The arc length s can be calculated as follows:

$$s = r\theta = 5 \cdot \frac{\pi}{3} = \frac{5\pi}{3} \text{ units}$$

Radian Measure

Radians are a unit of angular measure used in trigonometry. One radian is defined as the angle subtended at the center of a circle by an arc whose length is equal to the radius of the circle.

To convert between degrees and radians, you can use the following relationships:

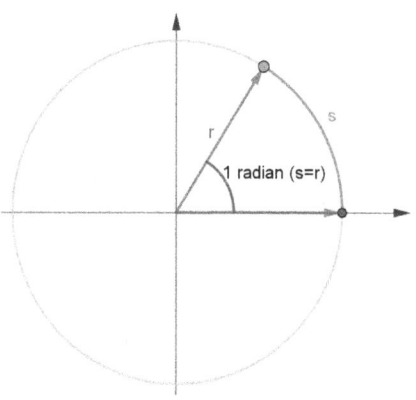

$$1 \text{ radian} = \frac{180°}{\pi}$$

$$1° = \frac{\pi}{180} \text{ radians}$$

Example: To convert 60° to radians:

$$60° = 60 \times \frac{\pi}{180} = \frac{\pi}{3} \text{ radians}$$

To convert $\frac{\pi}{4}$ radians to degrees:

$$\frac{\pi}{4} \text{ radians} = \frac{\pi}{4} \times \frac{180°}{\pi} = 45°$$

Unit Circle

The unit circle is a circle with a radius of 1 unit centered at the origin of the coordinate plane. The unit circle is essential for understanding trigonometric functions, as it allows angles to be represented in a standardized way.

Important Points on the Unit Circle

Here are some important angles and their corresponding points on the unit circle:

- 0° *or* 0 *radians*: (1,0)
- 90° *or* $\frac{\pi}{2}$ radians: (0,1)
- 180° *or* π radians: (−1,0)
- 270° *or* $\frac{3\pi}{2}$ radians: (0,−1)

Section 2: Introduction to Trigonometry

In this section, we will introduce the six trigonometric ratios, and how they apply to right-triangle and other special triangles.

Six Trigonometric Ratios

Trigonometry is the study of the relationships between the angles and sides of triangles. The six trigonometric ratios are defined for right-angled triangles and relate the angles to the lengths of the sides. The six trigonometric ratios are:

1. Sine (sin): $\sin(\theta) = \frac{\text{opposite}}{\text{hypotenuse}}$
2. Cosine (cos): $\cos(\theta) = \frac{\text{adjacent}}{\text{hypotenuse}}$
3. Tangent (tan): $\tan(\theta) = \frac{\text{opposite}}{\text{adjacent}}$
4. Cosecant (csc): $\csc(\theta) = \frac{1}{\sin(\theta)} = \frac{\text{hypotenuse}}{\text{opposite}}$
5. Secant (sec): $\sec(\theta) = \frac{1}{\cos(\theta)} = \frac{\text{hypotenuse}}{\text{adjacent}}$
6. Cotangent (cot): $\cot(\theta) = \frac{1}{\tan(\theta)} = \frac{\text{adjacent}}{\text{opposite}}$

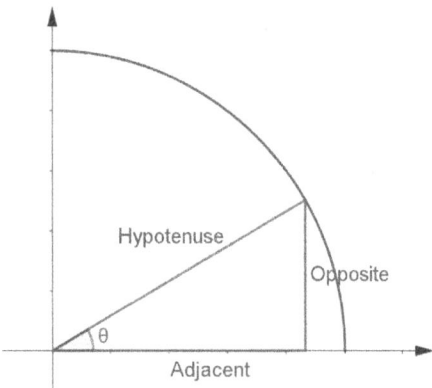

Remembering the Trigonometric Ratios

A common mnemonic to remember the basic trigonometric ratios (sine, cosine, tangent) is "SOH-CAH-TOA":

- SOH: Sine = Opposite / Hypotenuse
- CAH: Cosine = Adjacent / Hypotenuse
- TOA: Tangent = Opposite / Adjacent

A silly sentence to remember SOH-CAH-TOA is: "Some Old Hippie Caught Another Hippie Tripping On Apples." Each word in the sentence corresponds to a part of the mnemonic:

- Some (Sine) Old (Opposite) Hippie (Hypotenuse)
- Caught (Cosine) Another (Adjacent) Hippie (Hypotenuse)
- Tripping (Tangent) On (Opposite) Apples (Adjacent

Right-Triangle Trigonometry

Right-triangle trigonometry involves using the trigonometric ratios to solve problems involving right-angled triangles.

Example: Consider a right triangle with: θ = 30°, Opposite side = 3, Hypotenuse = 6. find the adjacent side and opposite side.

Solution: To find the adjacent side, we use the cosine ratio: $\cos(30°) = \frac{adjacent}{6}$.

Since $\cos(30°) = \frac{\sqrt{3}}{2}$, we have: $\frac{\sqrt{3}}{2} = \frac{adjacent}{6}$.

Solving for the adjacent side: $adjacent = 6 \times \frac{\sqrt{3}}{2} = 3\sqrt{3}$

Now, use tangent to find the length of the opposite side: $\tan(45°) = \frac{opposite}{adjacent}$, or $1 = \frac{opposite}{5}$.

Hence, opposite = 5.

Other Special Triangles

Two special right triangles are particularly important in trigonometry: the 45 − 45 − 90 triangle and the 30 − 60 − 90 triangle.

45-45-90 Triangle

In a 45-45-90 triangle, the angles are 45°, 45°, and 90°. The sides are in the ratio $1:1:\sqrt{2}$.

If the legs are x, then the hypotenuse is $x\sqrt{2}$.

Example: If each leg of a 45-45-90 triangle is 5 units, the hypotenuse is: $5\sqrt{2}$.

30-60-90 Triangle

In a 30-60-90 triangle, the angles are 30°, 60°, and 90°. The sides are in the ratio $1:\sqrt{3}:2$.

If the shortest leg is x, then the hypotenuse is $2x$ and the longer leg is $x\sqrt{3}$.

Example: If the shortest leg of a 30-60-90 triangle is 4 units, the hypotenuse is: $2 \times 4 = 8$ units, and the longer leg is: $4\sqrt{3}$ units.

Section 3: Evaluating Trigonometric Functions

In this section, we will learn how to evaluate trigonometric functions for given angles and explore equivalent trigonometric functions.

Evaluating Trigonometric Functions

To evaluate trigonometric functions, you need to know the values of sine, cosine, tangent, and their reciprocals (cosecant, secant, and cotangent) for specific angles. These angles are often found in special triangles or the unit circle.

Table: Special Triangle Facts

45 – 45 – 90 Triangle	30 – 60 – 90 Triangle	Unit Circle
Sides: $1:1:\sqrt{2}$ $$\sin(45°) = \cos(45°) = \frac{\sqrt{2}}{2}$$ $\tan(45°) = 1$	Sides: $1:\sqrt{3}:2$ $$\sin(30°) = \frac{1}{2}$$ $$\cos(30°) = \frac{\sqrt{3}}{2}$$ $$\tan(30°) = \frac{1}{\sqrt{3}} = \frac{\sqrt{3}}{3}$$ $$\sin(60°) = \frac{\sqrt{3}}{2}$$ $$\cos(60°) = \frac{1}{2}$$ $\tan(60°) = \sqrt{3}$	$\sin(0°) = 0$ $\cos(0°) = 1$ $\tan(0°) = 0$ $\sin(90°) = 1$ $\cos(90°) = 0$ $\tan(90°)$ *is undefined.*

Example: Evaluate $\sin(135°)$.

Using the unit circle, $\sin(135°)$ is the same as $\sin(180° - 45°)$, which is $\sin(45°)$ with a positive sign in the second quadrant: $\sin(135°) = \frac{\sqrt{2}}{2}$.

Example: Evaluate $\cos(210°)$.

Using the unit circle, $\cos(210°)$ is the same as $\cos(180° + 30°)$, which is $-\cos(30°)$ since cosine is negative in the third quadrant: $\cos(210°) = -\frac{\sqrt{3}}{2}$.

Equivalent Trigonometric Functions

Equivalent trigonometric functions arise from angle relationships and the properties of trigonometric functions. These equivalences often involve the use of identities and transformations.

Basic Trigonometric Identities

1. Reciprocal Identities:

$$\csc(\theta) = \frac{1}{\sin(\theta)}, \quad \sec(\theta) = \frac{1}{\cos(\theta)}, \quad \cot(\theta) = \frac{1}{\tan(\theta)}$$

2. Pythagorean Identities:

$$\sin^2(\theta) + \cos^2(\theta) = 1$$

$$1 + \tan^2(\theta) = \sec^2(\theta)$$
$$1 + \cot^2(\theta) = \csc^2(\theta)$$

3. Co-Function Identities (for complementary angles):

$$\sin(\theta) = \cos(90° - \theta), \quad \cos(\theta) = \sin(90° - \theta)$$
$$\tan(\theta) = \cot(90° - \theta), \quad \cot(\theta) = \tan(90° - \theta)$$
$$\sec(\theta) = \csc(90° - \theta), \quad \csc(\theta) = \sec(90° - \theta)$$

Example: Use the Pythagorean identity to find $\cos(\theta)$ *if* $\sin(\theta) = \frac{3}{5}$.

$$\sin^2(\theta) + \cos^2(\theta) = 1$$
$$\left(\frac{3}{5}\right)^2 + \cos^2(\theta) = 1$$
$$\frac{9}{25} + \cos^2(\theta) = 1$$
$$\cos^2(\theta) = 1 - \frac{9}{25} = \frac{16}{25}$$
$$\cos(\theta) = \pm\frac{4}{5}$$

Depending on the quadrant, $\cos(\theta)$ can be either $\frac{4}{5}$ *or* $-\frac{4}{5}$.

In this section, we've explored how to evaluate trigonometric functions using special triangles and the unit circle. We've also introduced equivalent trigonometric functions through basic identities. This foundational understanding is crucial for solving trigonometric equations and understanding more complex trigonometric relationships, which will be covered in the next sections.

§6 TSIA2 Mathematics Test Practice Questions

In this section, you'll apply the knowledge you've just learned to 45 practice questions. The actual TSIA2 Mathematics Test comprises 20 multiple-choice questions. This section has more questions than that to give you ample opportunities to practice.

Instructions

TSIA2 is a computer-adaptive exam designed to evaluate test takers' proficiency in a broad spectrum of mathematical subjects. All questions are presented in a multiple-choice format and appear individually throughout the test.

To answer each question, solve the problem and choose the correct option. Though a calculator isn't necessary for solving these problems, it's available for some of the questions. On the computer based TSIA2 test, if a calculator can be used, you'll see a calculator icon in the toolbar in the upper-right-hand corner of the screen. However, not all questions will provide this option.

Mathematics Practice Questions

Question 1: $(3+5)^2 - 12/3 =$

A) 58

B) 62

C) 60

D) 64

Question 2: $\frac{84}{28} =$

A) 2

B) 3

C) 4

D) 5

Question 3: A concert organizer charged $12 for each ticket. The organizer collected a total of $288 from ticket sales. How many tickets were sold?

A) 20

B) 22

C) 24

D) 26

Question 4: What is the product of 17 and 8?

A) 120

B) 136

C) 124

D) 138

174 | TSIA2 Study Guide

Question 5: What is the difference between 45.678 and 19.234, to the nearest integer?

A) 24

B) 26

C) 27

D) 28

Question 6: Solve the following problem and choose the best answer: $\frac{9.68}{2}$

A) 4.86

B) 4.84

C) 4.82

D) 4.87

Question 7: To the nearest integer, what is the product of 15.7 and 4.8?

A) 74

B) 75

C) 76

D) 77

Question 8: What is the sum of 23.85 and 2.155, to the nearest integer?

A) 26

B) 27

C) 25

D) 24

Question 9: The wholesale price of a chair is $80. The retail price of the chair is 15% more than the wholesale price. What is the retail price of the chair?

A) $90

B) $92

C) $94

D) $96

Question 10: If 35% of a number N is 14, what is the value of N?

A) 35

B) 40

C) 45

D) 50

Question 11: 72 is 30% of what number?

A) 210

B) 230

C) 240

D) 220

Question 12: Sara paid $45 for a jacket that was originally priced at $60. By what percent was the jacket discounted?

A) 15%

B) 20%

C) 25%

D) 30%

Question 13: 0.85, $\frac{2}{3}$, and 80%.

Which of the following correctly orders these numbers from least to greatest?

A) $\frac{2}{3}$, 0.85, 80%

B) 80%, $\frac{2}{3}$, 0.85

C) 0.85, 80%, $\frac{2}{3}$

D) $\frac{2}{3}$, 80%, 0.85

Question 14: Which of the following is equivalent to $\frac{68}{15}$?

A) $4\frac{2}{15}$

B) $4\frac{8}{15}$

C) $3\frac{13}{15}$

D) $3\frac{8}{15}$

Question 15: Which of the following has the least value?

A) 40% of 60

B) 60% of 40

C) 40% of 40

D) 60% of 60

Question 16: Which of the following fractions is greater than $\frac{1}{3}$ and less than $\frac{2}{3}$?

A) $\frac{1}{6}$

B) $\frac{2}{5}$

C) $\frac{3}{4}$

D) $\frac{5}{6}$

Question 17: Which of the following is equivalent to $\frac{3}{2} \times \frac{4}{5}$?

A) $\frac{7}{10}$

B) $\frac{6}{10}$

C) $\frac{3}{5}$

D) $\frac{6}{5}$

Question 18: Lucas bought a 24-pack of water bottles. The pack was $\frac{1}{3}$ full before Lucas decided to refill it with new bottles. Each new bottle cost $0.75. How much did Lucas spend, in dollars, to refill the pack to its full capacity?

A) $12.00

B) $10.50

C) $9.75

D) $11.25

Question 19: $\frac{7}{10} - \frac{2}{3} =$

A) $\frac{1}{30}$

B) $\frac{11}{30}$

C) $\frac{5}{30}$

D) $\frac{11}{21}$

Question 20: Which of the following is equivalent to $\frac{2}{5} \div \frac{4}{5}$?

A) $\frac{1}{2}$

B) $\frac{2}{4}$

C) $\frac{5}{4}$

D) $\frac{5}{2}$

Question 21: Which of the following points (x, y) lies on the graph of $7x + 3y = 26$?

A) (1,3)

B) (2,5)

C) (4,3)

D) (2,4)

Question 22: A cyclist traveled a distance of 45 kilometers in 3 hours. On average, how much distance did the cyclist cover each hour?

A) 12 km

B) 15 km

C) 18 km

D) 20 km

Question 23: A rocket traveled 160 kilometers in 360 seconds. On average, how much time did the rocket take to travel each 100 kilometers? (1 minute = 60 seconds)

A) 3 minutes and 45 seconds

B) 4 minutes and 30 seconds

C) 3 minutes and 40 seconds

D) 3 minutes and 45 seconds

Question 24: A circle has a diameter of 12 meters. What is the area, in square meters, of this circle? (The area of a circle with a radius of r, is equal to πr^2.)

A) 36π

B) 38π

C) 24π

D) 48π

Question 25: The cost of renting a bicycle is $10 per hour. In addition, a flat helmet rental fee of $5 is charged. Which of the following represents the total cost, in dollars, of the bicycle and helmet rental for h hours?

A) $10h + 5$

B) $10h + 15$

C) $15h$

D) $10h - 5$

Question 26: What is the value of $1.5 + 4 \times 3.2 - 10$?

A) 4.8

B) 5.3

C) 4.3

D) 6.3

Question 27: The box plot below summarizes the calories of food a group of lab mice consume per day. What could be the range of these mice's calorie intake per day?

A) 14

B) 15

C) 16

D) 17

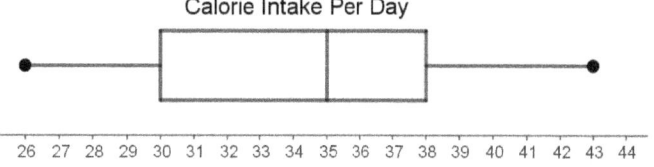

Question 28: The bar graph represents the number bags of each type of fruit in a grocery store. Which fruit has the most number of bags in the store?

A) Apple

B) Banana

C) Cherry

D) Date

Question 29: There are 24 books on a shelf. 8 of the books are fiction, and the rest are non-fiction. What is the ratio of fiction books to non-fiction books on the shelf?

A) 1 to 2

B) 1 to 3

C) 1 to 1

D) 2 to 3

Question 30: At a hardware store, nails cost $0.05 each and screws cost $0.10 each. Jenna spent less than $5.00 on 20 nails and x screws. Which inequality represents this situation?

A) $\left(\frac{0.05+0.10}{2}\right)x < 5.00$

B) $20(0.05) + 0.10x < 5.00$

C) $20(0.10) + 0.05x < 5.00$

D) $20(0.05 + 0.10)x < 5.00$

Question 31: Based on the relationship between elevation and temperature established in the graph, what's the temperature at 5,000 ft?

A) 35°

B) 36°

C) 37°

D) 38°

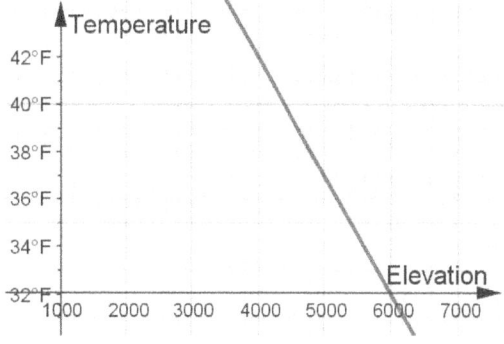

Question 32: A rectangular field has an area of 1500 square feet. If the width of the field is 20 feet less than the length, what is the perimeter, in feet, of the field?

A) 140

B) 150

C) 160

D) 185

Question 33: Which expression is equivalent to $5(d - 2^3) + 2d$?

A) $5d - 20$

B) $7d - 40$

C) $5d - 30$

D) $7d - 30$

Question 34: Which equation represents the line shown?

A) $y = -x + 2$

B) $y = x - 1$

C) $y = 2x + 2$

D) $y = 2x - 1$

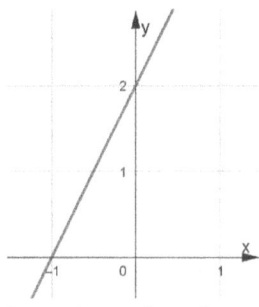

Question 35: Liam bought some apples for $1 each and some pineapples for $4 each. He bought 2 more apples than pineapples and spent a total of $17. How many pineapples did Liam buy?

A) 1

B) 2

C) 3

D) 4

Question 36: Which of the following is equivalent to $\left(\frac{3}{4}\right)^{-2}$?

A) $\frac{9}{16}$

B) $-\frac{9}{16}$

C) $\frac{16}{9}$

D) $-\frac{16}{9}$

Question 37: $1.25 \div 10^{-3} =$

A) 12.5

B) 125

C) 1250

D) 12500

Question 38: A jar contains 12 marbles, each marble containing a different number from 1 to 12. If you pull a marble at random from the jar, what's the probability that this number will be less than 5?

A) $\frac{1}{4}$

B) $\frac{1}{3}$

C) $\frac{1}{2}$

D) $\frac{5}{12}$

Question 39: At 7 a.m., a hiker at Death Valley National Park was at an elevation of -200 feet relative to sea level. By 3 p.m. on the same day, the hiker reached an elevation of 1300 feet above sea level. What was the change in elevation, in feet, for the hiker from 7 a.m. to 3 p.m.?

A) -100 feet

B) 1200 feet

C) 1300 feet

D) 1500 feet

Question 40: $2(x + 5)x^2 =$

A) $2x^3 + 5x^2$

B) $2x^3 + 10x^2$

C) $2x^3 + 5x$

D) $2x^3 + 10x$

Question 41: Which expression is equivalent to $3x^2 + 7x + 4$?

A) $(3x + 4)(x + 1)$

B) $(3x + 2)(x + 4)$

C) $(2x + 4)(x + 1)$

D) $(x + 4)(3x + 1)$

Question 42: Which expression is equivalent to $8x^{\frac{1}{3}}$?

A) $2\sqrt[3]{x}$

B) $4\sqrt[3]{x}$

C) $8\sqrt[3]{x}$

D) $\frac{1}{\sqrt[3]{8x}}$

Question 43: Which expression is a factor of both $x^2 - 16$ and $x^2 + x - 12$?

A) $x + 4$

B) $x - 4$

C) $x - 3$

D) $x + 2$

Question 44: What is the solution (x, y) to the given system of equations?

$$x + 2y = 9$$
$$2x - y = 3$$

A) $(-1, 6)$

B) $(2, 3.5)$

C) $(0, 4.5)$

D) $(3, 3)$

Question 45: $12x^2 + 5x - 2 = 0$

What are the solutions to the given quadratic equation?

A) $\frac{1}{3}, -2$

B) $-\frac{2}{3}, \frac{1}{4}$

C) $-\frac{5}{4}, \frac{2}{3}$

D) $\frac{1}{2}, -\frac{2}{3}$

ANSWER KEY

Q1: C) 60. Explanation: $(3+5)^2 - \frac{12}{3} = 64 - 4 = 60$

Q2: B) 3. Explanation: $\frac{84}{28} = 3$

Q3: C) 24. Explanation: $\frac{288}{12} = 24$

Q4: B) 136. Explanation: $17 \times 8 = 136$

Q5: B) 26. Explanation: $45.678 - 19.234 \approx 26.444 \approx 26$

Q6: B) 4.84. Explanation: $\frac{9.68}{2} = 4.84$

Q7: B) 75. Explanation: $15.7 \times 4.8 = 75.36 \approx 75$

Q8: A) 26. Explanation: $23.85 + 2.155 = 26.005 \approx 26$

Q9: B) $92. Explanation: $80 + 80 \times \frac{15}{100} = 80 + 12 = 92$

Q10: B) 40. Explanation: We know $0.35 \times N = 14$. Thus, solving the equation: $N = \frac{14}{0.35} = 40$.

Q11: C) 240. Explanation: We know $0.30 \times N = 72$. Hence, $N = \frac{72}{0.30} = 240$.

Q12: C) 25%. Explanation: $\frac{60-45}{60} \times 100 = \frac{15}{60} \times 100 = 25\%$

Q13: D) $\frac{2}{3}$, 80%, 0.85. Explanation: Convert Each to Decimals: $\frac{2}{3} \approx 0.6667$, $80\% = 0.80$. Order the Decimals from Least to Greatest: 0.6667, 0.80, 0.85.

Q14: B) $4\frac{8}{15}$. Explanation: $\frac{68}{15} = 4\frac{8}{15}$

Q15: C) 40% of 40. Explanation: A. $0.40 \times 60 = 24$. B. $0.60 \times 40 = 24$. C. $0.40 \times 40 = 16$. D. $0.60 \times 60 = 36$.

Q16: B) $\frac{2}{5}$. Explanation: Convert the Fractions to Decimals: $\frac{1}{3} \approx 0.3333$, $\frac{2}{3} \approx 0.6667$, $\frac{1}{6} \approx 0.1667$, $\frac{2}{5} = 0.4$, $\frac{3}{4} = 0.75$, $\frac{5}{6} \approx 0.8333$. Identify the Fraction Between $\frac{1}{3}$ and $\frac{2}{3}$: $0.3333 < 0.4 < 0.6667$.

Q17: D) $\frac{6}{5}$. Explanation: $\frac{3}{2} \times \frac{4}{5} = \frac{3 \times 4}{2 \times 5} = \frac{12}{10} = \frac{6}{5}$.

Q18: A) $12.00. Explanation: Calculate the Number of Bottles Needed: $24 \times \left(1 - \frac{1}{3}\right) = 24 \times \frac{2}{3} = 16$ bottles. Then calculate the Cost to Refill the Pack: $16 \times 0.75 = 12.00$.

Q19: A) $\frac{1}{30}$. Explanation: The least common denominator (LCD) of 10 and 3 is 30.

$\frac{7}{10} = \frac{7 \times 3}{10 \times 3} = \frac{21}{30}$, $\frac{2}{3} = \frac{2 \times 10}{3 \times 10} = \frac{20}{30}$. Subtract the Fractions: $\frac{21}{30} - \frac{20}{30} = \frac{1}{30}$.

Q20: A) $\frac{1}{2}$. Explanation: $\frac{2}{5} \div \frac{4}{5} = \frac{2}{5} \times \frac{5}{4} = \frac{2 \times 5}{5 \times 4} = \frac{2}{4} = \frac{1}{2}$.

Q21: D) (2,4). Explanation: When faced with such problems, try each pair of solutions in the equation to see if it is true. Here, $7 \times 2 + 3 \times 4 = 14 + 12 = 26$. So D is correct.

Q22: B) 15 km. Explanation: Total distance = 45 km, Total time = 3 hours. 45/3 = 15.

Q23: A) 3 minutes and 45 seconds. Explanation: Average speed $= \frac{160 \text{ kilometers}}{360 \text{ seconds}} = \frac{4}{9}$ km/second.

Convert average speed to time taken to travel 100 kilometers:

$$\text{Time for 100 km} = \frac{100 \text{ kilometers}}{\frac{4}{9} \text{ km/second}} = 225 \text{ seconds}$$

Convert 225 seconds into minutes and seconds: the integer portion of 225/60 is 3.

Seconds remaining $= 225 - (3 \times 60) = 45$. Therefore, the average time to travel 100 kilometers is: 3 minutes and 45 seconds.

Q24: A) 36π. Diameter = 12 meters, thus, Radius $= \frac{\text{Diameter}}{2} = \frac{12}{2} = 6$ meters.

Area $= \pi r^2 = \pi(6)^2 = \pi \times 36 = 36\pi$ square meters.

Q25: A) 10h + 5

Q26: C) 4.3. Explanation: $1.5 + 4 \times 3.2 - 10 = 1.5 + 12.8 - 10 = 1.5 + 2.8 = 4.3$

Q27: D) 17. Explanation: The range is the difference between the maximum and minimum values in a dataset. Range = Max − Min. So, $43 - 26 = 17$.

Q28: B) Banana. Explanation: The bar associated with banana is the tallest.

Q29: B) 1 to 2. Explanation: Total books = 24, Fiction books = 8, Non-fiction books $= 24 - 8 = 16$. Ratio of fiction books to non-fiction books $= \frac{8}{16} = \frac{1}{2}$.

Q30: B) $20(0.05) + 0.10x < 5.00$.

Q31: C) 37°. This can be observed in the graph: when elevation is at 5000, temperature is at 37°.

Q32: C) 160. Explanation: Let l = length of the field, w = width of the field. We know $w = l - 20$. Hence, Area $= l \times w \Rightarrow 1500 = l \times (l - 20) \Rightarrow 1500 = l^2 - 20l \Rightarrow$

$l^2 - 20l - 1500 = 0$.

Solve the quadratic equation: $l = \frac{-b \pm \sqrt{b^2 - 4ac}}{2a}$, where $a = 1$, $b = -20$, $c = -1500$.

So, $l = \frac{-(-20) \pm \sqrt{(-20)^2 - 4 \cdot 1 \cdot (-1500)}}{2 \cdot 1} = \frac{20 \pm \sqrt{400 + 6000}}{2} = \frac{20 \pm \sqrt{6400}}{2} = \frac{20 \pm 80}{2}$.

Hence, $l = \frac{20+80}{2}$ or $l = \frac{20-80}{2}$. Thus, $l = 50$ (since length cannot be negative).

$w = l - 20 \Rightarrow w = 50 - 20 = 30$. Perimeter $= 2(l + w) = 2(50 + 30) = 2 \times 80 = 160$ feet.

Q33: B) 7d − 40. Explanation: $5(d - 2^3) + 2d = 5(d - 8) + 2d \Rightarrow 5d - 40 + 2d \Rightarrow 7d - 40$.

Q34: C) $y = 2x + 2$. Explanation: From the graph, the line's slope is 2, while it intersects y-axis at (0,2). So, $y = 2x + 2$.

Q35: C) 3. Explanation: Let x be the number of pineapples. Then, $x + 2$ is the number of apples.

Hence, $1(x + 2) + 4x = 17 \Rightarrow x + 2 + 4x = 17 \Rightarrow 5x + 2 = 17 \Rightarrow 5x = 15 \Rightarrow x = 3$.

Thus, Liam bought 3 pineapples.

Q36: C) $\frac{16}{9}$. Explanation: $\left(\frac{3}{4}\right)^{-2} = \left(\frac{4}{3}\right)^2 = \frac{4^2}{3^2} = \frac{16}{9}$.

Q37: C) 1250. Explanation: $\frac{1.25}{10^{-3}} = 1.25 \times 10^3 = 1.25 \times 1000 = 1250$.

Q38: B) $\frac{1}{3}$. Explanation: Numbers less than 5: 1,2,3,4 (4 numbers).

Total numbers: 12. Probability $= \frac{4}{12} = \frac{1}{3}$.

Q39: D) 1500 feet. Explanation: Change in elevation $= 1300 - (-200) = 1500$.

Q40: B) $2x^3 + 10x^2$. Explanation: $2(x+5)x^2 = 2x \cdot x^2 + 2 \cdot 5 \cdot x^2 = 2x^3 + 10x^2$.

Q41: A) $(3x+4)(x+1)$. Explanation: Factor $3x^2 + 7x + 4 \Rightarrow 3x^2 + 7x + 4 = (3x+4)(x+1)$.

Q42: C) $8\sqrt[3]{x}$. Note that $(8x)^{\frac{1}{3}} = 2\sqrt[3]{x}$ while $8x^{\frac{1}{3}} = 8\sqrt[3]{x}$.

Q43: A) $x + 4$. Explanation: Factor $x^2 - 16$: $x^2 - 16 = (x-4)(x+4)$.

Factor $x^2 + x - 12$: $x^2 + x - 12 = (x-3)(x+4)$. The common factor is $x + 4$.

Q44: D) (3, 3). Explanation: Solve for y in the second equation: $2x - y = 3 \Rightarrow y = 2x - 3$

Substitute y into the first equation: $x + 2(2x - 3) = 9 \Rightarrow x + 4x - 6 = 9$
$$\Rightarrow 5x - 6 = 9 \Rightarrow 5x = 15 \Rightarrow x = 3$$

Substitute x back into the equation for y: $y = 2(3) - 3 \Rightarrow y = 3$. Solution: $(x, y) = (3,3)$.

Q45: B) $-\frac{2}{3}, \frac{1}{4}$. Explanation: Use formula: $x = \frac{-b \pm \sqrt{b^2 - 4ac}}{2a}$, where $a = 12, b = 5, c = -2$.

$$x = \frac{-5 \pm \sqrt{5^2 - 4 \cdot 12 \cdot (-2)}}{2 \cdot 12} = \frac{-5 \pm \sqrt{25 + 96}}{24} = \frac{-5 \pm \sqrt{121}}{24} = \frac{-5 \pm 11}{24}.$$ Hence, $x = \frac{1}{4}$ or $x = -\frac{2}{3}$.

PART V: PRACTICE TESTS

TSIA2 PRACTICE TEST 1

This TSIA2 practice exam includes two tests: English Language Arts and Reading (ELAR) and Mathematics. This sample test is paper-based. However, the actual TSIA2 is a computer-based exam. Keep in mind that with the computer-based test, you cannot skip questions and return to them later, nor can you change an answer once you have entered it into the computer and confirmed.

ENGLISH LANGUAGE ARTS AND READING (ELAR)

Directions for questions 1–15

Read the passage(s) below and then choose the best answer to each question. Answer the question on the basis of what is stated or implied in the passage(s).

> (1) Arthur Morel was growing up. (2) He was a quick, careless, impulsive boy, a good deal like his father. (3) He hated study, made a great moan if he had to work, and escaped as soon as possible to his sport again.
>
> (4) In appearance he remained the flower of the family, being well made, graceful, and full of life. (5) His dark brown hair and fresh coloring, and his exquisite dark blue eyes shaded with long lashes, together with his generous manner and fiery temper, made him a favorite. (6) But as he grew older his temper became uncertain. (7) He flew into rages over nothing, seemed unbearably raw and irritable.
>
> (8) His mother, whom he loved, wearied of him sometimes. (9) He thought only of himself. (10) When he wanted amusement, all that stood in his way he hated, even if it were she. (11) When he was in trouble he moaned to her ceaselessly.
>
> (12) "Goodness, boy!" she said, when he groaned about a master who, he said, hated him, "if you don't like it, alter it, and if you can't alter it, put up with it."
>
> (13) And his father, whom he had loved and who had worshipped him, he came to detest. (14) As he grew older Morel fell into a slow ruin. (15) His body, which had been beautiful in movement and in being, shrank, did not seem to ripen with the years, but to get mean and rather despicable. (16) There came over him a look of meanness and of paltriness. (17) And when the mean-looking elderly man bullied or ordered the boy about, Arthur was furious. (18) Moreover, Morel's manners got worse and worse, his habits somewhat disgusting. (19) When the children were growing up and in the crucial stage of adolescence, the father was like some ugly irritant to their souls. (20) His manners in the house were the same as he used among the colliers down pit.
>
> (21) "Dirty nuisance!" Arthur would cry, jumping up and going straight out of the house when his father disgusted him. (22) And Morel persisted the more because his children hated it. (23) He seemed to take a kind of satisfaction in disgusting them, and driving them nearly mad, while they were so irritably sensitive at the age of fourteen or fifteen. (24) So that Arthur, who was growing up when his father was degenerate and elderly, hated him worst of all. (*Sons and Lovers*, by D. H. Lawrence)

Question 1: Sentence 8 to 12 indicate Arthur's Mother's attitude towards Arthur is:

A) Supportive and encouraging

B) Loving but frustrated

C) Indifferent and distant

D) Strict and unforgiving

Question 2: Which of the following best describes Morel's character?

A) Generous and kind-hearted

B) Energetic and enthusiastic

C) Mean and despicable

D) Lazy and indifferent

Question 3: The narrator most strongly suggests how the father and son's relationship is evolving?

A) They are growing closer

B) Their relationship remains unchanged

C) They are becoming more distant and hostile

D) They are developing mutual respect

Question 4: As used in sentence 16, "paltriness" most nearly means:

A) Generosity

B) Insignificance

C) Cleanliness

D) Strength

Passage 1

Invasive plants, though often seen as harmful to native ecosystems, can sometimes play a positive role. In disturbed environments, they can fill ecological gaps left by lost species, provide food for wildlife, or stabilize soil in erosion-prone areas. These species often adapt better to climate change than native plants, helping preserve ecosystem functions. Removing them may do more harm than good by disrupting the soil and requiring chemical use. While invasive species require management, dismissing their potential ecological contributions overlooks the complexities of their role, which may be beneficial in some ecosystems.

Passage 2

Invasive plants pose significant threats to ecosystems by disrupting biodiversity and dominating native species. They outcompete native plants for resources, leading to monocultures and affecting soil and water dynamics, which can cause erosion. Without natural predators, they spread unchecked, undermining agriculture and local food chains. Controlling invasive species is expensive and labor-intensive, but essential for protecting ecosystems, preserving biodiversity, and maintaining the balance needed for native species to thrive.

Question 5: The authors of the two passages would most likely agree on which of the following?

A) Invasive plants should always be removed from ecosystems.

B) Invasive plants never provide any ecological benefits.

C) Invasive plants can have significant impacts on native ecosystems.

D) Invasive plants are essential for urban wildlife conservation.

Passage 1

Colonialism, though controversial, has left a legacy that some argue contributed to global development. Many former colonies benefitted from the introduction of modern infrastructure, including roads, railways, and schools. Colonial powers established administrative systems, legal frameworks, and improved healthcare in many regions. For example, British colonization led to the development of parliamentary systems in India and other countries, forming the foundation for their current democratic governance. In addition, trade networks established during colonialism opened up global markets, which allowed for economic growth in many regions. Supporters argue that these contributions have helped shape stable, modern nations, despite the undeniable negative aspects of colonization.

Passage 2

Colonialism is often criticized for its exploitative and violent impacts on indigenous populations. Many colonized regions experienced the destruction of native cultures, the imposition of foreign values, and the exploitation of natural resources for the benefit of colonial powers. Forced labor, slavery, and oppressive rule devastated local economies, leaving lasting inequalities. For instance, in Africa, colonial borders drawn without regard to ethnic groups contributed to ongoing conflicts and instability. Critics argue that the legacy of colonialism is seen in the deep economic, social, and political challenges faced by former colonies today. They contend that any benefits gained were outweighed by the profound human and cultural losses inflicted.

Question 6: The authors of the two passages would likely disagree on which of the following the most?

A) The influence of colonialism on modern infrastructure.

B) The long-term cultural effects of colonialism on indigenous populations.

C) Whether colonialism contributed to economic growth in former colonies.

D) The moral justification for colonial powers exploiting natural resources.

I hope I have made clear that the primary object of this journey with the dog-teams was to hurry Scott and his companions home so that they might be in time to catch the ship if possible, before she was compelled by the close of the season to leave McMurdo Sound. Another thing which made Scott anxious to communicate with the ship if possible before the season forced her to leave the Sound was his desire to send back news. From many remarks which he made, and also from the discussions in the hut during the winter, it was obvious that he considered it was of the first importance that the news of reaching the Pole, if it should be reached, be communicated to the world without the delay of another year. Of course he would also wish to send news of the safe return of his party to wives and relations as soon as possible. It is necessary to emphasize the fact that the dog-teams were intended to hasten the return of the Polar Party, but that they were never meant to form a relief journey.

But now Atkinson was left in a rather difficult position. I note in my diary, after we had reached the hut, that "Scott was to have sent back instructions for the dog party with us, but these have, it would seem, been forgotten"; but it may be that Scott considered that he had given these instructions in a conversation he had with Atkinson at the top of the Beardmore Glacier, when Scott said, "with the depot [of dog-food] which has been laid come as far as you can." (The Worst Journey in the World, by Apsley Cherry-Garrard)

Question 7: Which choice best describes the overall structure of the passage?

A) A detailed description of the challenges faced during the journey

B) A chronological recount of events leading to Scott's return

C) An explanation of the purpose of the journey followed by a discussion of a challenge encountered

D) A comparison between different exploration strategies

> Next morning I started out after the horse-thieves, being accompanied by Green, Jack Farley, and another scout. The mule track, marked by Green, was easily found, and with very little difficulty I followed it for about two miles into the timber and came upon a place where, as I could plainly see from numerous signs, quite a number of head of stock had been tied among the trees and kept for several days. This was evidently the spot where the thieves had been hiding their stolen stock until they had accumulated quite a herd. From this point it was difficult to trail them, as they had taken the stolen animals out of the timber one by one and in different directions, thus showing that they were experts at the business and experienced frontiersmen, for no Indian could have exhibited more cunning in covering up a trail than did they. (*The Life of Buffalo Bill*, William F. Cody)

Question 8: The passage most strongly suggests which characteristics of the horse thieves?

A) They were inexperienced and careless.

B) They were familiar with the local area.

C) They were cunning and skilled at covering their tracks.

D) They were frequently caught by authorities.

> And so we came back to our comfortable hut. Whatever merit there may be in going to the Antarctic, once there you must not credit yourself for being there. To spend a year in the hut at Cape Evans because you explore is no more laudable than to spend a month at Davos because you have consumption, or to spend an English winter at the Berkeley Hotel. It is just the most comfortable thing and the easiest thing to do under the circumstances.
>
> In our case the best thing was not at all bad, for the hut, as Arctic huts go, was as palatial as is the Ritz, as hotels go. Whatever the conditions of darkness, cold and wind, might be outside, there was comfort and warmth and good cheer within. (*The Worst Journey in the World*, by Apsley Cherry-Garrard)

Question 9: In the passage, the use of "Davos", "Berkeley Hotel" and "Ritz" is to emphasize

A) the importance of luxury in exploration

B) the discomfort of living conditions in the Antarctic

C) the contrast between different types of accommodations

D) the comfort and ease provided by the hut in the Antarctic

> Dark and high the war clouds were piling. Forked hatreds snaked flamingly across the blind gloom, and vengeance threatened in rumbling thunder growls. The red deluge was about to burst. Nothing now could hold back the storm.
>
> Swashbuckling Ike Clanton, unable to read the signs and portents of impending tragedy, drove alone into Tombstone on the afternoon of October 25th. Rash, blundering fellow, thus to venture single-handed into the stronghold of his enemies. But he believed in his soul the Earps were secretly afraid of him, would not dare to molest him, stood in awe of the banded outlaw strength that for years had been at his back. How quickly and cruelly was this proud freebooter to be stripped of his foolish illusions. So confident of his own safety was he that, as a law-abiding gesture, he left his Winchester rifle and six-shooter behind the bar at the Grand Hotel and sallied forth to tipple and take his pleasure in the saloons and gambling halls. (Tombstone, by Walter Noble Burns)

Question 10: The mention of the Winchester rifle and six-shooter in the passage conveys which of the following?

A) Ike Clanton's desire to show off his weapons

B) Ike Clanton's attempt to appear non-threatening

C) Ike Clanton's plan to attack his enemies

D) Ike Clanton's overconfidence in his safety

Our adventures and our troubles were alike over. We now experienced the incalculable contrast between descending a known and travelled river, and one that is utterly unknown. After four days we hired a rubber man to go with us as guide. We knew exactly what channels were passable when we came to the rapids, when the canoes had to unload, and where the carry-trails were. It was all child's play compared to what we had gone through. We made long days' journeys, for at night we stopped at some palm-thatched house, inhabited or abandoned, and therefore the men were spared the labor of making camp; and we bought ample food for them, so there was no further need of fishing and chopping down palms for the palm-tops. (*Through the Brazilian Wilderness*, by Theodore Roosevelt)

Question 11: Which of the following does the author offer as evidence to support the point that his adventures and troubles were over?

A) The river they were traveling on was known and traveled.

B) They encountered numerous rapids and had to unload the canoes.

C) They had to make camp every night.

D) They were frequently chopping down palms for food.

The difference of natural talents in different men is, in reality, much less than we are aware of, and the very different genius which appears to distinguish men of different professions when grown up to maturity is not upon many occasions so much the cause, as the effect of the division of labor. The difference between the most dissimilar characters, between a philosopher and a common street porter, for example, seems to arise not so much from nature, as from habit, custom, and education. When they came into the world, and for the first six or eight years of their existence, they were, perhaps, very much alike, and neither their parents nor playfellows could perceive any remarkable difference. (*The Wealth of Nations*, by Adam Smith)

Question 12: Which of the following statements would the author most likely agree with?

A) Natural talents are the primary reason for the differences in professions.

B) Education and environment play a significant role in shaping a person's abilities.

C) Differences in professions are mostly due to inherent genius.

D) Parents can easily distinguish the talents of their children from birth.

The possession of truth, so far from being here an end in itself, is only a preliminary means towards other vital satisfactions. If I am lost in the woods and starved, and find what looks like a cow-path, it is of the utmost importance that I should think of a human habitation at the end of it, for if I do so and follow it, I save myself. The true thought is useful here because the house which is its object is useful. The practical value of true ideas is thus primarily derived from the practical importance of their objects to us. Their objects are, indeed, not important at all times. I may on another occasion have no use for the house; and then my idea of it, however verifiable, will be practically irrelevant, and had better remain latent. Yet since almost any object may some day become temporarily important, the advantage of having a general stock of extra truths, of ideas that shall be true of merely possible situations, is obvious. (*Pragmatism*, by William James)

Question 13: What is the argument the author tried to make in this passage?

A) The possession of truth is always the ultimate goal.

B) Practical utility determines the value of true ideas.

C) All truths are equally important at all times.

D) Truths should be discarded if they are not immediately useful.

The first condition of universal freedom, that is to say, is a measure of universal restraint. Without such restraint some men may be free but others will be unfree. One man may be able to do all his will, but the rest will have no will except that which he sees fit to allow them. To put the same point from another side, the first condition of free government is government not by the arbitrary determination of the ruler, but by fixed rules of law, to which the ruler himself is subject. We draw the important inference that there is no essential antithesis between liberty and law. On the contrary, law is essential to liberty. Law, of course, restrains the individual; it is therefore opposed to his liberty at a given moment and in a given direction. But, equally, law restrains others from doing with him as they will. It liberates him from the fear of arbitrary aggression or coercion, and this is the only way, indeed, the only sense, in which liberty for an entire community is attainable. (*Liberalism*, L. T. Hobhouse)

Question 14: What is the author's view on the relationship between liberty and law?

A) Law is opposed to liberty and should be minimized.

B) Law and liberty are inherently contradictory.

C) Law is essential to achieving true liberty.

D) Liberty can only exist without any form of law.

It cannot absolutely be said that crowds do not reason and are not to be influenced by reasoning.

However, the arguments they employ and those which are capable of influencing them are, from a logical point of view, of such an inferior kind that it is only by way of analogy that they can be described as reasoning.

The inferior reasoning of crowds is based, just as is reasoning of a high order, on the association of ideas, but between the ideas associated by crowds there are only apparent bonds of analogy or succession. The mode of reasoning of crowds resembles that of the Eskimo who, knowing from experience that ice, a transparent body, melts in the mouth, concludes that glass, also a transparent body, should also melt in the mouth; or that of the savage who imagines that by eating the heart of a courageous foe he acquires his bravery; or of the workman who, having been exploited by one employer of labor, immediately concludes that all employers exploit their men.(The Crowd, Gustave Le Bon)

Question 15: How did the author illustrate a crowd's ability to reason?

A) By showing that crowds use logical arguments similar to those of individuals.

B) By comparing the reasoning of crowds to that of highly educated people.

C) By using examples of flawed reasoning based on superficial associations.

D) By demonstrating that crowds cannot be influenced by any reasoning.

Directions for questions 16–19

Read the following early draft of an essay and then choose the best answer to the question or the best completion of the statement.

> (1) Benjamin Franklin was born on January 17, 1706, in Boston, Massachusetts. (2) He was the fifteenth of seventeen children in a modest family. (3) His contributions spanned various fields, including science, politics, and literature. (4) Despite his humble beginnings, Franklin became one of the most influential figures in American history. (5) As a polymath, Franklin exhibited prodigious talent and intellect. (6) He is perhaps best known for his experiments with electricity, most famously the kite experiment. (7) Through this experiment, he had demonstrated that lightning is a form of electricity, which was a groundbreaking discovery at the time.
>
> (8) Franklin's ingenuity extended beyond science to practical inventions like the bifocal glasses and the Franklin stove. (9) His wisdom and wit were encapsulated in "Poor Richard's Almanack," a publication filled with proverbs and maxims. (10) Franklin's aphorisms, such as "A penny saved is a penny earned," reflects his prudence and sagacity.
>
> (11) Politically, Franklin played a pivotal role in the American Revolution. (12) He was a key figure in drafting the Declaration of Independence and the United States Constitution. (13) His diplomatic skills were instrumental in securing the Franco-American alliance, which was crucial for American victory in the Revolutionary War. (14) As an elder statesman, Franklin's counsel was highly esteemed by his contemporaries.
>
> (15) Franklin's life was also marked by his commitment to public service and civic improvement. (16) He founded the first public library in America and the University of Pennsylvania. (17) His establishment of the American Philosophical Society fostered intellectual exchange and advancement. (18) Franklin's contributions to the field of journalism were significant: particularly through his ownership and operation of The Pennsylvania Gazette. (19) His legacy is a testament to his relentless pursuit of knowledge and the betterment of society.
>
> (20) Franklin's life epitomizes the Enlightenment ideals of reason, progress, and empiricism. (21) His enduring influence continues to inspire generations to value education, innovation, and civic responsibility.

Question 16: Which of the following is the most logical placement of sentence 4 (reproduced below)?

Despite his humble beginnings, Franklin became one of the most influential figures in American history.

A) (As it is now)

B) After sentence 1

C) After sentence 2

D) After sentence 10

Question 17: Which is the best version of the underlined portion of sentence 7 (reproduced below)?

Through this experiment, he had demonstrated that lightning is a form of electricity, which was a groundbreaking discovery at the time.

A) (as it is now)

B) demonstrated

C) has demonstrated

D) demonstrates

Question 18: Which is the best version of the underlined portion of sentence 18 (reproduced below)?

Franklin's contributions to the field of journalism were significant: particularly through his ownership and operation of The Pennsylvania Gazette.

A) (as it is now)

B) significant; particularly

C) significant—particularly

D) significant, particularly

Question 19: Which is the best version of the underlined portion of sentence 5 (reproduced below)?

As a polymath, Franklin exhibited prodigious talent and intellect.

A) (as it is now)

B) ponderous

C) pensive

D) grotesque

Directions for questions 20–30

Select the best version of the underlined part of the sentence. If you think the original sentence is best, choose the first answer.

Question 20: While attending her sister's graduation, Lisa, who have been traveling around Europe for the past year, reflected on how much her family had changed during her absence.

A) have been traveling

B) was traveling

C) had been traveling

D) were traveling

Question 21: She read her book on the porch while her friend was enjoying playing the guitar.

A) was enjoying

B) was playing guitar

C) enjoyed playing the guitar

D) playing guitar

Question 22: The garden was filled with vibrant flowers, that attracted butterflies and bees throughout the summer.

A) that attracted

B) as they attracted

C) attracting

D) which attracted

Question 23: The students were mesmerized by the professor who giving a lecture on Greek mythology.

A) who giving

B) who is given

C) who had gave

D) who was giving

Question 24: The meeting was canceled due to a scheduling conflict, which resulting in many participants being unaware of the change until the last minute.

A) which resulting in

B) and resulting in

C) which result in

D) resulting in

Question 25: The lecture was so detailed that everyone <u>who were present</u> took notes throughout the session.

A) who were present

B) whom were present

C) that was present

D) who was present

Question 26: The employees proudly showed <u>his</u> dedication to the company by working long hours on the project.

A) his

B) their

C) its

D) one's

Question 27: The city is well known for <u>it's parks and landmarks</u>, which are popular with both residents and tourists.

A) it's parks and landmarks

B) their parks and landmarks

C) its parks and landmarks

D) the parks and landmarks

Question 28: The team continued with the project, <u>even the challenges</u> that arose during the early stages of development.

A) even the challenges

B) notwithstanding the challenges

C) although the challenges

D) withstanding the challenges

Question 29: With the growing demand for housing, <u>and many people moving</u> into the city for better job opportunities.

A) and many people moving

B) thus many people have moved

C) many people are moving

D) people being moved

Question 30: Birdwatching <u>being a popular pastime</u> for people who enjoy nature and wildlife observation.

A) being a popular pastime

B) is a popular pastime

C) which is a popular pastime

D) as a popular pastime

MATHEMATICS

Question 1: If $\frac{7}{3} + \frac{1}{5} = p$, then the value of p is between which of the following pairs of numbers?

A) 2 and 3

B) 4 and 5

C) 3 and 4

D) 1 and 2

Question 2: Which of the following inequalities is true?

A) $\frac{1}{2} > \frac{3}{5}$

B) $\frac{4}{7} < \frac{3}{6}$

C) $\frac{5}{8} > \frac{4}{5}$

D) $\frac{2}{3} < \frac{4}{5}$

Question 3: Sarah works at a library and a cafe. In a 30-day period, Sarah worked $\frac{1}{3}$ of the days at the library and did not work $\frac{1}{6}$ of the days. On the remaining days Sarah worked at the cafe. How many days did Sarah work at the cafe during the 30-day period?

A) 15

B) 10

C) 20

D) 5

Question 4: Which number in the list below has the greatest value? Given numbers: $\frac{8}{3}$, 2.28, $\frac{10}{12}$, 0.199.

A) $\frac{8}{3}$

B) 2.28

C) $\frac{10}{12}$

D) 0.199

Question 5: If a climber ascends 25% of a 1,300 ft mountain in a day, how many feet does the climber ascend?

A) 325 ft

B) 25 ft

C) 375 ft

D) 97.5 ft

Question 6: A conveyor belt is currently set to move at a speed of 5.921 meters per minute (MPM). The speed is increased to 6.088 MPM. By how much was the speed increased?

A) 0.167 MPM

B) 1.167 MPM

C) 1.833 MPM

D) 1.967 MPM

Question 7: 4x - 5y = 11, x = 2

The two lines given by the equations above intersect in the *xy*-plane. What is the value of the *y*-coordinate of the point of intersection?

A) -3

B) -0.6

C) 1

D) 0.5

Question 8: A faucet fills a bathtub at a rate of 2 gallons per minute. If the bathtub has a capacity of 160 gallons, how long will it take to fill the bathtub?

A) 10 minutes

B) 50 minutes

C) 80 minutes

D) 100 minutes

Question 9: The volume of a cube is given by the formula $V = s^3$, where s is the length of a side of the cube. If the volume of a cube is 64 cubic inches, what is the length of each side?

A) 4 inches

B) 8 inches

C) 16 inches

D) 32 inches

Question 10: Which of the following expressions is equivalent to $(y^3 \cdot y^2)^4$?

A) y^{12}

B) y^{16}

C) y^{20}

D) y^{25}

Question 11: What is the solution to the equation $\frac{1}{2}x + \frac{3}{4}(x+1) - \frac{1}{4} = 2$?

A) $\frac{3}{2}$

B) $\frac{6}{5}$

C) $\frac{15}{8}$

D) $\frac{17}{8}$

Question 12: The amount of money N, in dollars, Alice earns can be represented by the equation N = 15h + 20, where h is the number of hours Alice works. Which of the following is the best interpretation of the number 20 in the equation?

A) The amount of money, in dollars, Alice earns each hour

B) The total amount of money, in dollars, Alice earns after working for h hours

C) The total amount of money, in dollars, Alice earns after working for one hour

D) The amount of money, in dollars, Alice earns in addition to an hourly wage

Question 13: The table gives the population of the 5 largest cities in a state in the year 2020. Which of the following is closest to the mean population of these cities?

City	Approximate population (thousands)
City A	1,200
City B	800
City C	1,500
City D	900
City E	600

A) 1,200

B) 1,000

C) 800

D) 600

Question 14: A company's quarterly sales in the past 2 years are shown in the graph. Which quarter had the greatest increase in sales from Year 1 to Year 2?

A) Q1

B) Q2

C) Q3

D) Q4

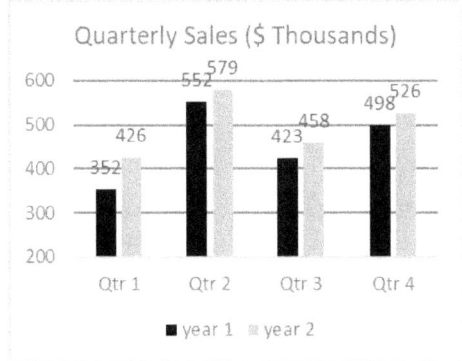

Question 15: The table below shows a survey of 60 students in a school. Each student was asked whether they planned to join the math club or the science club or both. If a student who plans to join the math club is randomly selected, what is the probability that student also plans to join the science club?

	Plans to join science club	Does not plan to join science club	Total
Plans to join math club	15	10	25
Does not plan to join math club	20	15	35
Total	35	25	60

A) 0.25

B) 0.35

C) 0.40

D) 0.60

Question 16: Factor $54x^4y^3z + 72x^2y^4$

A) $18x^2y^3(3x^2z + 4y)$

B) $18x^2y^3(3x^2z + 4y^2)$

C) $18x^3y^2(3x^2z + 4y)$

D) $18x^2y^2(3x^2z + 4y)$

Question 17: What are the solutions of the quadratic function $y = 4x^2 - 6x + 1$?

A) $\frac{3\pm\sqrt{5}}{4}$

B) $\frac{6\pm\sqrt{10}}{4}$

C) $\frac{6\pm\sqrt{5}}{8}$

D) $\frac{3\pm\sqrt{10}}{4}$

Question 18: In a right triangle, the two legs' length is 6 and 8. What's the value of AD, where AD is perpendicular to BC.

A) 6

B) 5.5

C) 4.8

D) 4

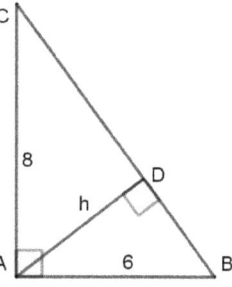

Question 19: In the figure on the right, the following relationship exists: $\angle \alpha + \angle \beta = 140°$, $\angle A - \angle \beta = 50°$. What is the value of $\angle \alpha$?

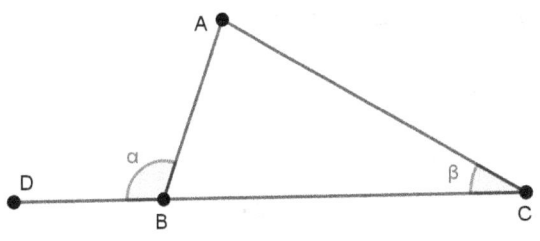

A) 100°

B) 110°

C) 120°

D) 130°

Question 20: A class has 12 students in Grade 8 and 18 students in Grade 9. The Grade 8 students averaged 80 on their final exam, and the Grade 9 students averaged 90. What was the average grade for the entire class?

A) 85

B) 88

C) 84

D) 86

PRACTICE TEST 1 ANSWER KEY

ELAR

Q1: B) Loving but frustrated.

Explanation: Arthur's mother loves him, as indicated by her concern, but she is also wearied and frustrated by his constant complaints and selfishness.

Q2: C) Mean and despicable

Explanation: As Morel ages, he becomes mean and despicable. His body and demeanor deteriorate, leading to a "look of meanness and paltriness," and his worsening manners disgust his family, particularly Arthur, who increasingly detests him.

Q3: C) They are becoming more distant and hostile

Explanation: The relationship between Arthur and his father deteriorates as Morel's behavior becomes more unpleasant and his manners worsen. Arthur's increasing disgust and fury towards his father, as well as his habit of leaving the house in anger, highlight their growing hostility.

Q4: B) Insignificance

Explanation: "Paltriness" means something trivial or of little value. In this context, it refers to Morel's diminishing physical presence and the overall perception of his worth, contributing to his characterization as mean and despicable.

Q5: C) Invasive plants can have significant impacts on native ecosystems.

Explanation: Both passages acknowledge that invasive plants significantly affect ecosystems, though they approach the topic from different perspectives (one positive and one negative). They agree on the impactful nature of invasive species.

Q6: C) Whether colonialism contributed to economic growth in former colonies.

Explanation: The first passage argues that colonialism contributed to economic growth through global trade and infrastructure, while the second passage emphasizes that colonialism exploited resources and left lasting economic challenges.

Q7: C) An explanation of the purpose of the journey followed by a discussion of a challenge encountered

Explanation: The passage first explains the purpose of the journey with the dog-teams and then discusses the challenge Atkinson faced due to the lack of clear instructions from Scott.

Q8: C) They were cunning and skilled at covering their tracks.

Explanation: The passage indicates that the horse thieves demonstrated expertise and cunning in hiding and moving the stolen animals in different directions to cover their trail, making it difficult to track them.

Q9: D) Comfort and ease provided by the hut in the Antarctic

Explanation: The passage uses "Davos", "Berkeley Hotel" and "Ritz" to draw a comparison, emphasizing that the hut at Cape Evans, although in the Antarctic, provides comfort and ease similar to well-known luxurious accommodations.

Q10: D) Ike Clanton's overconfidence in his safety

Explanation: Ike Clanton left his weapons behind because he believed that he was safe and that the Earps would not dare to attack him. This action shows his overconfidence and false sense of security.

Q11: A) The river they were traveling on was known and traveled.

Explanation: The author contrasts the current situation with the previous hardships by noting that they were now on a known and traveled river, making navigation easier and reducing the challenges they faced.

Q12: B) Education and environment play a significant role in shaping a person's abilities.

Explanation: The author argues that the differences in talents and abilities among individuals are largely due to habit, custom, and education rather than natural talents, suggesting that environment and upbringing significantly shape one's abilities.

Q13: B) Practical utility determines the value of true ideas.

Explanation: The author argues that the practical value of true ideas is derived from their usefulness in specific situations, implying that their importance is context-dependent and based on their practical application.

Q14: C) Law is essential to achieving true liberty.

Explanation: The author argues that law restrains individuals to prevent arbitrary aggression or coercion, thus enabling true liberty for the entire community by ensuring that everyone's freedom is protected under fixed rules.

Q15: C) By using examples of flawed reasoning based on superficial associations.

Explanation: The author illustrates the inferior reasoning of crowds with examples like the Eskimo believing glass melts like ice and the workman assuming all employers exploit their men, showing reasoning based on superficial associations rather than logic.

Q16: C) After sentence 2

Explanation: Placing sentence 4 after sentence 2 logically connects Franklin's humble beginnings and large family to his rise as one of the most influential figures, creating a coherent narrative flow from his early life to his achievements.

Q17: B) demonstrated

Explanation: The correct answer is "demonstrated" because it maintains the past tense consistent with the context of the passage, which describes historical events. "Had demonstrated" is unnecessary since the sequence of events is clear, and "demonstrates" and "has demonstrated" incorrectly shift the tense to present or present perfect.

Q18: D) significant, particularly

Explanation: The correct answer is D. The comma correctly separates the main clause from the modifying clause, providing a clear and grammatically correct structure. The other options either misuse punctuation or introduce unnecessary complexity.

Q19: A) (as it is now)

Explanation: The correct answer is A) (as it is now). "Prodigious" means remarkably or impressively great in extent, size, or degree, which accurately describes Franklin's exceptional talent and intellect. Ponderous: slow and clumsy because of great weight; dull, laborious, or excessively solemn. Pensive: engaged in, involving, or reflecting deep or serious thought. Grotesque: Comically or repulsively ugly or distorted; bizarre.

Q20: C) had been traveling

Explanation: The correct verb form "had been traveling" reflects the past perfect continuous tense, which indicates that her traveling occurred before the moment of reflection. The other options use incorrect tenses.

Q21: C) enjoyed playing the guitar

Explanation: "Enjoyed" matches the past tense of "read" and keeps the sentence fluid. The other options disrupt tense or structure.

Q22: D) which attracted

Explanation: "Which attracted" correctly introduces a non-restrictive relative clause and maintains proper subject-verb agreement. The other options either disrupt the sentence structure or incorrectly change the tense.

Q23: D) who was giving

Explanation: "Who was giving" correctly follows the past continuous tense to indicate an action in progress during the lecture. The other options either use incorrect verb forms or disrupt sentence flow.

Q24: D) resulting in

Explanation: "Resulting in" correctly follows the structure of the sentence, indicating the consequence of the cancellation. The other options create fragments or break the sequence of events.

Q25: D) who was present

Explanation: The subject "who" refers to "everyone," which is singular, so the correct verb should be "was." "Who was present" maintains proper subject-verb agreement.

Q26: B) their

Explanation: "Their" is the correct possessive pronoun to agree with "employees," which is plural. The other options use incorrect pronouns that do not match the subject in number or context.

Q27: C) its parks and landmarks

Explanation: "Its" is the correct possessive pronoun matching "the city," which is singular. The other options incorrectly use plural or contraction forms.

Q28: B) notwithstanding the challenges

Explanation: "Notwithstanding" means "in spite of," making it the appropriate word to convey that the team proceeded despite the difficulties. The other options either change the meaning or are grammatically incorrect in this context.

Q29: C) many people are moving

Explanation: The phrase "many people are moving" correctly completes the sentence, providing both the necessary subject-verb agreement and maintaining the present progressive tense that matches the ongoing action ("with the growing demand for housing"). Option A) creates a sentence fragment, while B) and D) introduce awkward or incorrect phrasing that breaks the flow of the sentence.

Q30: B) is a popular pastime

Explanation: "Is a popular pastime" properly completes the sentence with correct subject-verb agreement, creating a clear and complete statement. The other options either create fragments or do not correctly connect the subject and verb.

Mathematics

Q1: A) 2 and 3. Explanation: $\frac{7}{3} + \frac{1}{5} = \frac{35}{15} + \frac{3}{15} = \frac{38}{15} \approx 2.533$.

Q2: D) $\frac{2}{3} < \frac{4}{5}$. Explanation: $\frac{2}{3} \approx 0.6667, \frac{4}{5} = 0.8, \frac{2}{3} < \frac{4}{5}$.

Q3: B) 10. Explanation: Total days = 30. Days at the library = $\frac{1}{3} \times 30 = 10$. Days not worked = $\frac{1}{6} \times 30 = 5$. Remaining days = $30 - 10 - 5 = 15$. Days at the cafe = 15.

$$30 - \left(\frac{1}{3} \times 30\right) - \left(\frac{1}{6} \times 30\right) = 10$$

Q4: A) $\frac{8}{3}$. Explanation: $\frac{8}{3} \approx 2.6667$, bigger than all the other numbers.

Q5: A) 325 ft. Explanation: $0.25 \times 1300 = 325$ ft.

Q6: A) 0.167 MPM. Explanation: $6.088 - 5.921 = 0.167$ MPM

Q7: B) -0.6. Explanation: Substitute x = 2 into the first equation: $4(2) - 5y = 11$.

Thus, $8 - 5y = 11 \Rightarrow -5y = 3 \Rightarrow y = -\frac{3}{5} = -0.6$.

Q8: C) 80 minutes. Explanation: $\frac{160 \text{ gallons}}{2 \text{ gallons per minute}} = 80$ minutes.

Q9: A) 4 inches. Explanation: $s^3 = 64 \Rightarrow s = \sqrt[3]{64} = 4$.

Q10: C) y^{20}. Explanation: $(y^3 \cdot y^2)^4 = \left(y^{\{3+2\}}\right)^4 = (y^5)^4 = y^{\{5 \cdot 4\}} = y^{20}$.

Q11: B) $\frac{6}{5}$. Explanation: $\frac{1}{2}x + \frac{3}{4}(x+1) - \frac{1}{4} = 2 \Rightarrow \frac{1}{2}x + \frac{3}{4}x + \frac{3}{4} - \frac{1}{4} = 2 \Rightarrow \frac{1}{2}x + \frac{3}{4}x + \frac{1}{2} = 2$
$\Rightarrow \frac{5}{4}x + \frac{1}{2} = 2 \Rightarrow \frac{5}{4}x = 2 - \frac{1}{2} = \frac{3}{2} \Rightarrow x = \frac{6}{5}$

Q12: D) The amount of money, in dollars, Alice earns in addition to an hourly wage.

Explanation: Given $N = 15h + 20$, Alice makes $20 even when she works zero hours, or, just by showing up. So, 20 represents a set amount of money earned regardless of hours worked.

Q13: B) 1,000. Explanation: Mean population = $\frac{1,200 + 800 + 1,500 + 900 + 600}{5} = \frac{5,000}{5} = 1,000$.

Q14: A) Q1. Explanation: Increase in Q1 sales = $426 - 352 = 74$, which is greater than the increase for any other quarters.

Q15: D) 0.60. Explanation:

$$\text{Probability} = \frac{\text{Number of students who plan to join both clubs}}{\text{Number of students who plan to join math club}} = \frac{15}{25} = 0.60$$

Q16: A) $18x^2y^3(3x^2z + 4y)$. Explanation: Factor out the greatest common factor $18x^2y^3$, then we have: $54x^4y^3z + 72x^2y^4 = 18x^2y^3(3x^2z + 4y)$.

Q17: A) $\frac{3 \pm \sqrt{5}}{4}$. Explanation: Use quadratic formula: $x = \frac{-b \pm \sqrt{b^2 - 4ac}}{2a}$.

For $y = 4x^2 - 6x + 1 : a = 4, b = -6, c = 1$.

$$x = \frac{-(-6) \pm \sqrt{(-6)^2 - 4 \cdot 4 \cdot 1}}{2 \cdot 4} = \frac{6 \pm \sqrt{36 - 16}}{8} = \frac{6 \pm \sqrt{20}}{8} = \frac{6 \pm 2\sqrt{5}}{8} = \frac{3 \pm \sqrt{5}}{4}$$

Q18: C) 4.8. Explanation: First, determine the hypotenuse BC of the right triangle ABC using the Pythagorean theorem: $BC = \sqrt{6^2 + 8^2} = \sqrt{36 + 64} = \sqrt{100} = 10$. Now, use the area approach to find the length of AD. The area of $\triangle ABC$ can be calculated in two ways.

1. Using the legs: $Area = \frac{1}{2} \times 6 \times 8 = \frac{1}{2} \times 48 = 24$.

2. Using the hypotenuse and altitude AD : $Area = \frac{1}{2} \times BC \times AD$. Since $BC = 10$:

$$24 = \frac{1}{2} \times 10 \times AD$$
$$24 = 5 \times AD$$
$$AD = 4.8$$

Q19: B) 110°. Explanation: This is a system of equations problem in a geometry setting, with two equations and three unknowns.

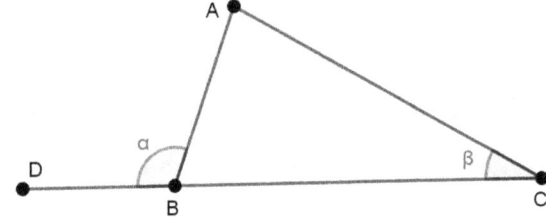

$\angle \alpha + \angle \beta = 140°$ (1)

$\angle A - \angle \beta = 50°$ (2)

We'll want to get rid of $\angle A$ first, so we have two unknowns with two equations. Because ABC is a triangle, its three internal angles add up to 180°: $\angle A + \angle \beta + (180° - \angle \alpha) = 180°$, where $(180° - \angle \alpha) = \angle ABC$. Hence,

$$\angle A = 180° - (180° - \angle \alpha) - \angle \beta$$
$$\angle A = \angle \alpha - \angle \beta$$

Given that: $\angle A - \angle \beta = 50°$, substitute $\angle A$: $\angle \alpha - \angle \beta - \angle \beta = 50° \Rightarrow \angle \alpha - 2\angle \beta = 50°$ (3)

From the first equation: $\angle \alpha + \angle \beta = 140° \Rightarrow \angle \alpha = 140° - \angle \beta$

Substitute $\angle \alpha$ into equation (3):

$$(140° - \angle \beta) - 2\angle \beta = 50°$$
$$140° - 3\angle \beta = 50°$$
$$3\angle \beta = 90°$$
$$\angle \beta = 30°$$

Now, substitute $\angle \beta$ back into equation (1) for $\angle \alpha$: $\angle \alpha = 140° - 30° = 110°$.

Q20: D) 86. Explanation: To find the overall average for the class, we calculate the weighted average based on the number of students in each grade:

$$Average = \frac{(12 \times 80) + (18 \times 90)}{12 + 18}$$

$$Average = \frac{960 + 1620}{30} = \frac{2580}{30} = 86$$

TSIA2 Practice Test 2

This TSIA2 practice exam includes two tests: English Language Arts and Reading (ELAR) and Mathematics. This sample test is paper-based. However, the actual TSIA2 is a computer-based exam. Keep in mind that with the computer-based test, you cannot skip questions and return to them later, nor can you change an answer once you have entered it into the computer and confirmed.

ENGLISH LANGUAGE ARTS AND READING (ELAR)

Directions for questions 1–15

Read the passage(s) below and then choose the best answer to each question. Answer the question on the basis of what is stated or implied in the passage(s).

---

(1) Scripps knew it was the factory. (2) They weren't going to fool him on that. (3) He walked up to the door. (4) There was a sign on it: Keep out. This means you.

(5) Can that mean me? Scripps wondered. (6) He knocked on the door and went in.

(7) "I'd like to speak to the manager," he said, standing quietly in the half-light.

(8) Workmen were passing him, carrying the new raw pumps on their shoulders. (9) They hummed snatches of songs as they passed. (10) The handles of the pumps flopped stiffly in dumb protest. (11) Some pumps had no handles. (12) They perhaps, after all, are the lucky ones, Scripps thought. (13) A little man came up to him. (14) He was well-built, short, with wide shoulders and a grim face.

(15) "You were asking for the manager?"

(16) "Yes, sir."

(17) "I'm the foreman here. (18) What I say goes."

(19) "Can you hire and fire?" Scripps asked.

(20) "I can do one as easily as the other," the foreman said.

(21) "I want a job."

(22) "Any experience?"

(23) "Not in pumps."

(24) "All right," the foreman said. (25) "We'll put you on piecework. (26) Here, Yogi," he called to one of the men, who was standing looking out of the window of the factory, "show this new chum where to stow his swag and how to find his way around these diggings." (27) The foreman looked Scripps up and down. (28) "I'm an Australian," he said. (29) "Hope you'll like the lay here." (30) He walked off.

(31) The man called Yogi Johnson came over from the window. (32) "Glad to meet you," he said. (33) He was a chunky, well-built fellow. (34) One of the sort you see around almost anywhere. (35) He looked as though he had been through things.

(36) "Your foreman's the first Australian I've ever met," Scripps said.

(37) "Oh, he's not an Australian," Yogi said. (38) "He was just with the Australians once during the war, and it made a big impression on him."

(39) "Were you in the war?" Scripps asked.

(40) "Yes," Yogi Johnson said. (41) "I was the first man to go from Cadillac."

> (42) "It must have been quite an experience."
>
> (43) "It's meant a lot to me," Yogi answered. (44) "Come on and I'll show you around the works."
>
> (*The Struggle for Life*, by Ernest Hemingway)

Question 1: What best describes Yogi's attitude towards Scripps?

A) Hostile

B) Indifferent

C) Welcoming

D) Suspicious

Question 2: What is the most likely reason the foreman introduced himself as Australian?

A) He wanted to confuse Scripps.

B) He was actually Australian.

C) He admired Australians from his war experience.

D) He wanted to sound exotic.

Question 3: In sentence 35, "He looked as though he had been through things," the word "things" most likely refers to something that is:

A) Pleasant

B) Stressful

C) Ordinary

D) Fun

Question 4: The way Scripps was greeted by the foreman can be described as:

A) Friendly

B) Indifferent

C) Formal

D) Hostile

Passage 1

Broader cancer screening can significantly reduce cancer-related mortality by enabling early detection and increasing the chances of successful treatment. Many cancers, like breast and colorectal cancers, are asymptomatic in early stages. Screening tests such as mammograms and colonoscopies can identify cancers earlier, improving prognosis. Additionally, screenings help identify precancerous conditions, such as polyps during colonoscopies, allowing for preventive measures. This reduces the cost and complexity of treating advanced cancers. Expanding cancer screening to the general population is vital for improving public health outcomes, reducing mortality, and promoting health equity, and public health policies should prioritize accessibility to these life-saving screenings.

Passage 2

While broader cancer screening is advocated for early detection, concerns exist regarding overdiagnosis and overtreatment. Screening can detect slow-growing cancers that might never cause harm, leading to unnecessary procedures. Additionally, screening tests can result in false positives, causing anxiety and invasive follow-ups, or false negatives, delaying real diagnoses. Widespread screening also poses financial challenges for healthcare systems, as resources might be better allocated to targeted screenings for high-risk groups. Ultimately, a more focused approach to screening, concentrating on high-risk individuals and improving healthcare access and education, may be more cost-effective and beneficial.

Question 5: Which choice best describes the relationship between Passage 1 and Passage 2?

A) Passage 1 supports broader cancer screening, while Passage 2 highlights concerns and drawbacks.

B) Passage 1 argues against cancer screening, and Passage 2 provides a solution.

C) Both passages fully agree on the benefits of cancer screening.

D) Passage 2 expands on the benefits discussed in Passage 1.

Passage 1

Gene editing, particularly through technologies like CRISPR, offers transformative possibilities for medicine. By targeting and modifying specific genes, scientists can potentially eliminate genetic disorders like cystic fibrosis and sickle cell anemia, improving the quality of life for millions. Additionally, gene editing holds promise in the fight against cancer, enhancing precision treatments tailored to individual genetic profiles. Beyond human health, gene editing can boost agricultural yields and address food shortages by creating crops that are more resistant to pests and climate change. Supporters argue that gene editing, when regulated ethically, offers a powerful tool for advancing human health, reducing suffering, and addressing global challenges.

Passage 2

Gene editing, while offering potential benefits, raises significant ethical and safety concerns. Modifying the human genome, especially in embryos, could lead to unforeseen and irreversible consequences, including off-target effects and genetic mutations passed to future generations. Critics argue that allowing gene editing in embryos risks creating a society of genetic inequality, where those who can afford enhancements could create a biological divide. Additionally, there are moral concerns about "playing God" and altering the natural course of human evolution. The potential for misuse of this technology—without strict regulation and oversight—poses significant risks to both individuals and society as a whole.

Question 6: Which of the following points about gene editing would the authors of the two passages be most unlikely to agree on?

A) Gene editing can help treat genetic diseases.

B) Gene editing could have unforeseen consequences.

C) Gene editing should be strictly regulated.

D) Gene editing offers primarily positive benefits to society.

When a species, owing to highly favorable circumstances, increases inordinately in numbers in a small tract, epidemics—at least, this seems generally to occur with our game animals—often ensue; and here we have a limiting check independent of the struggle for life. But even some of these so-called epidemics appear to be due to parasitic worms, which have from some cause, possibly in part through facility of diffusion among the crowded animals, been disproportionally favored: and here comes in a sort of struggle between the parasite and its prey. (*The Origin of Species*, by Charles Darwin)

Question 7: What purpose does the epidemics example serve in this passage?

A) To illustrate the natural balance of population control

B) To explain how parasites benefit their hosts

C) To argue against the existence of natural checks

D) To show that game animals are immune to epidemics

You must agree that a bird like this is an interesting beast, and when, seven months ago, we rowed a boat under those great black cliffs, and found a disconsolate Emperor chick still in the down, we knew definitely why the Emperor has to nest in midwinter. For if a June egg was still without feathers in the beginning of January, the same egg laid in the summer would leave its produce without practical covering for the following winter. Thus the Emperor penguin is compelled to undertake all kinds of hardships because his children insist on developing so slowly, very much as we are tied in our human relationships for the same reason. It is of interest that such a primitive bird should have so long a childhood. (*The Worst Journey in the World*, by Apsley Cherry-Garrard)

Question 8: What is the most likely reason the Emperor chick was "disconsolate"?

A) It was separated from its parents.

B) It was not yet fully feathered.

C) It was injured by predators.

D) It was hungry and unable to find food.

Mr. Beecher advised young men to get in debt if they could to a small amount in the purchase of land, in the country districts. "If a young man," he says, "will only get in debt for some land and then get married, these two things will keep him straight, or nothing will." This may be safe to a limited extent, but getting in debt for what you eat and drink and wear is to be avoided. Some families have a foolish habit of getting credit at "the stores," and thus frequently purchase many things which might have been dispensed with.

It is all very well to say; "I have got trusted for sixty days, and if I don't have the money the creditor will think nothing about it." There is no class of people in the world, who have such good memories as creditors. When the sixty days run out, you will have to pay. If you do not pay, you will break your promise, and probably resort to a falsehood. You may make some excuse or get in debt elsewhere to pay it, but that only involves you the deeper. (*The Art of Money Getting*, by P. T. Barnum)

Question 9: The primary purpose of the passage is to:

A) Advise young men on the importance of land ownership

B) Warn against the dangers of getting into debt for consumable goods

C) Encourage families to purchase goods on credit

D) Explain the benefits of getting married and owning land

When the shrapnel burst among us on the hillside we made up our minds that we had better settle down to solid siege work. All of the men who were not in the trenches I took off to the right, back of the Gatling guns, where there was a valley, and dispersed them by troops in sheltered parts. It took us an hour or two's experimenting to find out exactly what spots were free from danger, because some of the Spanish sharpshooters were in trees in our front, where we could not possibly place them from the trenches; and these were able to reach little hollows and depressions where the men were entirely safe from the Spanish artillery and from their trench-fire. Moreover, in one hollow, which we thought safe, the Spaniards succeeded in dropping a shell, a fragment of which went through the head of one of my men, who, astonishing to say, lived, although unconscious, for two hours afterward. Finally, I got all eight troops settled, and the men promptly proceeded to make themselves as much at home as possible. (*The Rough Riders*, by Theodore Roosevelt)

Question 10: The passage implies which action is most needed in the situation the soldiers were in?

A) Launch a counterattack against the Spanish sharpshooters

B) Find and eliminate the Spanish sharpshooters in the trees

C) Locate and occupy the safest positions for the soldiers

D) Request reinforcements to strengthen their position

The highest limit of conifers—in the middle Sierras, the white bark pine—is not along the water border. They come to it about the level of the heather, but they have no such affinity for dampness as the tamarack pines. Scarcely any bird-note breaks the stillness of the timberline, but chipmunks inhabit here, as may be guessed by the gnawed ruddy cones of the pines, and lowering hours the woodchucks come down to the water. On a little spit of land running into Windy Lake we found one summer the evidence of a tragedy; a pair of sheep's horns not fully grown caught in the crotch of a pine where the living sheep must have lodged them. The trunk of the tree had quite closed over them, and the skull bones crumbled away from the weathered horn cases. We hoped it was not too far out of the running of night prowlers to have put a speedy end to the long agony, but we could not be sure. I never liked the spit of Windy Lake again. (*The Land of Little Rain*, by Mary Austin)

Question 11: Based on the passage, the author's attitude toward Windy Lake can best be characterized as which of the following?

A) Admiring

B) Indifferent

C) Disdainful

D) Disturbed

> Nothing is more hallowing than the union of kindred spirits in art. At the moment of meeting, the art lover transcends himself. At once he is and is not. He catches a glimpse of Infinity, but words cannot voice his delight, for the eye has no tongue. Freed from the fetters of matter, his spirit moves in the rhythm of things. It is thus that art becomes akin to religion and ennobles mankind. It is this which makes a masterpiece something sacred. (*The Book of Tea*, Okakura Kakuzō)

Question 12: What does the author mean with the sentence "At once he is and is not."?

A) The art lover becomes physically invisible, merging with the artwork in such a way that his presence is no longer detectable by others in the room.

B) The art lover transcends the bounds of his individual identity and ego, experiencing a profound sense of connection with the universal and eternal aspects of the artwork.

C) The art lover experiences a psychological conflict, simultaneously recognizing his own existence while feeling an intense disconnection from his physical self due to the overwhelming impact of the art.

D) The art lover is so profoundly moved by the artwork that he enters a state where he no longer perceives the constraints of the physical world.

> Early in the session of the Congress which met in December, 1839, a bill was discussed abolishing the Military Academy. I saw in this an honorable way to obtain a discharge, and read the debates with much interest, but with impatience at the delay in taking action, for I was selfish enough to favor the bill. It never passed, and a year later, although the time hung drearily with me, I would have been sorry to have seen it succeed. My idea then was to get through the course, secure a detail for a few years as assistant professor of mathematics at the Academy, and afterwards obtain a permanent position as professor in some respectable college; but circumstances always did shape my course different from my plans. (*Personal Memoirs of Ulysses S. Grant*, by Ulysses S. Grant)

Question 13: Which of the following best summarizes the author's feeling towards the bill regarding abolishing the Military Academy?

A) He was indifferent to the bill and its potential outcomes.

B) He initially supported the bill but later felt relieved it did not pass.

C) He was strongly opposed to the bill from the beginning.

D) He believed the bill would significantly improve the Military Academy.

> Europe was so organized socially and economically as to secure the maximum accumulation of capital. While there was some continuous improvement in the daily conditions of life of the mass of the population, Society was so framed as to throw a great part of the increased income into the control of the class least likely to consume it. The new rich of the nineteenth century were not brought up to large expenditures, and preferred the power which investment gave them to the pleasures of immediate consumption. In fact, it was precisely the inequality of the distribution of wealth which made possible those vast accumulations of fixed wealth and of capital improvements which distinguished that age from all others. Herein lay, in fact, the main justification of the Capitalist System. If the rich had spent their new wealth on their own enjoyments, the world would long ago have found such a regime intolerable. But like bees they saved and accumulated, not less to the advantage of the whole community because they themselves held narrower ends in prospect.
> (*The Economic Consequences of the Peace*, by John Maynard Keynes)

Question 14: How did the author characterize the motivation of the new rich's actions and the results of their actions?

A) The rich sought immediate pleasure and their actions led to widespread consumption.

B) The rich aimed to maximize their power through investment, benefiting the community indirectly.

C) The rich were motivated by philanthropy and directly improved the lives of the poor.

D) The rich preferred to hoard wealth, leading to economic stagnation.

> Meanwhile the technological application of the complex apparatus which is science has revolutionized the conditions under which associated life goes on. This may be known as a fact which is stated in a proposition and assented to. But it is not known in the sense that men understand it. They do not know it as they know some machine which they operate, or as they know electric light and steam locomotives. They do not understand how the change has gone on nor how it affects their conduct. Not understanding its "how," they cannot use and control its manifestations. They undergo the consequences, they are affected by them. They cannot manage them, though some are fortunate enough—what is commonly called good fortune—to be able to exploit some phase of the process for their own personal profit. But even the most shrewd and successful man does not in any analytic and systematic way—in a way worthy to compare with the knowledge which he has won in lesser affairs by means of the stress of experience—know the system within which he operates.
> (*The Public and Its Problems*, John Dewey)

Question 15: How does the author view the relationship between the public and technological advancement?

A) The public possesses a comprehensive understanding and exerts full control over technological advancements.

B) The public remains largely unaffected by the profound changes brought about by technological advancements.

C) The public is influenced by technological advancements but does not fully understand or manage them.

D) The public benefits equally from technological advancements, regardless of their individual knowledge.

Directions for questions 16–19

Read the following early draft of an essay and then choose the best answer to the question or the best completion of the statement.

> (1) The Eskimo, or Inuit, people have developed ingenious methods for preserving meat, which is essential for survival in the harsh Arctic environment. (2) One of the primary techniques the Inuit use is freezing, which leverages the naturally cold temperatures of the Arctic. (3) Meat is often stored in ice cellars: deeply dug into the permafrost, where it remains frozen year-round. (4) This method not only preserves the meat but also prevents it from being scavenged by animals.
>
> (5) Another traditional method is drying or dehydrating the meat. (6) This process involves cutting the meat into thin strips and hanging it in the open air to dry. (7) The cold, dry Arctic air dehydrates the meat, preventing bacterial growth and spoilage. (8) Sometimes, smoke is used in conjunction with drying to enhance the preservation process and add flavor. (9) Smoke from burning wood or other materials contains chemicals that inhibit bacterial growth.
>
> (10) Fermentation is another traditional preservation method. (11) Fish, in particular is often fermented by placing it in a seal skin bag and burying it underground for several months. (12) This method relies on the natural fermentation process, which preserves the fish and enhances its nutritional value.

> (13) Seal oil is also used to preserve meat. (14) Meat is submerged in seal oil, which creates an anaerobic environment preventing the growth of spoilage bacteria. (15) This method is particularly effective for preserving small game and fish.
>
> (16) These preservation techniques reflect the Inuit's deep understanding of their environment. (17) They serve as a testament to the ingenuity and resilience of the Inuit people. (18) Regardless modern conveniences become more accessible, many Inuit communities continue to uphold these traditional practices, honoring their heritage and sustaining their way of life.

Question 16: Which is the best version of the underlined portion of sentence 3 (reproduced below)?

Meat is often stored in ice cellars: deeply dug into the permafrost, where it remains frozen year-round.

A) (as it is now)

B) cellars, deeply

C) cellars deeply

D) cellars; deeply

Question 17: Which is the best version of the underlined portion of sentence 11 (reproduced below)?

Fish, in particular is often fermented by placing it in a seal skin bag and burying it underground for several months.

A) (as it is now)

B) Fish, in particular, is

C) Fish in particular is

D) Fish in particular, is

Question 18: Which is the best version of the underlined portion of sentence 14 (reproduced below)?

Meat is submerged in seal oil, which creates an anaerobic environment preventing the growth of spoilage bacteria.

A) (as it is now)

B) environment prevents

C) environment which prevents

D) environment that prevents

Question 19: Which is the best version of the underlined portion of sentence 18 (reproduced below)?

Regardless modern conveniences become more accessible, many Inuit communities continue to uphold these traditional practices, honoring their heritage and sustaining their way of life.

A) (as it is now)

B) In spite of

C) Nevertheless

D) Even though

Directions for questions 20–30

Select the best version of the underlined part of the sentence. If you think the original sentence is best, choose the first answer.

Question 20:

The company's new marketing plan, which promotes sustainability, innovation, and reducing operational waste, is expected to drive significant growth in the upcoming fiscal year and help establish the brand as a leader in eco-friendly business practices.

A) promotes sustainability, innovation, and reducing

B) promotes sustainability, innovation, and reduce

C) promotes sustainability, innovation, and the reduction of

D) promotes sustainability, innovation, reducing

Question 21: As the sun set, the group hiked back to camp, where they prepare dinner and shared stories.

A) prepare dinner and shared stories

B) were sharing stories and prepared dinner

C) prepared dinner and shared stories

D) sharing stories while preparing dinner

Question 22: The teacher praised the student, who's essay received the highest score in the class.

A) who's essay

B) of whom the essay

C) whose essay

D) that essay had

Question 23: The scientists, who were attending the conference, shared their latest research on renewable energy technologies.

A) who were attending

B) who attend

C) who had been attended

D) whom attended

Question 24: Because of the maintenance issues, and the trains were delayed, affecting hundreds of commuters during rush hour.

A) and the trains were delayed

B) the trains were delayed

C) with the trains delaying

D) with the trains being delayed

Question 25: After hours of deliberation, the committee members finally made their decision and announce the results to the press.

A) made their decision and announce

B) made their decision and announced

C) making their decision and announcing

D) made their decisions and announces

Question 26: After finishing the race, each runner received their medal for participating in the marathon.

A) their

B) his

C) her

D) his or her

Question 27: The board of directors announced their decision to move forward with the merger after lengthy discussions.

A) their decision

B) its decision

C) it's decision

D) theirs decision

Question 28: The collaboration was shared across the three departments, ensuring each one played an important role in the success of the project.

A) across

B) between

C) among

D) around

Question 29: Nothing fuels the economy in Florida quite like orange farming, being the state's most prominent agricultural sector.

A) being the

B) it is the

C) and the

D) which is the

Question 30: Should I walk by the bakery in the morning, the smell of fresh bread is always in the air.

A) Should

B) As long as

C) When

D) If

MATHEMATICS

Question 1: Emily tracked her steps for a month and found that she walked 22 days out of the last 30 days. What percent of these days did she walk?

A) 62.5%

B) 73.33%

C) 72.5%

D) 80%

Question 2: In June, which has 30 days, Jamie worked 3 out of every 5 days at either a library or a café. He worked at the library for 12 days, and at the café for each of the remaining days that he worked. How many days did he work at the café?

A) 4 days

B) 5 days

C) 6 days

D) 8 days

Question 3: Which of the following inequalities is correct?

A) $\frac{6}{7} > \frac{5}{8}$

B) $\frac{7}{10} > \frac{8}{11}$

C) $\frac{9}{10} < \frac{8}{9}$

D) $\frac{5}{6} < \frac{4}{5}$

Question 4: What is 3.4567 rounded to the nearest hundredth?

A) 3.45

B) 3.46

C) 3.457

D) 3.456

Question 5: $\frac{4}{5} \div \frac{2}{3} =$

A) $\frac{4}{3}$

B) $\frac{6}{5}$

C) $\frac{5}{8}$

D) $\frac{5}{2}$

Question 6: On a flight from Paris to Tokyo, a total of 300 passengers each ordered a dinner whose main dish was beef, chicken, or fish. The number of passengers who ordered beef was 105, while 95 ordered fish. How many passengers ordered chicken?

A) 100

B) 95

C) 105

D) 110

Question 7: If you simplify (3x + 4)(2x - 3) - 4(x - 1), what's the result?

A) $6x^2 + 5x - 4$

B) $6x^2 - 5x - 4$

C) $6x^2 - 5x - 8$

D) $6x^2 + 5x - 8$

Question 8: If $14.8x - 3.4 = 15.3x + 1.6$, then x equals

A) 8

B) -7

C) 0.8

D) -10

Question 9: In a graph, the line intersects the points (1, 2) and (5, 8). What is the equation of this line?

A) $y = \frac{3}{4}x + \frac{5}{4}$

B) $y = \frac{3}{2}x + \frac{1}{2}$

C) $y = 2x - 1$

D) $y = \frac{3}{2}x - \frac{1}{2}$

Question 10: What is the greatest common factor of $18x^3y^2z$ and $24x^2yz^3$?

A) $3xy^2z$

B) $6x^2yz$

C) $6x^2yz^3$

D) $12xy^2z$

Question 11: If a = 2 and b = -4, then $5a^2 + 2ab - 3b^2 =$

A) -52

B) 52

C) -44

D) -92

Question 12: The following table lists data about the 40 employees in a company, dividing the group into departments and then dividing each of these two groups into those who are managers and those who are not. What percentage of the company are managers in the Marketing department?

	Managers	Non-Managers	Total
Marketing	5	15	20
Sales	10	10	20
Total	15	25	40

A) 10%

B) 12.5%

C) 15%

D) 25%

Question 13: If $y = mx + b$ is a linear function with a slope of 5 that intersects the point (2, -7), what are the values of m and b?

A) $m = 5, b = -10$

B) $m = 5, b = -17$

C) $m = -5, b = 17$

D) $m = -5, b = -7$

Question 14: A right triangle has one leg that is 3 units longer than the other leg. The hypotenuse is 15 units long. What are the lengths of the legs of the triangle?

A) 5 units and 12 units

B) 6 units and 13 units

C) 8 units and 15 units

D) 9 units and 12 units

Question 15: $(3x^2y^3)(4x^5)^2 =$

A) $36x^7y^3$

B) $48x^{10}y^6$

C) $72x^{11}y^3$

D) $72x^{13}y^6$

Question 16: The following graph shows the monthly production at a factory from January to December in 2020. In which month did the factory see the greatest increase in production compared with the previous month?

A) February

B) April

C) July

D) October

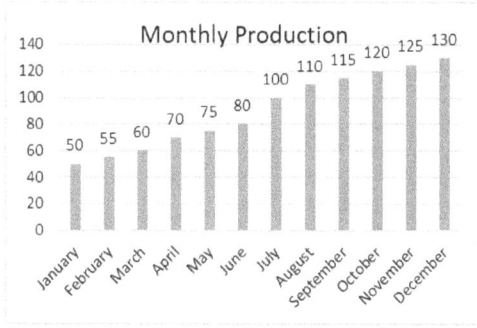

Mathematics | 217

Question 17: Thirty students took a 20-point pop quiz in their math class. Five students received scores of 18, seven got scores of 16, six got scores of 14, eight got scores of 12, and four got scores of 10. What was the difference between the mean score and the median score? Found the closest among the answers below.

A) about 0.1

B) about 2

C) about 2.5

D) about 3

Question 18: In a right-angled triangle, if $\sin \theta = \frac{4}{5}$, what is $\cos \phi$ where ϕ is the complementary angle to θ?

A) $\frac{3}{5}$

B) $\frac{4}{5}$

C) $\frac{5}{4}$

D) $\frac{3}{4}$

Question 19: Two triangles are shown to the right. Given DF=AB, which of the following condition can prove the two triangles are congruent.

A) $\angle D = \angle A$ and BC=EF

B) $\angle E = \angle C$

C) EF=BC

D) $\angle D = \angle A$ and $\angle F = \angle B$

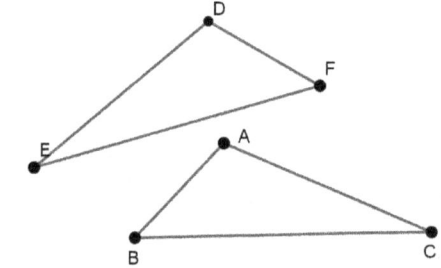

Question 20: The plot below identifies the number of hours students in a class spent studying for an exam. What fraction of the students studied for more than 3 hours (not including 3 hours)?

A) $\frac{2}{20}$

B) $\frac{1}{10}$

C) $\frac{1}{5}$

D) $\frac{2}{25}$

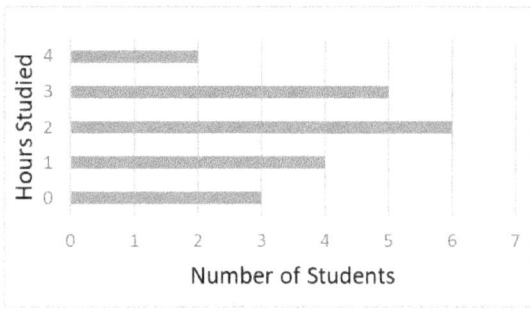

218 | TSIA2 Study Guide

Practice Test 2 Answer Key

ELAR

Q1: C) Welcoming

Explanation: Yogi Johnson greeted Scripps with "Glad to meet you" and offered to show him around the works, indicating a welcoming attitude.

Q2: C) He admired Australians from his war experience.

Explanation: Yogi explained that the foreman was with the Australians during the war, which made a big impression on him, leading him to identify as Australian.

Q3: B) Stressful

Explanation: The phrase "been through things" typically implies experiences that are challenging or stressful, suggesting Yogi had endured hardships.

Q4: C) Formal

Explanation: The foreman's interaction with Scripps was straightforward and business-like, indicating a formal rather than friendly or hostile greeting.

Q5: A) Passage 1 supports broader cancer screening, while Passage 2 highlights concerns and drawbacks.

Explanation: Passage 1 emphasizes the benefits of broader cancer screening for reducing mortality, while Passage 2 points out potential risks, such as overdiagnosis and financial costs, providing a counter-argument to the broader screening approach.

Q6: D) Gene editing offers primarily positive benefits to society.

Explanation: The author supporting gene editing emphasizes its potential benefits, while the opposing author highlights its ethical risks and potential negative consequences. Therefore, they would be unlikely to agree that gene editing offers only positive outcomes.

Q7: A) To illustrate the natural balance of population control

Explanation: The example of epidemics in the passage demonstrates how natural factors, such as diseases and parasites, serve as limiting checks on the overpopulation of species, thereby maintaining a balance independent of direct competition for resources.

Q8: B) It was not yet fully feathered.

Explanation: The passage explains that the chick was still in its down and not fully feathered, implying it was likely cold and uncomfortable, making it "disconsolate." This condition highlights the necessity for the Emperor penguin to nest in midwinter.

Q9: B) Warn against the dangers of getting into debt for consumable goods

Explanation: The passage advises against getting into debt for consumable goods, emphasizing the negative consequences of purchasing items on credit and the importance of avoiding unnecessary debt.

Q10: C) Locate and occupy the safest positions for the soldiers

Explanation: The passage describes the soldiers finding and settling in the safest positions to avoid danger from Spanish artillery and sharpshooters, indicating the primary need was to ensure the soldiers' safety by finding sheltered spots.

Q11: D) Disturbed

Explanation: The author describes a tragic scene involving a sheep's horns caught in a tree and expresses discomfort with the memory, stating they never liked the spit of Windy Lake again, indicating a disturbed attitude.

Q12: B) The art lover transcends the bounds of his individual identity and ego, experiencing a profound sense of connection with the universal and eternal aspects of the artwork.

Explanation: The phrase "At once he is and is not." suggests that in the moment of encountering great art, the lover of art transcends his personal, individual identity. He connects with something greater than himself, glimpsing infinity and experiencing a union with the universal essence of the art. This moment of transcendence elevates his spirit beyond the material world, aligning with the sacred and ennobling nature of a masterpiece, as discussed in the passage.

Q13: B) He initially supported the bill but later felt relieved it did not pass.

Explanation: The author initially favored the bill as a way to leave the Academy but later realized he would have regretted its passage, showing his change of heart.

Q14: B) The rich aimed to maximize their power through investment, benefiting the community indirectly.

Explanation: The author characterizes the rich's motivation as seeking power through investment rather than immediate consumption. This behavior led to the accumulation of capital, indirectly benefiting the community by enabling economic growth and improvements.

Q15: C) The public is influenced by technological advancements but does not fully understand or manage them.

Explanation: The author argues that while technological advancements revolutionize life, the public does not fully understand or control their effects. Instead, they experience the consequences without comprehending the underlying processes.

Q16: C) cellars deeply

Explanation: The correct answer is C) cellars deeply. This option removes unnecessary punctuation and integrates the clause smoothly, making the sentence clear and concise. The colon, comma, and semicolon in the other options are not needed in this context.

Q17: B) Fish, in particular, is

Explanation: The correct answer is B) Fish, in particular, is. The commas around "in particular" properly set off the phrase as a non-essential clause, improving the clarity and readability of the sentence.

Q18: D) environment that prevents

Explanation: The correct answer is D) environment that prevents. Using "that" properly connects the clause, making the sentence clear and grammatically correct. The use of "which" would be less appropriate in this restrictive clause.

Q19: D) Even though

Explanation: The correct answer is D) Even though. This choice correctly introduces the contrast between the increasing accessibility of modern conveniences and the continued practice of traditional methods by Inuit communities, maintaining the intended meaning and coherence of the sentence. "Regardless" is incorrect as it is missing the necessary preposition "of," and "Nevertheless" does not fit the context of the sentence as it suggests a contradiction rather than a contrast. "In spite of" is less formal and clear compared to "Even though."

Q20: C) promotes sustainability, innovation, and the reduction of

Explanation: The correct choice maintains parallelism with nouns in the series: "sustainability," "innovation," and "the reduction of." The other options mix verb forms and disrupt the parallel structure of the sentence.

Q21: C) prepared dinner and shared stories

Explanation: "Prepared" and "shared" maintain the past tense to match "hiked," ensuring sentence consistency. Other options disrupt the tense or meaning of the sentence.

Q22: C) whose essay

Explanation: "Whose essay" correctly introduces the possessive relative clause, indicating that the student owns the essay. Other options use awkward or incorrect phrasing that breaks the flow of the sentence.

Q23: A) who were attending

Explanation: "Who were attending" is correct as it indicates that the scientists were present at the conference. The other options use incorrect verb forms or break grammatical structure.

Q24: B) the trains were delayed

Explanation: "The trains were delayed" maintains the proper past tense to match "Because of the maintenance issues" and ensures clarity. The other choices introduce grammatical inconsistencies or incorrect tenses.

Q25: B) made their decision and announced

Explanation: Both actions "made" and "announced" occurred in the past, so the verbs must agree in tense. The correct answer uses the past tense form "announced."

Q26: D) his or her

Explanation: "His or her" is correct because "each runner" is singular. The use of "their" would be incorrect as it is plural, and the sentence refers to individual participants.

Q27: B) its decision

Explanation: "Its" is the correct singular possessive pronoun for "the board of directors." Though the board is composed of individuals, it is treated as a single entity in this context.

Q28: C) among

Explanation: "Among" is correctly used when referring to more than two entities (in this case, three departments). "Between" is used for two entities. The other options do not convey the intended meaning properly.

Q29: D) which is the

Explanation: "Which is the" properly completes the sentence by introducing a non-restrictive relative clause that describes orange farming as Florida's most prominent agricultural sector. The other options either create awkward phrasing or fail to smoothly connect the ideas.

Q30: C) When

Explanation: "When" is the correct conjunction for indicating a specific time, making the sentence clear and logical. The other options alter the meaning of the sentence or fail to make sense contextually.

Mathematics

Q1: B) 73.33%. Explanation: $\frac{22}{30} \times 100 = 73.33\%$.

Q2: C) 6 days. Explanation: $\frac{3}{5} \times 30 = 18$ days worked. $18 - 12 = 6$ days at the café.

Q3: A) $\frac{6}{7} > \frac{5}{8}$. Explanation: Using cross multiplication to compare $\frac{6}{7}$ and $\frac{5}{8}$: Cross multiply:

$$6 \times 8 \quad \text{and} \quad 7 \times 5$$

$$6 \times 8 = 48, 7 \times 5 = 35$$

Since: $48 > 35$, Therefore: $\frac{6}{7} > \frac{5}{8}$. Using cross multiplication to compare the other choices, none is true.

Q4: B) 3.46. Explanation: $3.4567 \approx 3.46$.

Q5: B) $\frac{6}{5}$. Explanation: $\frac{4}{5} \div \frac{2}{3} = \frac{4}{5} \times \frac{3}{2} = \frac{12}{10} = \frac{6}{5}$.

Q6: A) 100. Explanation: $300 - 105 - 95 = 100$.

Q7: C) $6x^2 - 5x - 8$.

Explanation: $(3x+4)(2x-3) - 4(x-1) = 6x^2 - 9x + 8x - 12 - 4x + 4 = 6x^2 - 5x - 8$.

Q8: D) -10. Explanation:

$$14.8x - 15.3x = 3.4 + 1.6$$
$$-0.5x = 5$$
$$x = -10$$

Q9: B) $y = \frac{3}{2}x + \frac{1}{2}$.

Explanation: 1. Find the slope m using the points $(x_1, y_1) = (1,2)$ and $(x_2, y_2) = (5,8)$:

$$m = \frac{y_2 - y_1}{x_2 - x_1} = \frac{8-2}{5-1} = \frac{6}{4} = \frac{3}{2}$$

2. Use the point-slope form $y - y_1 = m(x - x_1)$ with point $(1, 2)$ and slope $m = \frac{3}{2}$:

$$y - 2 = \frac{3}{2}(x - 1)$$
$$y - 2 = \frac{3}{2}x - \frac{3}{2}$$
$$y = \frac{3}{2}x + \frac{1}{2}$$

Q10: B) $6x^2yz$. Explanation: 1. Find the common factors for each term:

$$\text{Factors of } 18x^3y^2z = 2 \cdot 3^2 \cdot x^3 \cdot y^2 \cdot z$$

$$\text{Factors of } 24x^2yz^3 = 2^3 \cdot 3 \cdot x^2 \cdot y \cdot z^3$$

2. Identify the common factors: Common factors: $2 \cdot 3 \cdot x^2 \cdot y \cdot z$.

3. Multiply the common factors: $6x^2yz$. Thus, the greatest common factor is 6xyz.

Q11: C) -44. Explanation:

$$5a^2 + 2ab - 3b^2 = 5(2)^2 + 2(2)(-4) - 3(-4)^2$$

$$= 5(4) + 2(-8) - 3(16)$$
$$= 20 - 16 - 48$$
$$= -44$$

Q12: B) 12.5%. Explanation: Percentage of managers in Marketing $= \frac{5}{40} \times 100 = 12.5\%$.

Q13: B) $m = 5$, $b = -17$. Explanation: Step 1. Identify the given values: $m = 5$, point$(x_1, y_1) = (2, -7)$. Step 2. Substitute the point and slope into the equation y = mx + b to find b :

$$-7 = 5(2) + b$$
$$-7 = 10 + b$$
$$b = -17$$

Thus, the values are: $B) \ m = 5, \ b = -17$.

Q14: D) 9 units and 12 units. Explanation: Let x be the length of the shorter leg. Then, the longer leg is $x + 3$. Use the Pythagorean theorem: $x^2 + (x + 3)^2 = 15^2$, solve it:

$$x^2 + x^2 + 6x + 9 = 225$$
$$2x^2 + 6x - 216 = 0$$
$$x^2 + 3x - 108 = 0$$
$$x = \frac{-3 \pm \sqrt{3^2 + 4 \cdot 108}}{2}$$
$$x = \frac{-3 \pm \sqrt{9 + 432}}{2}$$
$$x = \frac{-3 \pm 21}{2}$$

Hence, $x = 9$, and we ignore the negative value. Therefore, the legs of the triangle are:

- Shorter leg = 9 units
- Longer leg 9+3=12 units

Q15: B) $48x^{10}y^6$. Explanation: 1. Apply the exponent to the term:

$$(4x^5)^2 : (4x^5)^2 = 4^2 \cdot (x^5)^2 = 16x^{10}$$

2. Multiply the terms: $(3x^2y^3)(16x^{10}) = 3 \cdot 16 \cdot x^{2+10} \cdot y^3 = 48x^{12}y^3$.

Q16: C) July. Explanation: Analyze the monthly production data and we can see the greatest increase is from June to July with 20. Thus, the month with the greatest increase is July.

Q17: A) about 0.1. Explanation: 1. Find the mean score:

Total score $= 5(18) + 7(16) + 6(14) + 8(12) + 4(10) = 90 + 112 + 84 + 96 + 40 = 422$

$$\text{Mean score} = \frac{422}{30} \approx 14.07$$

2. Find the median score: Observe that there are 12 students having scores of 18 and 16, and 12 students having scores of 10 and 12. Hence, the 6 students having scores of 14 rank between these 24 students with higher and lower scores. Hence, one can conclude that the median is 14.

3. Calculate the difference between the mean and median: $14.07 - 14 \approx 0.07$

Thus, the difference is 0.07, but since we need to match the choices available closely, an approximate choice is 0.1.

Q18: B) $\frac{4}{5}$. Explanation: The easiest way to solve this kind of problem is to draw a triangle, as follows. Because θ and φ are complementary, we know they are the two acute angles in the right-angle triangle. Once you have the triangle, it is easy to know derive that $\cos φ = \sin θ = \frac{4}{5}$.

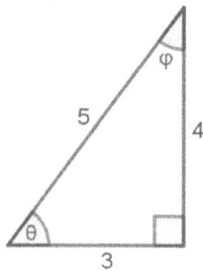

Q19: D) ∠D = ∠A and ∠F = ∠B. Explanation: A) This fits the SSA criteria, it cannot prove congruency. B) A single angle and one side are insufficient to prove congruency. C) Two sides are insufficient to prove congruency. D) This fits the ASA criteria; it is sufficient to prove congruency.

Q20: C) $\frac{1}{5}$

Explanation: From the plot, only the students who studied for more than 3 hours should be considered. According to the plot, 2 students studied for more than 3 hours. Since there are a total of 20 students, the fraction is:

$$\frac{2}{20} = \frac{1}{10}$$

Thus, the correct fraction is $\frac{1}{10}$.

Thank you!

Dear Reader,

Thank you for choosing Miller Test Prep as your guide in preparing for the TSIA2 test. We appreciate the trust you have placed in us, and we are honored to have been a part of your educational journey.

Congratulations on completing this test prep book! By diligently working through each section, practicing the exercises, and mastering the strategies provided, you have taken significant steps towards achieving great scores on the TSIA2 test.

We believe in your abilities and are confident that you are now well-prepared to tackle the exam. Remember, confidence and a positive mindset are key components of success. Trust in the effort and dedication you have put into your preparation.

Your feedback is incredibly valuable to us. If you found this book helpful, we would be grateful if you could take a moment to leave a review on Amazon. Your reviews help us to improve our materials and assist other students in their test preparation.

Thank you once again for choosing Miller Test Prep. We wish you the very best in your upcoming test and all your future academic endeavors.

Sincerely,

Steve H. Miller

Steve H. Miller
The Miller Test Prep Team
Email: MillerTestPrep@outlook.com

www.ingramcontent.com/pod-product-compliance
Lightning Source LLC
Chambersburg PA
CBHW081742100526
44592CB00015B/2266